the
fearless
organization

the
fearless
organization

Creating **Psychological Safety** in the Workplace for Learning, Innovation, and Growth

Amy C. Edmondson
HARVARD BUSINESS SCHOOL

WILEY

Published by John Wiley & Sons, Inc., Hoboken, New Jersey.
Published simultaneously in Canada.

For general information on our other products and services or for technical support, please contact our Customer Care Department within the United States at (800) 762-2974, outside the United States at (317) 572-3993 or fax (317) 572-4002.

Wiley publishes in a variety of print and electronic formats and by print-on-demand. Some material included with standard print versions of this book may not be included in e-books or in print-on-demand. If this book refers to media such as a CD or DVD that is not included in the version you purchased, you may download this material at http://booksupport.wiley.com. For more information about Wiley products, visit www.wiley.com.

Library of Congress Cataloging-in-Publication Data

Names: Edmondson, Amy C., author.
Title: The fearless organization : creating psychological safety in the
  workplace for learning, innovation, and growth / Amy C. Edmondson.
Description: Hoboken, New Jersey : John Wiley & Sons, Inc., [2019] | Includes
  index. |
Identifiers: LCCN 2018033732 (print) | LCCN 2018036160 (ebook) | ISBN
  9781119477228 (Adobe PDF) | ISBN 9781119477266 (ePub) | ISBN 9781119477242
  (hardcover)
Subjects: LCSH: Organizational behavior. | Organizational
  learning—Psychological aspects. | Psychology, Industrial.
Classification: LCC HD58.7 (ebook) | LCC HD58.7 .E287 2019 (print) | DDC
  658.3/82—dc23
LC record available at https://lccn.loc.gov/2018033732

Cover Design: Wiley

Printed in the United States of America

SKY10043086_022023

To George

Whose curiosity and passion make him a great scientist and leader — and who knows all too well that fear is the enemy of flourishing.

Brief Contents

Introduction   *xiii*

PART I   **The Power of Psychological Safety**   **1**

Chapter 1   The Underpinning   3

Chapter 2   The Paper Trail   25

PART II   **Psychological Safety at Work**   **51**

Chapter 3   Avoidable Failure   53

Chapter 4   Dangerous Silence   77

Chapter 5   The Fearless Workplace   103

Chapter 6   Safe and Sound   129

PART III   **Creating a Fearless Organization**   **151**

Chapter 7   Making it Happen   153

Chapter 8   What's Next?   187

Appendix: Variations in survey measures to Illustrate Robustness
of Psychological Safety   *213*

Acknowledgments   *217*

About the Author   *219*

Index   *221*

Contents

Introduction   *xiii*

    What It Takes to Thrive in a Complex, Uncertain
       World   *xiii*

    Discovery by Mistake   *xvi*

    Overview of the Book   *xviii*

    Endnotes   *xxi*

PART I   **The Power of Psychological Safety**   **1**

Chapter 1 The Underpinning   3

    Unconscious Calculators   4

    Envisioning the Psychologically Safe Workplace   6

    An Accidental Discovery   8

    Standing on Giants' Shoulders   12

    Why Fear Is Not an Effective Motivator   13

    What Psychological Safety Is Not   15

    Measuring Psychological Safety   19

    Psychological Safety Is Not Enough   21

    Endnotes   22

Chapter 2   The Paper Trail   25
                 Not a Perk   *26*
                 The Research   *29*
                 An Epidemic of Silence   *30*
                 A Work Environment that Supports Learning   *35*
                 Why Psychological Safety Matters for Performance *39*
                 Psychologically Safe Employees Are Engaged
                       Employees   *41*
                 Psychological Safety as the Extra Ingredient   *43*
                 Bringing Research to Practice   *45*
                 Endnotes   *46*

PART II   **Psychological Safety at Work**   **51**

Chapter 3   Avoidable Failure   53
                 Exacting Standards   *54*
                 Stretching the Stretch Goal   *60*
                 Fearing the Truth   *63*
                 Who Regulates the Regulators?   *66*
                 Avoiding Avoidable Failure   *68*
                 Adopting an Agile Approach to Strategy   *70*
                 Endnotes   *72*

Chapter 4   Dangerous Silence   77
                 Failing to Speak Up   *78*
                 What Was Not Said   *79*
                 Excessive Confidence in Authority   *83*
                 A Culture of Silence   *86*
                 Silence in the Noisy Age of Social Media   *92*
                 Endnotes   *97*

Chapter 5   The Fearless Workplace   103
Making Candor Real   104
Extreme Candor   109
Be a Don't Knower   113
When Failure Works   116
Caring for Employees   119
Learning from Psychologically Safe Work
Environments   123
Endnotes   124

Chapter 6   Safe and Sound   129
Use Your Words   130
One for All and All for One   135
Speaking Up for Worker Safety   138
Transparency by Whiteboard   142
Unleashing Talent   146
Endnotes   147

PART III   **Creating a Fearless Organization**   **151**

Chapter 7   Making it Happen   153
The Leader's Tool Kit   154
How to Set the Stage for Psychological Safety   158
How to Invite Participation So People Respond   167
How to Respond Productively to Voice – No Matter
Its Quality   173
Leadership Self-Assessment   181
Endnotes   183

Chapter 8   What's Next?   187
Continuous Renewal   187
Deliberative Decision-Making   189

Hearing the Sounds of Silence   *191*

When Humor Isn't Funny   *193*

Psychological Safety FAQs   *195*

Tacking Upwind   *208*

Endnotes   *209*

*Appendix: Variations in survey measures to Illustrate Robustness
    of Psychological Safety*   *213*

Acknowledgments   *217*

About the Author   *219*

Index   *221*

Introduction

"No passion so effectively robs the mind of all its powers of acting and reasoning as fear."

—Edmund Burke, 1756.[1]

Whether you lead a global corporation, develop software, advise clients, practice medicine, build homes, or work in one of today's state-of-the-art factories that require sophisticated computer skills to manage complex production challenges, you are a knowledge worker.[2] Just as the engine of growth in the Industrial Revolution was standardization, with workers as laboring bodies confined to execute "the one best way" to get almost any task done, growth today is driven by ideas and ingenuity. People must bring their brains to work and collaborate with each other to solve problems and accomplish work that's perpetually changing. Organizations must find, and keep finding, new ways to create value to thrive over the long term. And creating value starts with putting the talent you have to its best and highest use.

What It Takes to Thrive in a Complex, Uncertain World

While it's not news that knowledge and innovation have become vital sources of competitive advantage in nearly every industry, few managers stop to really think about the implications of this new reality – particularly when it comes to what it means for the kind of work environment that would help employees thrive and organizations succeed. The goal of this book is to help you do just that – and to equip you with some new ideas and practices to make knowledge-intensive organizations work better.

For an organization to truly thrive in a world where innovation can make the difference between success and failure, it is not enough to hire smart, motivated people. Knowledgeable, skilled, well-meaning people cannot always contribute what they know at that critical moment on the job when it is needed. Sometimes this is because they fail to recognize the need for their knowledge. More often, it's because they're reluctant to stand out, be wrong, or offend the boss. For knowledge work to flourish, the workplace must be one where people feel able to share their knowledge! This means sharing concerns, questions, mistakes, and half-formed ideas. In most workplaces today, people are holding back far too often – reluctant to say or ask something that might somehow make them look bad. To complicate matters, as companies become increasingly global and complex, more and more of the work is team-based. Today's employees, at all levels, spend 50% more time collaborating than they did 20 years ago.[3] Hiring talented individuals is not enough. They have to be able to work well together.

In my research over the past 20 years, I've shown that a factor I call *psychological safety* helps explain differences in performance in workplaces that include hospitals, factories, schools, and government agencies. Moreover, psychological safety matters for groups as disparate as those in the C-suite of a financial institution and on the front lines of the intensive care unit. My field-based research has primarily focused on groups and teams, because that's how most work gets done. Few products or services today are created by individuals acting alone. And few individuals simply do their work and then hand the output over to other people who do their work, in a linear, sequential fashion. Instead, most work requires people to talk to each other to sort out shifting interdependencies. Nearly everything we value in the modern economy is the result of decisions and actions that are interdependent and therefore benefit from effective teamwork. As I've written in prior books and articles, more and more of that teamwork is dynamic – occurring in constantly shifting configurations of people rather than in formal, clearly-bounded teams.[4] This dynamic collaboration is called *teaming*.[5] Teaming is the art of communicating and coordinating with people across boundaries of all kinds – expertise, status, and distance, to name the most important. But whether you're teaming with new colleagues all the time or working in a stable team, effective teamwork happens best in a psychologically safe workplace.

Psychological safety is not immunity from consequences, nor is it a state of high self-regard. In psychologically safe workplaces, people know they might fail, they might receive performance feedback that says they're not meeting expectations, and they might lose their jobs due to changes in the industry environment or even to a lack of competence in their role. These attributes of the modern workplace are unlikely to disappear anytime soon. But in a psychologically safe workplace, people are not hindered by *interpersonal* fear. They feel willing and able to take the inherent interpersonal risks of candor. They fear holding back their full participation *more* than they fear sharing a potentially sensitive, threatening, or wrong idea. The fearless organization is one in which interpersonal fear is minimized so that team and organizational performance can be maximized in a knowledge intensive world. It is not one devoid of anxiety about the future!

As you will learn in this book, psychological safety can make the difference between a satisfied customer and an angry, damage-causing tweet that goes viral; between nailing a complex medical diagnosis that leads to a patient's full recovery and sending a critically ill patient home too soon; between a near miss and a catastrophic industrial accident; or between strong business performance and dramatic, headline-grabbing failure. More importantly, you will learn crucial practices that help you build the psychologically safe workplaces that allow your organization to thrive in a complex, uncertain, and increasingly interdependent world.

Psychological safety is broadly defined as a climate in which people are comfortable expressing and being themselves. More specifically, when people have psychological safety at work, they feel comfortable sharing concerns and mistakes without fear of embarrassment or retribution. They are confident that they can speak up and won't be humiliated, ignored, or blamed. They know they can ask questions when they are unsure about something. They tend to trust and respect their colleagues. When a work environment has reasonably high psychological safety, good things happen: mistakes are reported quickly so that prompt corrective action can be taken; seamless coordination across groups or departments is enabled, and potentially game-changing ideas for innovation are shared. In short, psychological safety is a crucial source of value creation in organizations operating in a complex, changing environment.

Yet a 2017 Gallup poll found that only 3 in 10 employees strongly agree with the statement that their opinions count at work.[6] Gallup calculated that by "moving that ratio to six in 10 employees, organizations could realize a 27 percent reduction in turnover, a 40 percent reduction in safety incidents and a 12 percent increase in productivity."[7] That's why it's not enough for organizations to simply hire talent. If leaders want to unleash individual and collective talent, they must foster a psychologically safe climate where employees feel free to contribute ideas, share information, and report mistakes. Imagine what could be accomplished if the norm became one where employees felt their opinions counted in the workplace. I call that a fearless organization.

Discovery by Mistake

My interest in psychological safety began in the mid-1990s when I had the good fortune to join an interdisciplinary team of researchers undertaking a ground-breaking study of medication errors in hospitals. Providing patient care in hospitals presents a more extreme case of the challenges faced in other industries – notably, the challenge of ensuring teamwork in highly-technical, highly-customized, 24/7 operations. I figured that learning from an extreme case would help me develop new insights for managing people in other kinds of organizations.

As part of the study, trained nurse investigators painstakingly gathered data about these potentially devastating human errors over a six-month period, hoping to shed new light on their actual incidence in hospitals. Meanwhile, I observed how different hospital units worked, trying to understand their structures and cultures and seeking to gain insight into the conditions under which errors might happen in these busy, customized, occasionally chaotic operations, where coordination could be a matter of life-or-death. I also distributed a survey to get another view of how well the different patient care units worked as teams.

Along the way, I accidentally stumbled into the importance of psychological safety. As I will explain in Chapter 1, this launched me on a new research program that ultimately provided empirical evidence that validates the ideas developed and presented in this book. For now, let's just say I didn't set out to study psychological safety but rather to study teamwork and its relationship to mistakes. I thought that how people work together was an important element of what allows organizations to learn in a changing world. Psychological safety showed up unexpectedly – in what I would later describe as a blinding flash of the obvious – to explain some puzzling results in my data. Today, studies of psychological safety can be found in sectors ranging from business to healthcare to K–12 education. Over the past 20 years, a burgeoning academic literature has taken shape on the causes and consequences of psychological safety in the workplace, some of which is my own work but a great deal of which has been done by other researchers. We have learned a lot about what psychological safety is, how psychological safety works, and why psychological safety matters. I'll summarize key findings from these studies in this book.

Recently, the concept of psychological safety has taken hold among practitioners as well. Thoughtful executives, managers, consultants, and clinicians in a variety of industries are seeking to help their organizations make changes to create psychological safety as a strategy to promote learning, innovation, and employee engagement. Psychological safety received a significant boost in popularity in the managerial blogosphere after Charles Duhigg published an article in the *New York Times Magazine* in February 2016, reporting on a five-year study at Google that investigated what made the best teams.[8] The study examined several possibilities: Did it matter if teammates have similar educational backgrounds? Was gender balance important? What about socializing outside of work? No clear set of parameters emerged. Project Aristotle, as the initiative was code-named, then turned to studying norms; that is, the behaviors and unwritten rules to which a group adheres often without much conscious attention. Eventually, as Duhigg wrote, the researchers "encountered the concept of psychological safety in academic papers [and] everything suddenly fell into place."[9] They concluded, "psychological safety was far and away the most important of the five dynamics we found."[10] Other behaviors were also important, such as setting clear goals and reinforcing mutual accountability, but unless team members felt psychologically safe, the other behaviors were insufficient. Indeed, as the study's lead researcher, Julia Rozovsky, wrote, "it's the underpinning of the other four."[11] Reflecting her wonderfully concise conclusion, Chapter 1 of this book is titled "The Underpinning."

Overview of the Book

This book is divided into three parts. *Part I: The Power of Psychological Safety* consists of two chapters that introduce the concept of psychological safety and offer a brief history of the research on this important workplace phenomenon. We'll look at why psychological safety matters, as well as why it's not the norm in many organizations.

Chapter 1, "The Underpinning," opens with a disguised true story taking place in a hospital that shows at once the ordinariness of an employee holding back at work – not sharing a concern or a question – as well as the profound implications this human reflex can have for the quality of work in almost any organization. I will also recall the story of how I stumbled into psychological safety by accident early in my academic career.

Chapter 2, "The Paper Trail," presents key findings from a systematic review of academic research on psychological safety. I don't provide many details of individual studies but rather give an overview of how research on psychological safety has provided evidence supporting the central argument in this book – that no twenty-first century organization can afford to have a culture of fear. *The Fearless Organization* is not only a better place for employees, it's also a place where innovation, growth, and performance take hold. If readers want to skim this evidence and move quickly to Part II, they will be rewarded by a series of case studies that clearly illuminate first the costs of not having psychological safety and next the rewards of investing in building it.

The four chapters in *Part II: Psychological Safety at Work* present real-world case studies of workplaces in both private and public-sector organizations to show how psychological safety (or its absence) shapes business results and human safety performance.

Chapter 3, "Avoidable Failure," digs into cases in which workplace fear allowed an illusion of business success, postponing inevitable discoveries of underlying problems that had gone unreported and unaddressed for a period of time. Here we will see iconic companies that appeared to be industry stars only to suffer dramatic and highly-publicized falls from grace. Chapter 4, "Dangerous Silence," highlights workplaces where employees, customers, or communities suffered avoidable physical or emotional harm because employees, living in a culture of fear, were reluctant to speak up, ask questions, or get help.

Chapters 5 and 6 take us into organizations that have worked diligently to create an environment where speaking up is enabled and expected. These organizational portraits allow us to see what a fearless organization looks and feels like. They are strikingly different from those highlighted in Chapters 3 and 4, but importantly they are also very different from each other. There is more than one way to be fearless! Chapter 5 ("The Fearless Workplace") presents companies (like Pixar) where creative work is directly and obviously critical to business performance and where leaders understood the need to create psychological safety early in their tenure, as well as companies like Barry-Wehmilller, an industrial equipment manufacturer that underwent a transformational journey to discover that the business thrives when employees thrive. Chapter 6 ("Safe and Sound") examines workplaces where psychological safety helps to ensure employee and client safety and dignity.

Part III: Creating a Fearless Organization presents two chapters that build on the stories and research presented so far to focus on the question of *what leaders must do* to create a fearless organization – an organization where everyone can bring his or her full self to work, contribute, grow, thrive, and team up to produce remarkable results.

Chapter 7, "Making It Happen," tackles the question of what you need to do to build psychological safety – and how to get it back if it's lost. It contains the leader's tool kit. I present a framework with three simple (but not always easy) activities that leaders – at the top and throughout an organization – can use to create a more engaged and vital workforce. We'll see that creating psychological safety takes effort and skill, but the effort pays off when expertise or collaboration matter to the quality of the work. We will also see that the leader's work is never done. It's not a matter of checking the psychological safety box and moving on. Building and reinforcing the work environment where people can learn, innovate, and grow is a never-ending job, but a deeply meaningful one. Chapter 8, "What's Next," concludes the book, updates a few stories, and offers answers to some of the questions I am most frequently asked by people in companies around the world.

★★★★★

In an era when no individual can know or do everything needed to carry out the work that serves customers, it's more important than ever for people to speak up, share information, contribute expertise, take risks, and work with each other to create lasting value. Yet, as Edmund Burke wrote more than 250 years ago, fear limits our ability for effective thought and action – even for the most talented of employees. Today's leaders must be willing to take on the job of driving fear out of the organization to create the conditions for learning, innovation, and growth. I hope this book will help you do just that.

Endnotes

1. Burke, E. *A Philosophical Inquiry into the Origin of Our Ideas of the Sublime and Beautiful.* Dancing Unicorn Books, 2016. Print.
2. Selingo, J.J. "Wanted: Factory Workers, Degree Required." *The New York Times.* January 30, 2017. https://www.nytimes.com/2017/01/30/education/edlife/factory-workers-college-degree-apprenticeships.html Accessed June 13, 2018.
3. Cross, R., Rebele, R., & Grant, A. "Collaborative Overload." *Harvard Business Review.* January 1, 2016. https://hbr.org/2016/01/collaborative-overload Accessed June 13, 2018.
4. Edmondson, A.C. "Teamwork on the fly." *Harvard Business Review 90*.4, April 2012. 72–80. Print.
5. Edmondson, A.C. *Teaming: How Organizations Learn, Innovate, and Compete in the Knowledge Economy.* San Francisco: Jossey-Bass, 2012. Print.
6. Gallup. *State of the American Workplace Report.* Gallup: Washington, D.C, 2017. http://news.gallup.com/reports/199961/state-american-workplace-report-2017.aspx Accessed June 13, 2018.
7. Gallup, *State of the American Workplace Report.* 2012: 112
8. Duhigg, C. "What Google Learned From Its Quest to Build the Perfect Team" *The New York Times Magazine.* February 25, 2016. https://www.nytimes.com/2016/02/28/magazine/what-google-learned-from-its-quest-to-build-the-perfect-team.html Accessed June 13, 2018.
9. *Ibid.*
10. Rozovsky, J. "The five keys to a successful Google team." *re:Work Blog.* November 17, 2015. https://rework.withgoogle.com/blog/five-keys-to-a-successful-google-team/ Accessed June 13, 2018.
11. *Ibid.*

PART

I

The Power of Psychological Safety

1 | The Underpinning

"Psychological safety was by far the most important of the five key dynamics we found. It's the underpinning of the other four."

—Julia Rozovsky,
"The five keys to a successful Google team."[1]

The tiny newborn twins seemed healthy enough, but their early arrival at only 27 weeks' gestation meant they were considered "high risk." Fortunately, the medical team at the busy urban hospital where the babies were delivered included staff from the Neonatal Intensive Care Unit (NICU): a young Neonatal Nurse Practitioner named Christina Price* and a silver-haired neonatologist named Dr. Drake. As Christina looked at the babies, she was concerned. Her recent training had included, as newly established best practice, administering a medicine that promoted lung development as soon as possible for a high-risk baby. Babies born very prematurely often arrive with lungs not quite ready for fully independent breathing

---

*Names in this story are pseudonyms.

outside the womb. But the neonatologist had not issued an order for the medicine, called a prophylactic surfactant. Christina stepped forward to remind Dr. Drake about the surfactant and then caught herself. Last week she'd overheard him publicly berate another nurse for questioning one of his orders. She told herself that the twins would probably be fine – after all, the doctor probably had a reason for avoiding the surfactant, still considered a judgment call – and she dismissed the idea of bringing it up. Besides, he'd already turned on his heel, off for his morning rounds, white coat billowing.

Unconscious Calculators

In hesitating and then choosing not to speak up, Christina was making a quick, not entirely conscious, risk calculation – the kind of micro-assessment most of us make numerous times a day. Most likely she was not even aware that she had weighed the risk of being belittled or berated against the risk that the babies might in fact need the medication to thrive. She told herself the doctor knew better than she did, and she was not confident he would welcome her input. Inadvertently, she had done something psychologists call discounting the future – underweighting the more important issue of the patients' health, which would take some time to play out, and *over*weighting the importance of the doctor's possible response, which would happen immediately. Our spontaneous tendency to discount the future explains the prevalence of many unhelpful or unhealthy behaviors – whether eating that extra piece of chocolate cake or procrastinating on a challenging assignment – and the failure to speak up at work is an important and often overlooked example of this problematic tendency.

Like most people, Christina was spontaneously managing her image at work. As noted sociologist Erving Goffman argued in his seminal 1957 book, *The Presentation of the Self in Everyday Life*, as humans, we are constantly attempting to influence others' perceptions of us by regulating and controlling information in social interactions.[2] We do this both consciously and subconsciously.

Put another way, no one wakes up in the morning excited to go to work and look ignorant, incompetent, or disruptive. These are called interpersonal risks, and they are what nearly everyone seeks to avoid, not always consciously.[3] In fact, most of us want to look smart, capable, or helpful in the eyes of others. No matter what our line of work, status, or gender, all of us learn how to manage interpersonal risk relatively early in life. At some point during elementary school, children start to recognize that what others think of them matters, and they learn how to lower the risk of rejection or scorn. By the time we're adults, we're usually really good at it! So good, we do it without conscious thought. Don't want to look ignorant? Don't ask questions. Don't want to look incompetent? Don't admit to mistakes or weaknesses. Don't want to be called disruptive? Don't make suggestions. While it might be acceptable at a social event to privilege looking good over making a difference, at work this tendency can lead to significant problems – ranging from thwarted innovation to poor service to, at the extreme, loss of human life. Yet avoiding behaviors that might lead others to think less of us is pretty much second nature in most workplaces.

As influential management thinker Nilofer Merchant said about her early days as an administrator at Apple, "I used to go to meetings and see the problem so clearly, when others could not." But worrying about being "wrong," she "kept quiet and learned to sit on my hands lest they rise up and betray me. I would rather keep my job by staying within the lines than say something and risk looking stupid."[4] In one study investigating employee experiences with speaking up, 85% of respondents reported at least one occasion when they felt unable to raise a concern with their bosses, even though they believed the issue was important.[5]

If you think this behavior is limited to those lower in the organization, consider the chief financial officer recruited to join the senior team of a large electronics company. Despite grave reservations about a planned acquisition of another company, the new executive said nothing. His colleagues seemed uniformly enthusiastic, and he went along with the decision. Later, when the takeover had clearly failed, the executives gathered with a consultant for a post-mortem. Each was asked to reflect on what he or she might have done to contribute to or avert the failure. The CFO, now less of an outsider, shared his earlier concerns, acknowledging that he had let the team down by not speaking up. Openly apologetic and emotional, he lamented that the others' enthusiasm had left him afraid to be "the skunk at the picnic."

The problem with sitting on our hands and staying within the lines rather than speaking up is that although these behaviors keep us personally safe, they can make us underperform and become dissatisfied. They can also put the organization at risk. In the case of Christina and the newborns, fortunately, no immediate damage was done, but as we will see in later chapters, the fear of speaking up can lead to accidents that were in fact avoidable. Remaining silent due to fear of interpersonal risk can make the difference between life and death. Airplanes have crashed, financial institutions have fallen, and hospital patients have died unnecessarily because individuals were, for reasons having to do with the climate in which they worked, afraid to speak up. Fortunately, it doesn't have to happen.

Envisioning the Psychologically Safe Workplace

Had Christina worked in a hospital unit where she felt psychologically safe, she would not have hesitated to ask the neonatologist whether or not he thought treating the newborns with prophylactic lung medicine was warranted. Here too, she might not even be aware of making a conscious decision to speak up; it would simply seem natural to check. She would take for granted that her voice was appreciated, even if what she said didn't lead to a change in the patient's care. In a climate characterized by psychological safety – which blends trust and respect – the neonatologist might quickly agree with Christina and call the pharmacy to put in a request, or he might have explained why he thought it wasn't warranted in this case. Either way, the unit would be better off as a result. The patients would have received life-saving medication, or the team would have learned more about the subtleties of neonatal medicine. Before leaving the room, the doctor might thank Christina for her intervention. He'd be glad he could rely on her to speak up in case he slipped up, missed a detail, or was simply distracted.

Finally, as she gave the medicine to the babies, Christina might come up with the idea that the NICU could institute a protocol to make sure that that all babies who need a surfactant would get it. She might seek out her manager to make this suggestion during a break in the action. And because psychological safety exists in work groups, rather than between specific individuals (such as Christina and Dr. Drake), it's likely her nurse manager would be receptive to her suggestion.

Speaking up describes back-and-forth exchanges people have at work – from volunteering a concern in a meeting to giving feedback to a colleague. It also includes electronic communication (for example, sending an extra email to ask a coworker to clarify a particular point or seek help with a project). Valuable forms of speaking up include raising a different point of view in a conference call, asking a colleague for feedback on a report, admitting that a project is over budget or behind schedule, and so on – the myriad verbal interactions that make up the world of twenty-first century work.

There is, of course, a range of interpersonal riskiness involved in speaking up. Some cases of speaking up occur after significant trepidation; others feel reasonably straightforward and feasible. Still others simply don't occur – as in the case of Christina in the NICU – because one has weighed the risk (consciously or not) and come out on the side of silence. The free exchange of ideas, concerns or questions is routinely hindered by interpersonal fear far more often than most managers realize. This kind of fear cannot be directly seen. Silence – when voice was possible – rarely announces itself! The moment passes, and no one is the wiser except the person who held back.

I have defined psychological safety as the belief that the work environment is safe for interpersonal risk taking.[6] The concept refers to the experience of feeling able to speak up with relevant ideas, questions, or concerns. Psychological safety is present when colleagues trust and respect each other and feel able – even obligated – to be candid.

In workplaces with psychological safety, the kinds of small and potentially consequential moments of silence experienced by Christina are far less likely. Speaking up occurs instead, facilitating the open and authentic communication that shines the light on problems, mistakes, and opportunities for improvement and increases the sharing of knowledge and ideas.

As you will see, our understanding of interpersonal risk management at work has advanced since Goffman studied the fascinating micro-dynamics of face-saving. We now know that psychological safety emerges as a property of a group, and that groups in organizations tend to have very interpersonal climates. Even in a company with a strong corporate culture, you will find pockets of both high and low psychological safety. Take, for instance, the hospital where Christina works. One patient care unit might be a place where nurses readily speak up to challenge or inquire about care decisions, while in another it feels downright impossible. These differences in workplace climate shape behavior in subtle but powerful ways.

An Accidental Discovery

As much as I'm passionate about the ideas in this book, I didn't set out to study psychological safety on purpose. As a first-year doctoral student in the process of clarifying my research interests for my eventual dissertation, I had been fortunate to join a large team studying medical error in several hospitals. This was a great way to gain research experience and to sharpen my general interest in how organizations can learn and succeed in an increasingly challenging, fast-paced world. I had long been interested in the idea of learning from mistakes for achieving excellence.

My role in the research team was to examine the effects of teamwork on medical error rates. The team had numerous experts, including physicians who could judge whether human error had occurred and trained nurse investigators who would review medical charts and interview frontline caregivers in patient care units in two hospitals to obtain error rates for each of these teams. These experts were, in effect, getting the data for what would be the dependent variable in my study – the team-level error rates. This was a great arrangement for me, for at least two reasons. First, I lacked the medical expertise to identify medical errors on my own. Second, from a research methods perspective, it meant that my survey measures of team effectiveness would not be subject to experimenter bias – the cognitive tendency for a researcher to see what she wants to see rather than what is actually there. So the independence of our data collection activities was an important strength of the study.[7]

The nurse investigators collected error data over a six-month period. During the first month, I distributed a validated instrument called the *team diagnostic survey* to everyone working in the study units – doctors, nurses, and clerks – slightly altering the language of the survey items to make sure they would make sense to people working in a hospital, and adding a few new items to assess people's views about making mistakes. I also spent time on the floor (in the patient care units) observing how each of the teams worked.

Going into the study, I hypothesized, not surprisingly, that the most effective teams would make the fewest errors. Of course, I had to wait six months for the data on the dependent variable (the error rates) to be fully collected. And here is where the story took an unexpected turn.

First, the good news (from a research perspective anyway). There was variance! Error rates across teams were strikingly different; indeed, there was a 10-fold difference in the number of human errors per thousand patient days (a standard measure) from the best to the worst unit on what I sincerely believed was an important performance measure. A wrong medicine dosage, for example, might be reported every three weeks on one ward but every other day on another. Likewise, the team survey data also showed significant variance. Some teams were much stronger – their members reported more mutual respect, more collaboration, more confidence in their ability to deliver great results, more satisfaction, and so on – than others.

When all of the error and survey data were compiled, I was at first thrilled. Running the statistical analysis, I immediately saw that there was a significant correlation between the independently collected error rates and the measures of team effectiveness from my survey. But then I looked closely and noticed something wrong. The direction of the correlation was exactly the opposite of what I had predicted. Better teams were apparently making *more* – not fewer – mistakes than less strong teams. Worse, the correlation was statistically significant. I briefly wondered how I could tell my dissertation chair the bad news. This was a problem.

No, it was a puzzle.

Did better teams *really* make more mistakes? I thought about the need for communication between doctors and nurses to produce safe, error-free care. The need to ask for help, to double-check each other's work to make sure, in this complex and customized work environment, that patients received the best care. I knew that great care meant that clinicians had to team up effectively. It just didn't make sense that good teamwork would lead to more errors. I wondered for a moment whether better teams got overconfident over time and then became sloppy. That might explain my perplexing result. But why *else* might better teams have higher error rates?

And then came the eureka moment. What if the better teams had a climate of openness that made it easier to report and discuss error? The good teams, I suddenly thought, don't *make* more mistakes; they *report* more. But having this insight was a far cry from proving it.

I decided to hire a research assistant to go out and study these patient care teams carefully, with no preconceptions. He didn't know which units had made more mistakes, or which ones scored better on the team survey. He didn't even know my new hypothesis. In research terms, he was "blind" to both the hypothesis and the previously collected data.[8]

Here is what he found. Through quiet observation and open-ended interviews about all aspects of the work environment, he discovered that the teams varied wildly in whether people felt able to talk about mistakes. And these differences were almost perfectly correlated with the detected error rates. In short, people in the better teams (as measured by my survey, but unbeknownst to the research assistant) talked openly about the risks of errors, often trying to find new ways to catch and prevent them. It would take another couple of years before I labeled this climate difference psychological safety. But the accidental finding set me off on a new and fruitful research direction: to find out how interpersonal climate might vary across groups in other workplaces, and whether it might matter for learning and speaking up in other industries – not just in healthcare.

Over the years, in studies in companies, hospitals, and even government agencies, my doctoral students and I have found that psychological safety does indeed vary, and that it matters very much for predicting both learning behavior and objective measures of performance. Today, researchers like me have conducted dozens of studies showing greater learning, performance, and even lower mortality as a result of psychological safety. In Chapter 2, I will tell you about some of the studies.

In that initial study over two decades ago, I learned that psychological safety varies across groups *within* hospitals. Since that time, I have replicated this finding in many industry settings. The data are consistent in this simple but interesting finding: psychological safety seems to "live" at the level of the group. In other words, in the organization where you work, it's likely that different groups have different interpersonal experiences; in some, it may be easy to speak up and bring your full self to work. In others, speaking up might be experienced as a last resort – as it did in some of the patient-care teams I studied. That's because psychological safety is very much shaped by local leaders. As I will elaborate later in this book, subsequent research has borne out my initial, accidental discovery.

Standing on Giants' Shoulders

I might have stumbled into psychological safety by accident, but understanding of its importance traces back to organizational change research in the early 1960s. Massachusetts Institute of Technology professors Edgar Schein and Warren Bennis wrote about the need for psychological safety to help people cope with the uncertainty and anxiety of organizational change in a 1965 book.[9] Schein later noted that psychological safety was vital for helping people overcome the defensiveness and "learning anxiety" they face at work, especially when something doesn't go as they'd hoped or expected.[10] Psychological safety, he argued, allows people to focus on achieving shared goals rather than on self-protection.

Later seminal work by Boston University professor William Kahn in 1990 showed how psychological safety fosters employee engagement.[11] Drawing from rich case studies of a summer camp and an architecture firm, Kahn explored the conditions in which people at work can engage and express themselves rather than disengage or defend themselves. Meaningfulness and psychological safety both mattered. But Kahn further noted that people are more likely to believe they'll be given the benefit of the doubt – a wonderful way to think about psychological safety – when they experience trust and respect at work.

Next, my dissertation introduced and tested the idea that psychological safety was a group-level phenomenon.[12] Building on the unexpected insights into interpersonal climate from the hospital error study, I studied 51 teams in a manufacturing company in the Midwest, measuring psychological safety on purpose this time. Published in 1999 in a leading academic journal, this research – which later influenced Google's celebrated Project Aristotle, discussed in Chapter 2 – showed that psychological safety differed substantially across teams in the company and that it enabled both team learning behaviors and team performance.[13]

A key insight from this work was that psychological safety is not a personality difference but rather a feature of the workplace that leaders can and must help create. More specifically, in every company or organization I've since studied, even some with famously strong corporate cultures, psychological safety has been found to differ substantially across groups. Nor was psychological safety the result of a random or elusive group chemistry. What was clear was that leaders in some groups had been able to effectively create the conditions for psychological safety while other leaders had not. This is true whether you're looking across floors in a hospital, teams in a factory, branches in a retail bank, or restaurants in a chain.

The results of my dissertation research bolstered my confidence that all of us are subject to subtle interpersonal risks at work that can be mitigated. Whether explicitly or implicitly, when you're at work, you're being evaluated. In a formal sense, someone higher up in the hierarchy is probably tasked with assessing your performance. But informally, peers and subordinates are sizing you up all the time. Our image is perpetually at risk. At any moment, we might come across as ignorant, incompetent, or intrusive, if we do such things as ask questions, admit mistakes, offer ideas, or criticize a plan. Unwillingness to take these small, insubstantial risks can destroy value (and often does, as you will see in Chapters 3 and 4). But they can also be overcome. People at work do not need to be crippled by interpersonal fear. It is possible to build environments, such as those showcased in Chapters 5 and 6, where people are more afraid of failing the customer than of looking bad in front of their colleagues.

Why Fear Is Not an Effective Motivator

Fear may have once acted to motivate assembly line workers on the factory floor or farm workers in the field – jobs that reward individual speed and accuracy in completing repetitive tasks. Most of us have been exposed to, and internalized, the figure of a villainous boss who rules by fear. Indeed, popular culture has exaggerated the stereotype to become comical, as in the animated Pixar film *Ratatouille,* where Remy the rat, the story's cartoon hero, must first overcome the tyrannical restaurant chef who rules the kitchen if he is to realize his dream of becoming a chef.

Worse, many managers – both consciously and not – still believe in the power of fear to motivate. They assume that people who are afraid (of management or of the consequences of underperforming) will work hard to avoid unpleasant consequences, and good things will happen. This might make sense if the work is straightforward and the worker is unlikely to run into any problems or have any ideas for improvement. But for jobs where learning or collaboration is required for success, fear is not an effective motivator.

Brain science has amply demonstrated that fear inhibits learning and cooperation. Early twentieth century behavioral scientist Ivan Pavlov, who housed dozens of dogs in his laboratory, found their ability to learn behavioral tasks was inhibited after they'd been frightened in the Leningrad flood of 1924. The lab workers who swam in to rescue the animals reported that water had filled the cage, with only the dogs' noses visible above water.[14] Since then, neuroscientists have discovered that fear activates the amygdala, the section of the brain that is responsible for detecting threats. If you've ever felt your heart pound your palms sweat before making an important presentation, that's due to the automatic responses of your amygdala.

Fear inhibits learning. Research in neuroscience shows that fear consumes physiologic resources, diverting them from parts of the brain that manage working memory and process new information. This impairs analytic thinking, creative insight, and problem solving.[15] This is why it's hard for people to do their best work when they are afraid. As a result, how psychologically safe a person feels strongly shapes the propensity to engage in learning behaviors, such as information sharing, asking for help, or experimenting. It also affects employee satisfaction. Hierarchy (or, more specifically, the fear it creates when not handled well) reduces psychological safety. Research shows that lower-status team members generally feel less safe than higher-status members. Research also shows that we are constantly assessing our relative status, monitoring how we stack up against others, again mostly subconsciously. Further, those lower in the status hierarchy experience stress in the presence of those with higher status.[16]

Psychological safety describes a belief that neither the formal nor informal consequences of interpersonal risks, like asking for help or admitting a failure, will be punitive. In psychologically safe environments, people believe that if they make a mistake or ask for help, others will not react badly. Instead, candor is both allowed and expected. Psychological safety exists when people feel their workplace is an environment where they can speak up, offer ideas, and ask questions without fear of being punished or embarrassed. Is this a place where new ideas are welcomed and built upon? Or picked apart and ridiculed? Will your colleagues embarrass or punish you for offering a different point of view? Will they think less of you for admitting you don't understand something?

What Psychological Safety Is Not

As more and more consultants, managers, and other observers of organizational life are talking about psychological safety, the risk of misunderstanding what the concept is all about has intensified. Here are some common misconceptions, along with clarifications.

Psychological Safety Is Not About Being Nice

Working in a psychologically safe environment does not mean that people always agree with one another for the sake of being nice. It also does not mean that people offer unequivocal praise or unconditional support for everything you have to say. In fact, you could say it's the opposite. Psychological safety is about candor, about making it possible for productive disagreement and free exchange of ideas. It goes without saying that these are vital to learning and innovation. Conflict inevitably arises in any workplace. Psychological safety enables people on different sides of a conflict to speak candidly about what's bothering them.

In many companies in which I've consulted or conducted research, I'll hear a variation of the following: "We have a problem with '[Company Name] Nice'." They go on to describe the common experience of being "polite" to one another in meetings, only to disagree later when people talk privately in the hallway, along with a tendency to not actually implement that which was discussed in the meeting. Nice, in short, is not synonymous with psychologically safe. In a related vein, psychological safety does not imply ease or comfort. In contrast, psychological safety is about candor and willingness to engage in productive conflict so as to learn from different points of view.

Psychological Safety Is Not a Personality Factor

Some have interpreted psychological safety as a synonym for extroversion. They might have previously concluded that people don't speak up at work because they're shy or lack confidence, or simply prefer to keep to themselves. However, research shows that the experience of psychological safety at work is not correlated with introversion and extroversion.[17] This is because psychological safety refers to the work climate, and climate affects people with different personality traits in roughly similar ways. In a psychologically safe climate, people will offer ideas and voice their concerns regardless of whether they tend toward introversion or extroversion.

Psychological Safety Is Not Just Another Word for Trust

Although trust and psychological safety have much in common, they are not interchangeable concepts. A key difference is that psychological safety is experienced at a group level. People working together tend to have similar perceptions of whether or not the climate is psychologically safe. Trust, on the other hand, refers to interactions between two individuals or parties; trust exists in the mind of an individual and pertains to a specific target individual or organization. For instance, you might trust one colleague but not another. Or, to illustrate trust in an organization, you might trust a particular company to uphold high standards.

Further, psychological safety describes a temporally immediate experience. Whereas trust describes an expectation about whether another person or organization can be counted on to do what it promises to do in some future moment, the psychological experience of safety pertains to expectations about immediate interpersonal consequences. For example, when Christina fails to ask a physician about a medication she believes might be warranted, she is worried about the immediate consequence of asking her question – the risk of being berated or humiliated. Trust pertains instead to whether Christina believes the doctor can and will do the right thing for patients. One way to put this is that trust is about giving others the benefit of the doubt, and psychological safety relates to whether others will give you the benefit of the doubt when, for instance, you have asked for help or admitted a mistake.

Psychological Safety Is Not About Lowering Performance Standards

Psychological safety is not an "anything goes" environment where people are not expected to adhere to high standards or meet deadlines. It is not about becoming "comfortable" at work. This is particularly important to understand because many managers appreciate the appeal of error-reporting, help-seeking, and other proactive behavior to help their organizations learn. At the same time, they implicitly equate psychological safety with relaxing performance standards – that is, with an inability to, in their words, "hold people accountable." This conveys a misunderstanding of the nature of the

	Low Standards	High Standards
High Psychological Safety	*Comfort Zone*	*Learning & High Performance Zone*
Low Psychological Safety	*Apathy Zone*	*Anxiety Zone*

Figure 1.1   How Psychological Safety Relates to Performance Standards.[18]

phenomenon. Psychological safety enables candor and openness and, as such, thrives in an environment of mutual respect. It means that people believe they can – and must – be forthcoming at work. In fact, psychological safety is conducive to setting ambitious goals and working toward them together. Psychological safety sets the stage for a more honest, more challenging, more collaborative, and thus also more effective work environment. As Chapter 2 will explain, researchers around the world have found that psychological safety promotes high performance in a wide range of work environments and industries. In short, as depicted in Figure 1.1, psychological safety and performance standards are two separate, equally important dimensions – both of which affect team and organizational performance in a complex interdependent environment.

When both psychological safety and performance standards are low (lower left), the workplace becomes a kind of "apathy zone." People show up at work, but their hearts and minds are elsewhere. They choose self-protection over exertion every time. Discretionary effort might be spent perusing social media or on making each other's lives miserable.

Next, in workplaces with high psychological safety but low performance standards (upper left), people generally enjoy working with one another; they are open and collegial but not challenged by the work. Let's call this the "comfort zone." Today, fewer workplaces around the world than ever fall into this quadrant, and it's just as well. When employees are comfortable being themselves but don't see a compelling reason to seek additional challenge, there won't be much learning or innovation – nor will there be much engagement or fulfillment.

But it's not the comfort or apathy zones that worry me most. What keeps me up at night is the lower right-hand quadrant. When performance standards are high but psychological safety is low – a situation far too common in today's workplace – employees are anxious about speaking up, and both work quality and workplace safety suffer. In Chapters 3 and 4, you will see many such workplaces. Managers in these organizations have unfortunately confused setting high standards with good management. High standards in a context where there is uncertainty or interdependence (or both) combined with a lack of psychological safety comprise a recipe for suboptimal performance. And sometimes, as you will see in the chapters ahead, it's a recipe for disaster. I call this the "anxiety zone." Here I'm not referring to anxiety about being able to accomplish a demanding goal or about the competitive business environment but rather to interpersonal anxiety. The experience of having a question or an idea but not feeling able to share it can be deeply unsatisfying at work. And it is a serious risk factor in any company facing volatility, uncertainty, complexity, and ambiguity, or VUCA – the acronym introduced by the U.S. Army War College and widely used in the business world today.[19]

Finally, when standards and psychological safety are both high (upper right in Figure 1.1), I call this the learning zone. If the work is uncertain, interdependent, or both, this is also the high-performance zone. Here, people can collaborate, learn from each other, and get complex, innovative work done. In a VUCA world, high performance occurs when people are actively learning as they go.

Measuring Psychological Safety

Researchers and managers have useful tools at their disposal to measure psychological safety, and these are in the public domain. Surveys are certainly the most popular of these, and Figure 1.2 presents seven survey items, introduced in my dissertation and widely used in

1. If you make a mistake on this team, it is often held against you. (R)

2. Members of this team are able to bring up problems and tough issues.

3. People on this team sometimes reject others for being different. (R)

4. It is safe to take a risk on this team.

5. It is difficult to ask other members of this team for help. (R)

6. No one on this team would deliberately act in a way that undermines my efforts.

7. Working with members of this team, my unique skills and talents are valued and utilized.

Figure 1.2   A Survey Measure of Psychological Safety.[20]

the research community ever since. I use a seven-point Likert scale (from strongly agree to strongly disagree) to obtain responses, but a five-point scale works as well. Note that three of the seven items are expressed positively, such that agreement indicates greater psychological safety, and three are expressed negatively (represented in Figure 1.2 with an "R" for reverse), such that disagreement is consistent with higher psychological safety. In analyzing the data, therefore, it is important to "reverse score" data from the negatively worded items, where a 1 in the data set is converted to a 7, a 7 to a 1, a 2 to a 6, and so on.

Fortunately, the psychological safety measure has proven to be robust despite variations in both the number and the wording of the items used. By robust, I mean that the collected data demonstrate the necessary statistical properties, such as inter-item reliability as measured by Chronbach's alpha and predictive validity, as measured by correlations with other variables of interest. The appendix at the back of the book shows some of the survey item variations of which I am aware. The measure has also been translated into numerous other languages, including German, Spanish, Russian, Japanese, Chinese, and Korean, all of which have yielded robust research findings.

In purely qualitative case-study research, interview data can be coded to detect the presence or absence of psychological safety.

Several examples of research where this approach has been taken are found in Chapter 2. Another fruitful approach is to provide interviewees with hypothetical scenarios that fall into gray areas at work and ask them what they or their colleagues might do in that situation. When people trust that their answers will be kept confidential, they will be quite open in reporting that they would hold back unless they were extremely confident that what they want to say will be well received. Well-designed vignettes, with questions asking about how people would respond, can also be used to collect data from a larger number of employees than individual interviews will allow. I will mention examples of both approaches in Chapter 2.

Psychological Safety Is Not Enough

I do not mean to imply that psychological safety is all you need for high performance. Not even close. I like to say that psychological safety takes off the brakes that keep people from achieving what's possible. But it's not the fuel that powers the car. In any challenging industry setting, leaders have two vital tasks. One, they must build psychological safety to spur learning and avoid preventable failures; two, they must set high standards and inspire and enable people to reach them. Setting high standards remains a crucial management task. So does sharing, sharpening, and continually emphasizing a worthy purpose.

The key insight to take away from this chapter is that in most workplaces today it's simply not possible to ensure excellence by inspecting proverbial widgets. In knowledge work, excellence cannot be measured easily and simply along the way. More to the point, it's almost impossible to determine whether people have failed to hit the highest possible standards. It takes time for the results of uncertain programs to become clear, and reliably measuring good process is difficult. In other words, today's leaders must motivate people to do their very best work by inspiring them, coaching them, providing feedback, and making excellence a rewarding experience. Motivating and coaching both receive substantial attention already. What I hope you will take away from this chapter is that making the environment safe for open communication about challenges, concerns, and opportunities is one of the most important leadership responsibilities in the twenty-first century.

Chapter 1 Takeaways

- People constantly manage interpersonal risk at work, consciously and not, inhibiting the open sharing of ideas, questions, and concerns.
- When people don't speak up, the organization's ability to innovate and grow is threatened.
- Psychological safety describes a climate where people feel safe enough to take interpersonal risks by speaking up and sharing concerns, questions, or ideas.
- Leaders of teams, departments, branches, or other groups within companies play an important role in shaping psychological safety.

Endnotes

1. Rozovsky, J. "The five keys to a successful Google team." *re:Work Blog.* November 17, 2015. https://rework.withgoogle.com/blog/five-keys-to-a-successful-google-team/ Accessed June 13, 2018.
2. Goffman, E. *The Presentation of Self in Everyday Life.* Overlook Press, 1973. Print.
3. Edmondson, A.C. "Managing the risk of learning: Psychological safety in work teams." *International Handbook of Organizational Teamwork and Cooperative Working.* Ed. M. West. London: Blackwell, 2003, 255–276.
4. Merchant, N. "Your Silence is Hurting Your Company." *Harvard Business Review.* September 7, 2011. https://hbr.org/2011/09/your-silence-is-hurting-your-company Accessed June 13, 2018.

5. Milliken, F.J., Morrison, E.W., & Hewlin, P.F. "An Exploratory Study of Employee Silence: Issues that Employees Don't Communicate Upward and Why." *Journal of Management Studies* 40.6 (2003): 1453–1476.

6. Edmondson, A.C. "Psychological Safety and Learning Behavior in Work Teams." *Administrative Science Quarterly* 44.2 (1999): 350–83.

7. Edmondson, A.C. "Learning from Mistakes Is Easier Said Than Done: Group and Organizational Influences on the Detection and Correction of Human Error." *The Journal of Applied Behavioral Science* 32.1 (1996): 5–28.

8. The research assistant, Andy Molinsky, is now an accomplished scholar and Professor of International Management and Organizational Behavior at Brandeis University.

9. Schein, E.H. & Bennis, W.G. *Personal and Organizational Change through Group Methods: The Laboratory Approach.* Wiley, 1965. Print.

10. Schein, E.H. "How Can Organizations Learn Faster? The Challenge of Entering the Green Room." *Sloan Management Review* 34.2 (1993): 85–92. Print.

11. Kahn, W.A. "Psychological Conditions of Personal Engagement and Disengagement at Work." *Academy of Management Journal* 33.4 (1990): 692–724.

12. Edmondson, A.C. "Learning from Mistakes Is Easier Said Than Done: Group and Organizational Influences on the Detection and Correction of Human Error." *The Journal of Applied Behavioral Science* 32.1 (1996): 5–28.

13. Edmondson, A.C. (1999), op cit.

14. Todes, D.P. *Ivan Pavlov: A Russian Life in Science.* Oxford University Press, 2014. Print.

15. Rock, D. "Managing with the Brain in Mind." *strategy+business.* August 27, 2009. https://www.strategy-business.com/article/09306?gko=5df7f Accessed June 13, 2018.

16. Zink, C.F., Tong, Y., Chen, Q., Bassett, D.S., Stein, J.L., & Meyer-Lindenberg, A. "Know Your Place: Neural Processing of Social Hierarchy in Humans." *Neuron* 58.2 (2008): 273–83.

17. Edmondson, A.C. & Mogelof, J.P. "Explaining Psychological Safety in Innovation Teams: Organizational Culture, Team Dynamics, or Personality?" *Creativity and Innovation in Organizational Teams.* Ed. L. Thompson & H. Choi. Mahwah, NJ: Lawrence Erlbaum Associates Press, 2005: 109–36.

18. This is a modified version of the framework first published by Edmondson, A.C. "The Competitive Imperative of Learning." *Harvard Business*

Review. July–August, 2008. Print. It was later published in Edmondson, A.C. *Teaming: How Organizations Learn, Innovate, and Compete in the Knowledge Economy*. San Francisco: Jossey-Bass, 2012. Print.

19. Stiehm, J.H. & Townsend, N.W. *The U.S. Army War College: Military Education in a Democracy*. Temple University Press, 2002. Print.

20. See Edmondson, A.C. "Psychological Safety and Learning Behavior in Work Teams." *Administrative Science Quarterly* 44.2 (1999): 350–83.

2 | The Paper Trail

"Your greatest fear as a CEO is that people aren't telling you the truth."

—Mark Costa[1]

Mark Costa, CEO of Eastman Chemical Company, was speaking to a classroom full of second-year MBA students at the Harvard Business School in the late spring of 2018. The students were paying unusually close attention; there was something about his confidence, his energy – and indeed his taking the time to share his insights with them – that exuded "role model." An alumnus of the school, Costa had spent many years in strategy consulting before taking an executive role at Eastman – from which he was later promoted to run the company. Now four years into his tenure as CEO, he clearly relished both the opportunity and the responsibility of leading the $10 billion-dollar global specialty chemical manufacturer headquartered in Kingsport, Tennessee. Under Costa's leadership, the portion of sales accounted for by innovative specialty products rather than commodity products had steadily risen, consistent with a crucial strategic goal he'd articulated for the company. Financial performance was correspondingly strong. To accomplish this, engaging the expertise, ideas, and market knowledge of Eastman's 15 000 employees around the world had been mission critical.

For the benefit of the students for whom diplomas and new jobs were imminent, Costa reflected on what he had learned in the quarter century since he'd graduated from business school. As the quote at the opening of the chapter conveys, he stated – likely surprising many of them – that his greatest fear as CEO was of not knowing what's really going on. He worked hard to make it clear to his employees that he wanted the truth—good, bad, ugly, or disappointing. He explained to the class that, as a leader, you have to "be willing to be vulnerable and be open about your mistakes so others feel safe" to report their own.[2] Alluding to the risk of hubris, Costa added, "If you think you have all the answers, you should quit. Because you're going to be wrong."[3]

In today's organizations, psychological safety is not a "nice-to-have." It's not an employee perk, like free lunch or game rooms, that you might care about so as to make people happy at work. In contrast, I'll argue that psychological safety is *essential* to unleashing talent and creating value. Hiring talent simply isn't enough anymore. People have to be in workplaces where they are able and willing to *use* their talent. In any organization that requires knowledge – and especially in one that requires integrating knowledge from diverse areas of expertise – psychological safety is a requirement for success. In short, when companies rely on knowledge and collaboration for innovation and growth, whether or not to invest in building a climate of psychological safety is no longer a choice. Every manager must follow Mark Costa's lead.

Not a Perk

In any company confronting conditions that might be characterized as volatility, uncertainty, complexity, and ambiguity (VUCA), psychological safety is directly tied to the bottom line. This is because

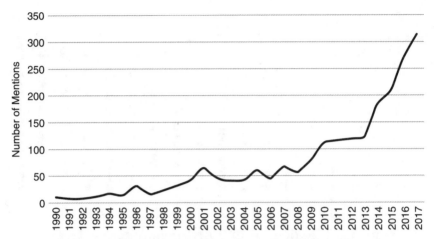

Figure 2.1 Mentions of Psychological Safety in Popular Media.[4]

employee observations, questions, ideas, and concerns can provide vital information about what's going on – in the market and in the organization. Add to that today's growing emphasis on diversity, inclusion, and belonging at work, and it becomes clear that psychological safety is a vital leadership responsibility. It can make or break an employee's ability to contribute, to grow and learn, and to collaborate.

One measure of practitioner interest in psychological safety can be found in the term's use frequency in the popular media. To gauge the popularity of the concept, I used Factiva to see how many times the term had been mentioned in newspapers, articles, blogs, and other news media. The graph in Figure 2.1 depicts the results, indicating mentions of "psychological safety" and its variants (i.e. psychologically safe) each year since 1990.

The uptick in mentions in recent years reflects, I believe, growing recognition that psychological safety matters in any environment in which people are attempting to do something novel or challenging. From leading a project team in the office[5] to caring for patients in the hospital ward,[6] from coaching a cricket squad on the pitch[7] to teaching and counseling young students at school,[8] from encouraging

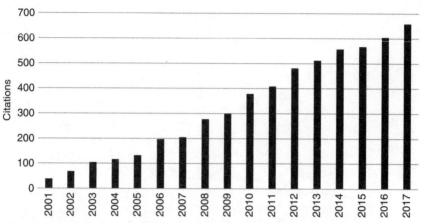

Figure 2.2   Citations of 1999 Article Introducing Team Psychological Safety.[12]

others to speak out about wrong-doing[9] to even reaching Mars(!),[10] psychological safety is essential for communicating, collaborating, experimenting, and ensuring the well-being of others in a wide variety of team and organizational settings.

Another measure of interest on the part of researchers can be found in academic citations to the article that introduced the concept and measure of team psychological safety.[11] As shown in Figure 2.2, the article has been frequently cited, with each year since its publication in 1999 showing more citations than the year before. This is a quick and simple index of the degree to which academic research has found that the psychological safety variable explains outcomes of interest.

This chapter reviews the evidence for psychological safety's benefits from two decades of research, laying the foundation for the real-world stories of low and high psychological safety workplaces that lie ahead in Part II. Over the past 20 years, scholars, consultants, and company insiders have published dozens of rigorous studies showing effects of psychological safety in a variety of industry settings. By sharing some of the highlights, I hope to give the reader confidence in the importance of psychological safety in the modern workplace. My hope is that knowing that the ideas and stories in this book are backed up by data will motivate many readers to act on this knowledge.

The Research

My colleagues and I reviewed the academic literature on psychological safety. We were surprised by the number of studies we found and by the range of settings in which psychological safety has been examined. Studies conducted in companies, government organizations, nonprofits, school systems, hospitals, and classrooms highlight the growing cross-sector interest in psychological safety.

Reading more than 100 articles, we found plenty of evidence that psychological safety matters. It affects measurable outcomes ranging from employee error reporting[13] to company return on investment.[14] Unfortunately, the research also makes clear that many workplaces lack psychological safety, cutting themselves off from the kinds of employee input, engagement, and learning that are so vital to success in a complex and turbulent world.

I organized the studies into five categories. Group 1 reveals the extent to which psychological safety is lacking in many workplaces. Group 2, which is the largest, investigates relationships between psychological safety and learning. In these studies, we find the evidence that psychological safety leads to, among others, creativity, error reporting, and knowledge sharing, as well as behaviors that detect the need for change or that help teams and organizations make change. Group 3 finds positive relationships between psychological safety and performance, and Group 4 finds positive relationships between psychological safety and employee engagement.

Lastly, Group 5 encompasses what researchers call "moderator studies," in which psychological safety alters a relationship between another team attribute and an outcome, such as team performance. A team attribute might be diverse expertise, which would naturally challenge the team to figure out how to work effectively. Similarly, a team with members located in multiple geographic regions might struggle to coordinate. Studies show that psychological safety makes it easier for teams to manage such challenges. When people can speak up, ask questions, and get the help they need from each other to sort things out, they are more likely to overcome the barriers created by working together across diverse disciplines or time zones.

1. An Epidemic of Silence

Chances are you've had the experience at work when you did not ask a question you really wanted to ask. Or you may have wanted to offer an idea but stayed quiet instead. Several studies show that these types of silence are painfully common. Collecting and analyzing data from interviews with employed adults, studies have investigated when and why people feel unable to speak up in the workplace. From this work we learn, first and foremost, *that people often hold back even when they believe that what they have to say could be important for the organization, for the customer, or for themselves.*

There is a poignancy in these discoveries. No one gains from the silence. Teams miss out on insights. Those who fail to speak up often report regret or pain. Some wish they had spoken up. Others recognize they could be experiencing more fulfillment and meaning in their jobs were they more able to contribute. Those deprived of hearing a colleague's comments may not know what they are missing, but the fact is that problems go unreported, improvement opportunities are missed, and occasionally, tragic failures occur that could have been avoided.

In an early study of workplace silence, New York University management researchers Frances Milliken, Elizabeth Morrison, and Patricia Hewlin interviewed 40 full-time employees working in consulting, financial services, media, pharmaceuticals, and advertising, to understand why employees failed to speak up at work and what issues they failed to raise most often.[15] When pressed to explain why they remained silent, people often said they did not want to be seen in a bad light. Another common reason was not wanting to embarrass or upset someone. Still others expressed a sense of futility – along the lines of, "it won't matter anyway; why bother?" A few mentioned fear of retaliation. But the two most frequently mentioned reasons for remaining silent were one, fear of being viewed or labeled negatively, and two, fear of damaging work relationships. These fears, which are definitionally the opposite of psychological safety, have no place in the fearless organization.

What issues employees wanted to speak up about were both organizational and personal. They ranged from concerns that are understandably difficult to raise: for example, about harassment, a supervisor's competence, or having made a mistake. More surprisingly, however, they also held back on suggestions for improving a work process. In short, as later research would demonstrate more systematically, people at work are not only failing to speak up with potentially threatening or embarrassing content, they are also withholding ideas for improvement. Notably, every individual interviewee reported failing to speak up on at least one occasion. Most had found themselves in situations where they were very concerned about an issue and yet still did not raise it to a supervisor.

A later and larger study conducted in a manufacturing company used survey data to identify very similar reasons for silence.[16] Specifically, employees who did not feel psychologically safe to speak up cited reasons that included fear of damaging a relationship, lack of confidence, and self-protection. In another study, social psychologist Renee Tynan surveyed business school students about their relationships with a prior boss to gain insight into when and why people do (or don't) communicate their thoughts upward. She found that when people felt psychologically safe, they spoke up to their bosses. They were able to ask for help and admit errors, despite interpersonal risk. When they did not feel psychologically safe, they tended to keep quiet or to distort their message so as not to upset their bosses.

A few years ago, University of Virginia Professor Jim Detert and I interviewed more than 230 employees in a large multinational high-tech company.[17] We asked interviewees, who spanned all levels, regions, and functions, to describe instances in which they did and did not speak up at work to their managers or anyone else higher in the company. Here too, all individuals could readily describe a time in which they failed to speak up about something they believed mattered. Jim and I combed through the thousands of pages of accumulated responses to find out what drove people to speak up – and, perhaps more importantly, what drove them to hold back.

Consider the manufacturing technician in a US plant who told us he didn't share an idea he had for speeding up the production process. When we asked why, he replied, "I have kids in college." At first glance, a nonsensical reply. But his meaning was clear; he felt he could not take the risk of speaking up because he could not afford to lose his job. When we probed further, hoping to hear a story about someone losing a job related to speaking up, the associate admitted that it really didn't work that way. In fact, he replied, "Oh, everyone knows we never fire anybody." He was not speaking sarcastically; he was admitting that his reticence to rock the boat with what he believed was a good idea was irrational, and deep down he understood that. Yet the gravitational pull of silence – even when bosses are well-meaning and don't think of themselves as intimidating – can be overwhelming. People at work are vulnerable to a kind of implicit logic in which safe is simply better than sorry. Many have simply inherited beliefs from their earliest years of schooling or training. If they stop to think more deeply, they may realize they've erred too far on the side of caution. But that kind of reflection is rarely prompted.

Ultimately, we discovered a small set of common, largely taken-for-granted beliefs about speaking up at work. We called them *implicit theories of voice*. Shown in Table 2.1, they are essentially beliefs about when it is and isn't appropriate to speak to higher ups in an organization. To test these implicit theories, gleaned from one company, Jim and I conducted a vignette study with managers from many other companies. We designed fictional vignettes to test when and if people would employ specific decision rules in determining whether or not to speak up. For example, one vignette involved an important correction an employee wanted to share with the boss; in

Table 2.1   Taken-for-granted Rules for Voice at Work.

Taken-for-granted Rule Governing when to Speak or Remain Silent	Examples from Interviews
Don't criticize something the boss may have helped create.	"It's inherently risky since bosses may feel personal ownership of the tasks I am suggesting are problematic." "The boss may have created these processes and may be offended because he's attached to them."
Don't speak unless you have solid data.	"I think that presenting an under-developed, under-researched idea is never a good idea." "You are questioning their ideas and had better have proof to back up your statements."
Don't speak up if the boss's boss is present.	"If there is a higher level individual present it is risky because you would be afraid that your direct boss would feel as if you were going over their head." "My boss would see [speaking up to his boss] as undermining and insubordinate."
Don't speak up in a group with anything negative about the work to prevent boss from losing face.	"Managers hate to be put on the spot in front of others. It is best to brief them one-on-one so the boss doesn't look bad in front of the group." "You should pass it by the boss in private first, so you don't 'cut his legs out from under him.'"
Speaking up brings career consequences.	"To stop or criticize a project would be a career ender at our place." "The long-term consequences are bad because [higher ups] will resent being put on the spot."

one of the versions of the vignette, the boss's boss was present. In the other vignette, only the boss was present. The managers we studied were significantly more likely to point out the correction if the boss's boss was not present.

By and large, these beliefs (taken-for-granted rules) about speaking up make it harder to achieve productivity, innovation, or employee engagement. It's an old truism that bad news doesn't travel up the hierarchy. But what we found is that people err so far on the side of caution at work that they routinely hold back great ideas – not just bad news. They intuitively recognize what Jim and I call the asymmetry of voice and silence. Consider the automatic calculus that governs speaking up. As depicted in Table 2.2, voice is effortful and might (but might not) make a real difference in a crucial moment. Unfortunately, much of the time the potential benefit will take a while to materialize and might not even happen at all. Silence is instinctive and safe; it offers self-protection benefits, and these are both immediate and certain.

Table 2.2   Why Silence Wins in the Voice–Silence Calculation.

	Who Benefits	When Benefit Occurs	Certainty of Benefit
Voice	The organization and/ or its customers	After some delay	Low
Silence	Oneself	Immediately	High

Another way to think about the voice-silence asymmetry is captured in the phrase "no one was ever fired for silence." The instinct to play it safe is powerful. People in organizations don't spontaneously take interpersonal risks. We don't want to stumble into a sacred cow. We can be completely confident that we'll be safe if we are silent, and we lack confidence that our voices will really make a difference – a voice inhibiting combination.

Another of the implicit theories of voice that Jim and I found that explains why people hold back on good ideas, not just bad news, is related to a fear of insulting someone higher up in the organization by implying that the current systems or processes are problematic. What if the current system is effectively the boss's baby? By suggesting a change, we might be calling the boss's baby ugly. Better to stay silent.

In failing to challenge these widely held taken-for-granted speaking rules, employees around the world at this particular company (which, ironically, was dependent on employee expertise and ideas for its future success) were depriving their colleagues of their ideas and ingenuity. They were depriving themselves as well – missing out on the satisfaction of the chance to act on their ideas and create change. Instead of helping to create a learning organization, they were just showing up and doing their jobs.

2. A Work Environment that Supports Learning

Given this well-documented tendency for people in the workplace to choose silence over voice, sometimes it seems surprising that anyone ever speaks up at all with potentially sensitive or interpersonally threatening content. This is where psychological safety comes in. A growing number of studies find that psychological safety *can* exist at work and, when it does, that people do in fact speak up, offer ideas, report errors, and exhibit a great deal more that we can categorize as "learning behavior."

Learning from Mistakes

For example, in a study of nurses in four Belgian hospitals, a team of researchers led by Hannes Leroy explored how head nurses encouraged other nurses to report errors, while also enforcing high standards for safety.[18] The challenge here is one of asking people to perform the highest quality (arguably, error-free) work yet still be willing to talk about the errors that do occur. Leroy and his colleagues surveyed the nurses in 54 departments, measuring a set of interrelated factors.

These were psychological safety, error reporting, the actual number of errors made, and nurses' beliefs about how much the department prioritized patient safety and about whether the head nurse practiced the safety protocols.

Leroy found that groups with higher psychological safety reported more errors to head nurses. That finding was consistent with what I had seen back in graduate school in my study of medication errors.[19] More interestingly, they found that when nurses thought patient safety was a high priority in the department *and* when psychological safety was high, fewer errors were made. In contrast, when psychological safety was low, despite believing in the department's professed commitment to patient safety, staff made more errors. In short, psychologically safe teams made fewer errors and spoke up about them more often. What I have found in similar settings is that good leadership (for instance, on the part of head nurses who demonstrate a commitment to safety and to openness), together with a clear, shared understanding that the work is complex and interdependent, can help groups build psychological safety, which in turn enables the candor that is so essential to ensuring the quality of patient care in modern hospitals.

Quality Improvement: Learn-What and Learn-How

Nearly every organization wants quality improvement. Hospitals, especially, constantly pursue efforts to improve the innumerable processes of patient care. Does it make a difference whether a unit supervisor creates the conditions for psychological safety or simply commands staff to work on improvement projects?

With Wharton Professor Ingrid Nembhard and Boston University Professor Anita Tucker, I studied over a hundred quality improvement (QI) project teams in neonatal intensive care units (NICUs) in 23 North American hospitals.[20] By asking the QI team members to report on what they did to improve unit processes, we found that these clustered into two distinct sets of learning behavior, which we called *learn-what* and *learn-how*. Learn-what described largely independent activities like reading the medical literature to get caught up with the latest research findings. Learn-how, in contrast, was team-based learning that included sharing knowledge, offering suggestions, and brainstorming better approaches.

We were intrigued to find that psychological safety predicted an uptick in learn-how behaviors (those that came with interpersonal risk) but had no statistical relationship whatsoever with the more independent behaviors captured by learn-what activities. This result provided a reassuring demonstration that psychological safety does promote learning by helping people overcome interpersonal risk for engaging in learn-how behaviors. Not surprisingly, for the kinds of learning that you can do alone (read a book, take an online course), psychological safety is not essential. The results also offer support for why psychological safety was not as important in days of yore when work might consist primarily of well-defined tasks such as typing letters for the boss, or passing the surgeon the correct scalpel.

Reducing Workarounds

"Workarounds," a phenomenon identified by Anita Tucker in her remarkable ethnographic study of nurses in the early 2000s, are short-cuts that people take at work when they confront a problem that disrupts their ability to carry out a required task.[21] A workaround accomplishes the immediate goal, but does nothing to diagnose or solve the problem that triggered the workaround in the first place.

The problem with workarounds is that well they, work. They seem to get the job done, but, in so doing, they create new, subtle, problems. First, workarounds sometimes create unintended risks or problems in other areas. For example, confronted with a shortage of a needed material input (say, linens in a hospital unit), a worker might simply find a supply of linens in another unit, thereby getting what she needs but depleting her colleagues who will encounter a shortage later. Second, workarounds delay or prevent process improvement. The problems that trigger workarounds can be seen as small signals of a need for change in a system or process. The workaround bypasses the problem, thereby silencing the signal by getting the immediate job done – but getting it done in a way that is inefficient over the longer term. More difficult, because it would require working across silos, would be for nurses to devise a new linen supply system for all units.

Workarounds can occur when workers do not feel safe enough to speak up and make suggestions to improve the system. Indeed, in another study of hospitals, Jonathon Halbesleben and Cheryl Rathert found that cancer teams with low psychological safety relied more on workarounds, while teams with high psychological safety focused more on diagnosing the problem and improving the process that caused it so it didn't happen again.[22] Halbesleben and Rathert gave us additional evidence that psychological safety is important for organizations interested in achieving process improvement. Their work shows that psychological safety makes it easier for people to speak up about problems and to alter and improve work processes rather than engaging in the counterproductive workarounds.

Another study of process improvement projects, this time in a manufacturing company, also found that projects with greater psychological safety were more successful. Here the researchers studied 52 process-improvement teams following principles of total quality management (TQM). They found that even when employing a highly-structured process improvement technique, interpersonal climate matters for success.[23]

Sharing Knowledge When Confidence Is Low

You might think that speaking up with creative ideas is easier than speaking up about errors. Now, imagine you're at work and you've got an idea you're 95% confident is creative or interesting. You'll probably have no trouble speaking up. Now imagine that same situation but you're only 40% confident of your idea. Most people will hesitate, perhaps trying to size up the receptivity of their colleagues. Stated another way, when you feel extremely confident in the value or veracity of something you want to say, you are more likely to simply open your mouth and say it. But when your confidence in your idea or your knowledge is low, you might hold back.

In a particularly compelling study in several US manufacturing and service companies, University of Minnesota Professor Enno Siemsen and his colleagues found an intuitively interesting relationship between confidence and psychological safety.[24] As expected, the more confident people were in their knowledge, the more they spoke up. More interestingly, a psychologically safe workplace helped people overcome a lack of confidence. In other words, if your workplace is psychologically safe, you're more able to speak up even when you have less confidence. Given that an individual's confidence and the value of his idea are not always tightly linked, the usefulness of psychological safety for facilitating knowledge sharing can be immense. Communication frequency among coworkers also led to psychological safety. In other words, the more we talk to each other, the more comfortable we become doing so.

3. Why Psychological Safety Matters for Performance

To understand why psychological safety promotes performance, we have to step back to reconsider the nature of so much of the work in today's organizations. With routine, predictable, modular work on the decline, more and more of the tasks that people do require judgment, coping with uncertainty, suggesting new ideas, and coordinating and communicating with others. This means that voice is mission critical. And so, for anything but the most independent or routine work, psychological safety is intimately tied to freeing people up to pursue excellence.

When I set out to study 50 teams – including sales, production, new product development, and management teams – in a manufacturing company in the mid 1990s, my goal had been to establish a relationship between psychological safety and learning behavior. While I was at it, I measured performance. I did this in two ways:

The first was self-report, meaning team members confidentially rated their team's performance on a scale of one to seven. The other was somewhat more objective. I asked managers who evaluated the team's work, along with (internal) customers who received the work, to rate each team's performance on a similar scale, also with complete confidentially. Happily, the data showed that teams with psychological safety also had higher performance – a result that held for both types of performance measures.[25]

Researchers Markus Baer and Michael Frese took this question up to the next level of analysis by showing that psychological safety increased company performance in a sample of 47 mid-size German firms in both industrial and services industries. Performance was measured in two ways: longitudinal change in return on assets (holding prior return on assets constant) and executive ratings of company goal achievement.[26] All of the companies were engaged in process innovations. But process innovation efforts only led to higher performance when the organization had psychological safety. In short, process innovation can be a good way to boost firm performance, but a psychologically safe environment helps the investment pay off.

Research also shows a relationship between psychological safety and innovation. For instance, Chi-Cheng Huang and Pin-Chen Jiang collected survey data from 245 members of 60 Research and Development (R&D) teams in several Taiwanese technology firms and found that psychologically safe teams outperformed others.[27] Without psychological safety, the researchers explained, team members were unwilling to offer their ideas or knowledge because of the fear of being rejected or embarrassed. They emphasized the particular importance of psychological safety for teams in R&D because they necessarily have to take risks and confront failure before they achieve success.

Finally, a multi-year study of teams at Google, code-named Project Aristotle, found that psychological safety was the critical factor explaining why some teams outperformed others, as reported in a detailed feature article by Charles Duhigg in the *New York Times Magazine* in 2016, and widely discussed in the blogosphere.[28] Google researchers from the company's sophisticated "people analytics" group reviewed the academic literature on team effectiveness. Their first line of attack was to consider team composition – a variable considered important in historical research on teams, primarily in terms of whether the skills team members hold are a good match for the work they're expected to do.

Led by Julia Rozovsky, the researchers considered people's educational backgrounds, hobbies, friends, personality traits and more, in their analysis a set of 180 teams from all over the company. They found nothing. No mix of personality types or skills or backgrounds emerged that helped explain which teams performed well and which didn't. It seemed like there was no answer to the question of why some teams thrive and others fail. And then, as Duhigg wrote, "When Rozovsky and her Google colleagues encountered the concept of psychological safety in academic papers, it was as if everything suddenly fell into place."[29] What they had discovered was that even the extremely smart, high-powered employees at Google needed a psychologically safe work environment to contribute the talents they had to offer. The team also found four other factors that helped explain team performance – clear goals, dependable colleagues, personally meaningful work, and a belief that the work has impact. As Rozovsky put it, however, reiterating the quote at the start of Chapter 1, "psychological safety was by far the most important . . . it was the underpinning of the other four."[30]

4. Psychologically Safe Employees Are Engaged Employees

Executive interest in employee engagement has taken hold in recent years, building on the longtime focus on employee satisfaction as an important measure for predicting turnover. Today, most managers understand that employee satisfaction is important but incomplete. Satisfaction, which refers to how happy or content employees are, doesn't capture emotional commitment to the work, or motivation to pour oneself into doing a good job. Engagement, defined as the extent to an employee feels passionate about the job and committed to the organization, is seen as an index of willingness to put discretionary effort into one's work. Validated measures of employee engagement are widely available, and most executives recognize employee engagement as a vital element of strong company performance.

Recent studies of employee engagement include attention to psychological safety. For instance, a study in a Midwestern insurance company found that psychological safety predicted worker engagement. In turn, psychological safety was fostered by supportive relationships with coworkers.[31] Another study looked at the relationship between employee trust in top management and employee engagement. With survey data from 170 research scientists working in six Irish research centers, the authors showed that trust in top management led to psychological safety, which in turn promoted work engagement.[32] Finally, a study of Turkish immigrants employed in Germany found that psychological safety was associated with work engagement, mental health, and turnover intentions. Moreover, they found that the positive effects of psychological safety were higher for the immigrants than for the German employees in the same company.[33]

One place where worker engagement really matters is healthcare delivery. Frontline staff confront high stress and emotionally laden work with life and death consequences. Disengaged employees lead to safety risks and to staff turnover. Turnover means higher recruiting and training costs, as well as a higher percentage of less experienced workers on staff. Experts' concerns about staff turnover have thus given rise to interest in improving the healthcare work environment as a strategy for employee retention. In one recent study, a survey of clinical staff at a large metropolitan hospital found that psychological safety was related to commitment to the organization and to patient safety. The authors noted that a work environment in which workers felt safe to speak up about problems was especially important in healthcare for helping people feel able to provide safe care and stay engaged in the work.[34]

5. Psychological Safety as the Extra Ingredient

The fifth and final group of studies emphasizes psychological safety's role in altering the strength of relationships between other variables. In these studies, psychological safety acts (using statistical language) as a moderator that makes other relationships weaker or stronger. Psychological safety has been found to help teams overcome the challenges of geographic dispersion, put conflict to good use, and leverage diversity.

Overcoming Geographic Dispersion

It's increasingly common for teams to have members working in different locations around the world who may not even have met in person. These so-called virtual teams face the related challenges of communicating through electronic media, managing national cultural diversity, coping with time zone differences, and dealing with shifting membership over time. Psychological safety has been shown to help such teams manage these challenges. For instance, in an ambitious study of 14 innovation teams with members dispersed across 18 nations, University of Western Australia Professor Cristina Gibson and Rutgers University Professor Jennifer Gibbs showed that psychological safety helped these dispersed teams navigate the challenges of dispersion.[35] With psychological safety, team members felt less anxious about what others might think of them and were better able to communicate openly.

Putting Conflict to Good Use

Conflict is another challenge most teams confront – whether they work face to face or spread around the globe. In theory, conflict promotes better decision-making and fosters innovation because it ensures consideration of diverse views and perspectives. In practice, however, people are not always good at navigating conflict and putting it to good use.[36] It's easy to get upset or dig in one's heels, effectively squandering the opportunity to improve the work by working through differences. Some recent research has found that psychological safety can make the difference between conflict being put to good use and conflict getting in the way of team performance. For instance, in a study of 117 student project teams, Bret Bradley and his colleagues showed that psychological safety moderated the relationship between conflict and performance such that conflict led to good team performance when teams had high psychological safety and low performance otherwise.[37] They attributed this result to the ability to express relevant ideas and critical discussion without embarrassment or excessive personal conflict between team members.

As you can see, studies that look at psychological safety have been done in many settings, including factories, hospitals, and classrooms. Yet it is also the case that executives wrestling with strategic decisions can benefit from attention to creating a climate of curiosity and candor – in other words, psychological safety. When I studied top management teams with action scientist Diana Smith, we analyzed detailed transcripts of their conversations to show how a psychologically safe climate for candid discussion of strategic disagreement can be created, even in high-level teams confronting strategic challenges, and how this can enable productive decision-making.[38]

Gaining Value from Diversity

Teams are often put together to leverage diverse expertise. But too often, the challenge of integrating diverse knowledge, perspectives, and skills is underestimated, and the hoped-for synergy never materializes. One recent study showed that psychological safety can make or break achievement of team performance in diverse teams. The researchers surveyed master's students participating in 195 teams in a French university and found that expertise-diverse teams performed well when psychological safety was high and badly otherwise.[39]

Finally, a number of studies have investigated effects of demographic diversity on team performance. Some have shown that diversity helps performance, while others have found a negative relationship between diversity and performance. When different studies show conflicting results like this, it's usually a sign of a missing moderator. In this case, psychological safety could be that missing ingredient – the factor that could make or break a diverse team's ability to put its different perspectives to good use. Indeed, in one study in a Midwestern mid-size manufacturing company, a positive climate for diversity and psychological safety together led to more discretionary effort. These relationships were stronger for minorities than for whites, suggesting that psychological safety may be playing an especially crucial role for minorities in creating engagement and a feeling of being valued at work.[40]

Bringing Research to Practice

The research summarized here, which is steadily growing with consistent observations across diverse industry settings, provides further confidence that psychological safety truly offers benefits for organizations and countries around the world. No longer confined to academic interest, psychological safety has garnered attention from practitioners in almost every industry – especially in the aftermath of Google's Project Aristotle, with its feature pieces in the *New York Times* and on *Fareed Zakaria GPS* on CNN.[41] More and more professionals – consultants, managers, physicians, nurses, engineers – can be found talking about psychological safety. Yet few may be aware of the full weight of supporting evidence that it matters. And fewer still may have stopped to reflect on what their companies lose when psychological safety is missing.

One of the most important things to keep in mind, wherever you work, is that the failure of an employee to speak up in a crucial moment cannot be seen. This is true whether that employee is on the front lines of customer service or sitting next to you in the executive board room. And because *not* offering an idea is an invisible act, it's hard to engage in real-time course correction. This means that psychologically safe workplaces have a powerful advantage in competitive industries.

The four chapters ahead in Part II vividly portray the consequences of workplace fear (Chapters 3 and 4) and the benefits of psychological safety (Chapters 5 and 6) for both organizational performance and human safety. We'll visit more than 20 organizations – old and new, large and small, private and public sector, domestic and overseas. Examining events that transpired in companies as diverse as Volkswagen and Wells Fargo, I hope to convey a visceral understanding of what is lost in fear-based workplaces, which are, alas, all too often still the default in organizations around the world, even after two decades of research providing evidence of its costs. Taking a look inside a range of fearless organizations, such as Pixar Animation Studios and DaVita Kidney Centers, I also hope to convey all that is gained.

Chapter 2 Takeaways

- Psychological safety is not a perk; it's essential to producing high performance in a VUCA world.
- Psychological safety is too often missing in today's organizations
- Twenty years of research on psychological safety finds positive benefits for learning, engagement, and performance in a wide range of organizations.

Endnotes

1. Mark Costa, CEO of Eastman Chemical, HBS class comments, April 18, 2018.
2. *Ibid.*
3. *Ibid.*
4. The data in this chart comes from a Factiva search, conducted May 25, 2018. Factiva, Inc. is a business information and research tool owned

Dow Jones & Company. Factiva provides access to more than 30,000 sources, such as newspapers, journals, magazines, and more from nearly every country in the world. Thus, the search was quite comprehensive.

5. Corcoran, S. "A good boss makes for a happy team." *The Sunday Times*. September 24, 2017. https://www.thetimes.co.uk/article/a-good-boss-makes-for-a-happy-team-r30ndjjfv Accessed June 13, 2018.

6. Blumental, D. & Ganguli, I. "Patient Safety: Conversation to Curriculum." *The New York Times*. January 26, 2010. https://www.nytimes.com/2010/01/26/health/26error.html Accessed June 13, 2018.

7. "Six and Out? What Australia's cricket scandal tells us about the six golden rules of integrity." *The Mandarin*, March 28, 2018. https://www.themandarin.com.au/90552-australian-cricket-scandal-six-golden-rules-integrity/ Accessed June 13, 2018.

8. Vander Ark, T. "Promoting Psychological Safety in Classrooms for Student Success." *GettingSmart.com*, December 29, 2016. http://www.gettingsmart.com/2016/12/promoting-psychological-safety-in-classrooms/ Accessed June 13, 2018.

9. Wallace, K. "After #MeToo, more women feeling empowered." *CNN Wire*, December 27, 2017. https://www.cnn.com/2017/12/27/health/sexual-harassment-women-empowerment/index.html Accessed June 13, 2018.

10. Landon, L.B., Slack, K.J., & Barrett, J.D. "Teamwork and Collaboration in Long-Duration Space Missions: Going to Extremes." *American Psychologist* 73.4 (2018): 563–575.

11. Edmondson, A.C. "Psychological Safety and Learning Behavior in Work Teams." *Administrative Science Quarterly* 44.2 (1999): 350–83.

12. This citation data was obtained from Google Scholar, accessed May 25, 2018.

13. Frese, M. & Keith, N. "Action Errors, Error Management, and Learning in Organizations." *Annual Review of Psychology* 66.1 (2015): 661–87.

14. Baer, M. & Frese, M. "Innovation Is Not Enough: Climates for Initiative and Psychological Safety, Process Innovations, and Firm Performance." *Journal of Organizational Behavior* 24.1 (2003): 45–68.

15. Milliken, F.J., Morrison, E.W., & Hewlin, P.F. "An Exploratory Study of Employee Silence: Issues That Employees Don't Communicate Upward and Why." *Journal of Management Studies* 40.6 (2003): 1453–76.

16. Brinsfield, C.T. "Employee Silence Motives: Investigation of Dimensionality and Development of Measures." *Journal of Organizational Behavior* 34.5 (2013): 671–97.

17. Detert, J.R. & Edmondson, A.C. "Implicit Voice Theories: Taken-for-Granted Rules for Self-Censorship at Work." *The Academy of Management Journal* 54.3 (2011): 461–88.

18. Leroy, H., Dierynck, B., Anseel, F., Simons, T., Halbesleben, J.R.B., McCaughey, D., Savage, G.T., & Sels, L. "Behavioral Integrity for Safety, Priority of Safety, Psychological Safety, and Patient Safety: A Team-Level Study." *Journal of Applied Psychology* 97.6 (2012): 1273–81.

19. Edmondson, A.C. "Learning from Mistakes Is Easier Said Than Done: Group and Organizational Influences on the Detection and Correction of Human Error." *The Journal of Applied Behavioral* Science 32.1 (1996): 5–28.

20. Tucker, A.L., Nembhard, I.M., & Edmondson, A.C. "Implementing New Practices: An Empirical Study of Organizational Learning in Hospital Intensive Care Units." *Management Science* 53.6 (2007): 894–907.

21. Tucker, A.L. & Edmondson, A.C. "Why hospitals don't learn from failures: Organizational and psychological dynamics that inhibit system change." *California Management Review* 45.2 (2003): 55–72.

22. Halbesleben, J.R.B. & Rathert, C. "The Role of Continuous Quality Improvement and Psychological Safety in Predicting Work-Arounds." *Health Care Management Review* 33.2 (2008): 134–144.

23. Arumugam, V., Antony, J., & Kumar, M. "Linking Learning and Knowledge Creation to Project Success in Six Sigma Projects: An Empirical Investigation." *International Journal of Production Economics* 141.1 (2013): 388–402.

24. Siemsen, E., Roth, A.V., Balasubramanian, S., & Anand, G. "The Influence of Psychological Safety and Confidence in Knowledge on Employee Knowledge Sharing." *Manufacturing & Service Operations Management* 11.3 (2009): 429–47.

25. Edmondson, A.C. (1999), op cit.

26. Baer, M. & Frese, M. (2003), op cit.

27. Huang, C., & Jiang, P. "Exploring the Psychological Safety of R&D Teams: An Empirical Analysis in Taiwan." *Journal of Management & Organization* 18.2 (2012): 175–92.

28. Duhigg, C. "What Google Learned From Its Quest to Build the Perfect Team." *The New York Times Magazine*, February 25, 2016. https://www.nytimes.com/2016/02/28/magazine/what-google-learned-from-its-quest-to-build-the-perfect-team.html Accessed June 13, 2018.

29. *Ibid.*

30. Rozovsky, J. "The five keys to a successful Google team." *re:Work Blog.* November 17, 2015. https://rework.withgoogle.com/blog/five-keys-to-a-successful-google-team/ Accessed June 13, 2018.

31. May, D.R., Gilson, G.L., & Harter, L.M. "The Psychological Conditions of Meaningfulness, Safety and Availability and the Engagement of the Human Spirit at Work." *Journal of Occupational and Organizational Psychology* 77.1 (2004): 11–37.

32. Chughtai, A. A. & Buckley, F. "Exploring the impact of trust on research scientists' work engagement." *Personnel Review* 42.4 (2013): 396–421.

33. Ulusoy, N., Mölders, C., Fischer, S., Bayur, H., Deveci, S., Demiral, Y., & Rössler, W. "A Matter of Psychological Safety: Commitment and Mental Health in Turkish Immigrant Employees in Germany." *Journal of Cross-Cultural Psychology* 47.4 (2016): 626–645.

34. Rathert, C., Ishqaidef, G., May, D.R. "Improving Work Environments in Health Care: Test of a Theoretical Framework." *Health Care Management Review* 34.4 (2009): 334–343.

35. Gibson, C.B. & Gibbs, J.L. "Unpacking the Concept of Virtuality: The Effects of Geographic Dispersion, Electronic Dependence, Dynamic Structure, and National Diversity on Team Innovation." *Administrative Science Quarterly* 51.3 (2006): 451–95.

36. Edmondson, A.C. & Smith, D.M. "Too Hot to Handle? How to Manage Relationship Conflict." *California Management Review* 49.1 (2006): 6–31.

37. Bradley, B.H., Postlethwaite, B.E., Hamdani, M.R., & Brown, K.G. "Reaping the Benefits of Task Conflict in Teams: The Critical Role of Team Psychological Safety Climate." *Journal of Applied Psychology* 97.1 (2012): 151–58.

38. Edmondson, A.C. & Smith, D.M. (2006), op cit.

39. Martins, L.L., Schilpzand, M.C., Kirkman, B.L., Ivanaj, S., & Ivanaj, V. "A Contingency View of the Effects of Cognitive Diversity on Team Performance: The Moderating Roles of Team Psychological Safety and Relationship Conflict." *Small Group Research* 44.2 (2013): 96–126.

40. Singh, B., Winkel, D.E., & Selvarajan, T.T. "Managing Diversity at Work: Does Psychological Safety Hold the Key to Racial Differences in Employee Performance?" *Journal of Occupational and Organizational Psychology* 86.2 (2013): 242–63.

41. "How to Build the Perfect Team." *Fareed Zakaria GPS.* CNN, April 17, 2016. https://archive.org/details/CNNW_20160417_170000_Fareed_Zakaria_GPS Accessed June 1, 2018.

PART II

Psychological Safety at Work

3 | Avoidable Failure

In May 2015, the Volkswagen Group had every reason to feel proud.[3] It had sold over 10 million vehicles the previous year, thereby laying claim to the title of world's largest automaker. One of the largest employers in Germany, the company was credited with helping the country recover from the global financial crisis of 2008. Ironically, as it would turn out, its Jetta TDI Clean Diesel won the Green Car of the Year at the 2008 Los Angeles Auto Show. A firm with a 78-year history in Germany, made famous by the iconic Beetle of the 1960s, and with a pristine reputation for engineering prowess, Volkswagen's star shone bright enough to be blinding.

As the saying goes, pride cometh before the fall. Merely months later, Volkswagen (VW), the world's largest automotive company, was facing unimaginable scandal. The clean diesel engines that had anchored its impressive US sales were discovered to have been – essentially – a hoax. German officials raided the company headquarters in Wolfsburg, searching for incriminating evidence. Criminal investigations were opened by the United States and the European Union to figure out who knew what, when, and how. The company halted sales, reported its first quarterly loss in 15 years, and witnessed a third of its market value vanish. CEO Martin Winterkorn resigned in September of 2015, taking "full responsibility" while denying "wrongdoing," and at least nine senior managers were suspended or put on leave.[4]

In the following years, prosecutors in the United States and Germany would identify more than 40 people, "spread out across at least four cities and working for three VW brands" involved an elaborate scheme to defraud government regulators.[5] "Dieselgate," as the scandal was dubbed, referred to VW's deceptiveness in complying with the regulations required by the US Environmental Protection Agency (EPA) to sell automobiles in the United States.

Exacting Standards

How could this have happened? When Winterkorn had taken the helm in 2007, he'd set a goal that was both precise and ambitious: to triple the company's US sales within 10 years, thereby surpassing rivals Toyota and General Motors to become the world's largest automobile maker. The company's so-called clean diesel vehicles, touted for their high performance and excellent fuel economy, were essential to this strategy. There was only one problem: diesels produced more nitrous oxide (NOx) than gasoline engines and would not pass the United States environmental regulations. As VW manager-engineer Wolfgang Hatz admitted in 2007 about the challenge to create clean diesel for the US market, "The CARB [California Air Resources Board] is not realistic. We can do quite a bit, and we will do quite a bit. But impossible we cannot do."[6]

Hatz and his engineering colleagues then went to work. Somewhere in the millions of lines of software code they wrote for what became the "clean diesel" vehicles, they embedded instructions that would enable the cars to pass the strict US emissions tests. Conceptually, the trick was simple enough. The engineers designed and implemented software that could determine when a vehicle was undergoing standard emissions testing in a lab, in which case only two wheels rotated, as opposed to four wheels when the vehicle was driven on the road. When tested in a lab, the diesel engines complied with acceptable NOx levels. However, that compliance sacrificed performance and fuel economy, which made the cars unacceptable to consumers. That's why the software directed the exhaust control equipment to stop working once the vehicle was off the regulators' test beds. On the road, the so-called clean diesel engines spewed into the atmosphere as much as 40 times the level of NOx permitted by regulations.[7]

For nearly 10 years, all appeared to be going well. The defeat devices, as they were later called, enabled VW to reach its ambitious sales goals four years ahead of its target date.[8] In 2013, an international nonprofit group, partnering with engineers at West Virginia University's Center for Alternative Fuels, Engines, and Emissions, along with California environmental regulators, became interested in how diesel engines performed. They decided to compare in-lab and on-road emissions and mileage performances on several types of diesel vehicles, including those of Volkswagen. Soon enough, the defeat device came to light. For the next two years, the US environmental agencies presented their findings, VW denied, covered up, and finally confessed. Winterkorn then resigned, saying, "I am not aware of any wrongdoing on my part."[9] Across VW's brands, about 11 million of the diesel vehicles worldwide would be discovered to have the cheating device installed.

How could this failure have been avoided? It's natural to want to point a finger at someone, or at a small group, to hold responsible for, at the very least, the 59 unnecessary deaths and 30 cases of chronic bronchitis that researchers estimated are the result of VW's deceptive emissions practices.

Martin Winterkorn is certainly a good candidate to be cast as the villain. He had a reputation as an arrogant, perfectionistic martinet with an obsessive attention to detail. As one executive at VW told reporters, "There was always a distance, a fear and a respect . . . If he [Winterkorn] would come and visit or you had to go to him, your pulse would go up. If you presented bad news, those were the moments that it could become quite unpleasant and loud and quite demeaning." Other managers cited instances when Winterkorn blamed engineers for paint that exceeded regulations by less than a millimeter, or for not offering a specific shade of red that was selling well on competitors' models.[10] A video shot at the Frankfurt motor show in 2011 and widely viewed on YouTube shows Winterkorn's irritation at discovering that Hyundai, a so-called lesser automotive brand, had managed to engineer a steering wheel that was silent when adjusted from the driver's seat – a feat VW had been unable to master.[11] "Bischoff!" barks Winterkorn, as if to lay the blame on his design chief, Klaus Bischoff, and voices displeasure that a rival company managed to get rid of the "clonking sound."

Yet, there are reasons to question this temptingly simple explanation with its singular villain. First, many organizational leaders genuinely believe that "no news" means that things are going well. They assume that if people were struggling to implement some directive or another, they would speak up and push back. They take for granted that their own voices are welcome and fail to appreciate that others might feel unable to bring bad news up the chain of command. For sure, this kind of blindness does not constitute effective leadership, but it also cannot be called villainous. Second, and more specific to this case, Winterkorn's leadership was not born in a vacuum. He was the protégé of the immensely powerful Ferdinand Piech, VW's former chairman, CEO, and top shareholder. A brilliant and visionary automotive engineer, Piech had been convinced that terrorizing subordinates was the way to achieve profitable design. Chrysler executive Bob Lutz recounted a conversation he had with Piesch at an industry dinner in the 1990s. When Lutz expressed admiration for the exterior design of Volkswagen's new model Golf and wished for similar success at Chrysler, Piech offered up an explanation that might serve as a textbook example of how to create a psychologically unsafe environment while seeking to motivate:

> I'll give you the recipe. I called all the body engineers, stamping people, manufacturing, and executives into my conference room. And I said, "I am tired of all these lousy body fits. You have six weeks to achieve world-class body fits. I have all your names. If we do not have good body fits in six weeks, I will replace all of you. Thank you for your time today.[12]

Writing soon after VW's fall, Lutz speculated that Piech was "more than likely the root cause of the VW diesel-emissions scandal" because he instigated "a reign of terror and a culture where performance was driven by fear and intimidation."[13] Although perhaps an extreme case, the fact is that many managers are sympathetic to the use of power to insist that people achieve certain goals – offering clear metrics and deadlines. The belief that people may not push themselves hard enough without a clear understanding of the negative consequences of failing to do so is widespread and even taken for granted by many in management roles, along with just as many casual onlookers contemplating human motivation at work. What many people do not realize is that motivation by fear is indeed highly effective – effective at creating the *illusion* that goals are being achieved. It is not effective in ensuring that people bring the creativity, good process, and passion needed to accomplish challenging goals in knowledge-intensive workplaces.

But even Piech was not, as Lutz remarked, the "root cause" of Dieselgate. Just as CEO Martin Winterkorn's beliefs about how best to motivate people were learned from his mentor, Ferdinand Piech, Piech's management beliefs were learned from his mentor – his grandfather, Ferdinand Porsche, who had been the brilliant lead engineer for the Beetle. Nor was Herr Porsche the root cause. Porsche, for his part, was hugely inspired in his efforts by Henry Ford and in the mid-1930s traveled to Detroit to study Ford's River Rouge factory complex, eventually using what he'd learned to build the first automotive assembly line in Germany.[14] This was still the golden age for the manufacturing industry, when fear and intimidation were, arguably, a proven managerial technique to motivate speed and accuracy in factory workers. When authoritative demands, combined with process improvements, could reduce an automobile's assembly line production time from 12 hours to 3, as Ford's factory did, the company's profits were real.

The root cause of VW's Dieselgate scandal in 2015 cannot be located in the personality or leadership of any single person or small group. Perhaps one could say the failure was caused by holding fast to an outdated belief about what motivates workers. A scene in Charlie Chaplin's classic film *Modern Times* parodies what such old-fashioned motivation-by-fear can look like. Chaplin plays an assembly line worker who fails to keep pace tightening the widgets as they appear before him on the moving belt, only to be kicked by a coworker, chastised and hit by a manager, and ordered to increase speed by an executive.[15] Today, when simple tasks have increasingly become automated and knowledge workers do not tighten widgets but rather collaborate, synthesize, make decisions, and continually learn, such methods seem especially comedic.

Interestingly, Bischoff, the designer who was chastised by Winterkorn for the clonking steering shaft, defended this management style, telling a reporter, "Of course [Winterkorn] went through the roof when something went wrong . . ." and excused the behavior by pointing out that his boss could also be "extremely human with a soft spot for people's personal fates."[16] What's at stake here isn't whether or not a CEO is extremely human or not. Winterkorn's kindness and "soft spots" were likely within a normal range when measured against other human beings. What's at stake is what he believed was the best way to motivate employees – and the relevance of these beliefs for today's work. Given what we now know about the relationship between psychological safety and learning, a leader who threatens to fire managers and engineers if they do not come up with world–class body fits in six weeks seems best cast in a silent film.

Like the noxious fumes the faulty VW diesel engines emitted, low psychological safety affects everyone who breathes it in. As Professor

Ferdinand Dudenhoffer, an automotive expert of at the University of Duisburg-Essen, put it " . . . there is a special pressure at VW."[17] The company's governance dynamics contributed to that special pressure. According to Dudenhoffer, unlike at other German automobile manufacturers, where the supervisory board ultimately controlled the CEO, at VW the board held "no such authority."[18] That may be because relatives of the founding Porsche family held a quarter of the 20 board seats; two seats were held by regional politicians, eager to do whatever it took to keep jobs in the region, and two were held by representatives of Qatar's sovereign wealth fund.

Given this insidious culture of fear, it's unsurprising that when faced with a seemingly insurmountable technical obstacle – to produce a diesel engine that could pass US environmental testing – and pressed for a solution that could meet the company's target goals, engineers and regulatory officials at VW decided to find a way. However clever and lucrative the idea may have seemed at the time, and however much VW's sales and reputation soared, history has shown us that it was not, in the long run, a viable solution.

At least one member of the supervisory board was unafraid to speak up. Bernd Osterloh, 1 of the 10 elected members who represented employees (comparable to union representatives in the US), sent a telling letter to the VW staff on September 24, 2015, shortly after the US regulators revealed the cheating. As if citing central tenets of psychological safety, Osterloh wrote, "we need in the future a climate in which problems aren't hidden but can be openly communicated to superiors. We need a culture in which it's possible and permissible to argue with your superior about the best way to go."[19]

After the emissions scandal broke, Winterkorn claimed the company needed stricter rules to make sure this kind of deceit did not happen again. But it's unclear how stricter rules would have engineered an environmentally safe diesel engine or enabled the company to reach its goal to become the world's largest car company. In retrospect, the goal itself seems suspect. Could failure have been avoided if the engineers, working in a psychologically safer environment, could report back the "bad news" that attaining a clean diesel engine under the terms demanded was simply not feasible?

Perhaps most stunning thing about the VW emissions debacle is that it's by no means a singular event. The same script – unreachable target goals, a command-and-control hierarchy that motivates by fear, and people afraid to lose their jobs if they fail – has been repeated again and again. In part that's because it's a script that was useful in the past, when goals were reachable, progress directly observable, and tasks largely individually executed. Under those conditions, people could be compelled to reach them simply by fear and intimidation. The problem is that, in today's volatile, uncertain, complex, and ambiguous (VUCA) world, this is no longer a script that's good for business. Rather than success, it's a playbook that invites avoidable, and often painfully public, failure.

In the rest of this chapter, we will see a similar script play out in three other organizations: Wells Fargo, Nokia, and the Federal Reserve Bank of New York. In each of these cases, a psychologically unsafe culture appeared to be working *for some period of time,* but, like a ticking bomb, it eventually exploded from within, decimating reputations of once-venerated companies.

Stretching the Stretch Goal

A year before its notorious fall, Wells Fargo could still call itself the most valuable bank, ranking first in market value among all US banks and serving roughly one in three American households.[20] Rated by *Barron's* as one of the "world's most respected companies," the lion's share of Wells Fargo's success stemmed from its Community Banking division; in 2015, with over 6000 local branches across the US, the division accounted for over half the company's revenue.[21] Community Banking provided a range of financial services, including checking and savings accounts, loans, and credit cards, to households and small businesses.

Community Banking relied heavily on cross-selling, the practice of selling existing customers additional products, for its growth strategy. Wells Fargo believed it could gain a competitive advantage in the banking industry by becoming a one-stop shop for all of its customers' financial needs. The bank took pride in its ability to sell its customers additional products. In fact, in his 2010 letter to shareholders, CEO John Stumpf boasted that the company was "the king of cross-sell."[22] By 2015, Wells Fargo's claim to that title seemed strong: it was averaging 6.11 products per customer, compared to the industry average of 2.71.[23]

Yet superior cross-selling was to Wells Fargo what clean diesel was to the Volkswagen Group: involving an ultimately unattainable target goal that was nonetheless demanded of employees by the company's top leaders upon penalty of job loss.

By September 8, 2016, it was all over. The ticking time bomb had exploded from within, shattering the king of cross-sell's illusory one-stop shop. After having been found guilty of widespread misconduct in sales practices in its Community Banking division, Wells Fargo announced a $185 million settlement with the Consumer Financial Protection Bureau (CFPB) and two other US regulatory agencies. John Stumpf resigned the following month.[24]

What happened at Wells Fargo was both predictable and avoidable. And it could not have persisted as long as it did without a psychologically unsafe culture. Let's look more closely at how events unfolded.

In the early 2000s, Wells Fargo had adopted a cross-selling campaign called "Going for Gr-Eight," meant to motivate Community Banking employees to sell, on average, a previously unheard of eight products per customer. To accomplish this, incentive schemes were put in place up and down the hierarchy: personal bankers and tellers were given a percentage commission for each sale, district managers were required to hit specific sales numbers to earn bonuses, and cross-selling success was factored into top executives' annual bonuses.[25]

Metrics tracking was strict and unforgiving. Branch personnel were assigned ambitious sales numbers and their progress was tracked closely in a daily "Motivator Report."[26] Each branch was required to report daily sales four times per day: at 11 a.m., 1 p.m., 3 p.m., and 5 p.m.[27] One area president told employees to "do whatever it takes" to sell.[28] At some branches, employees reportedly could not leave until they reached their daily sales goal.[29]

Bank personnel who did not meet sales goals were coached to increase their numbers, including "objection-handling" training to coerce people into buying more products. If they could still not hit their numbers, they were terminated from the company. Managers who did not do well enough were publicly criticized or fired.[30]

Beginning in 2013, reports began to surface that Wells Fargo employees had engaged in, and were still currently engaging in, questionable practices to hit their sales numbers. A former employee reported that members of his Los Angeles branch opened accounts or credit cards for customers without their consent, saying a computer glitch had occurred if customers complained. He also reported that employees lied to customers-saying that certain products could only be purchased together-to hit their numbers.[31] Other tactics to meet sales goals included encouraging customers to open unnecessary multiple checking accounts – one for groceries, one for travel, one for emergencies, and so on[32] – and creating fake email addressees to enroll customers in online banking.[33]

Before the scandal went public, Wells Fargo made a number of changes that seemed to try to address its problems. The company fired over 5300 employees for ethics violations between 2011 and 2016,[34] rolled out a "Quality of Sale" Report Card that set limits on the terms of a sale,[35] expanded ethics training, and explicitly told employees not to create fake accounts.[36] There was, however, one glaring omission: no changes were made to "Going for Gr-Eight." Just as VW engineers were unable to design a clean diesel engine in ways that were "permissible," Wells Fargo employees were unable to meet sales goals without engaging in shady practices. There was simply a limit to how many products any one customer's wallet could allow. As one former banker put it, "They [the higher ups] warned us about this [unethical] type of behavior . . . but the reality was that people had to meet their goals. They needed a paycheck."[37]

Eventually, federal and state regulators opened an investigation into the bank's practices. Their report found that from 2011 to 2016, employees in the Community Banking division, in order to boost sales figures, opened two million unauthorized customer accounts and credit cards and sold products and services to customers under false pretenses.[38] The investigation also found that several employees who witnessed the unethical behavior had reported it to their supervisors or to the ethics hotline. One even claimed to have emailed Stumpf about it. Some employees were later terminated for blowing the whistle.[39]

Like Volkswagen, Wells Fargo's avoidable failure was not the result of one bad apple but of a system that demanded hitting targets so ambitious they could only be met by deceit. Employees operated in a culture of fear that brooked no dissent. Rather than manifesting interest in salespeople's experiences while executing the cross-selling strategy and using what was being learned in the field to shift or sharpen the company's strategy,[40] managers sent a clear message: produce – or else.

Fearing the Truth

A similar script to that of VW and Wells Fargo was followed years earlier – across the ocean and in another industry. Nokia, which traces its origins as a company to an 1865 paper mill in the town of Nokia, Finland,[41] had become, by the 1980s, a pioneering telecom company in the world's burgeoning cellular networks. Led by CEO Kari Kairamo, by the late 1990s Nokia was the world's leading mobile phone manufacturer, with a 23% market share.[42] By the early 2000s, as a developer of the Symbian operating system, the company seemed well poised to ride what would become the smartphone's exponential rise.

Instead, Nokia became another casualty of avoidable failure. By June 2011, the company's share of the smartphone market had fallen far, and by 2012, its market value had dropped by over 75%.[43] The company had lost its innovative edge, its lead as a handset manufacturer, and over two billion euros. In September 2013, the company, conceding defeat, announced the sale of its Device and Services business to Microsoft.[44]

Although it was not a tangled web of deceit that destroyed Nokia, as at Volkswagen and Wells Fargo, all three companies were handicapped by a culture of fear. For instance, an in-depth investigation of Nokia's rise and fall in the smartphone industry between 2005 and 2010, which included interviews with 76 managers and engineers at Nokia, concluded that the company lost the smartphone battle not as a result of poor vision or a few bad managers but at least partly due to a "fearful emotional climate" that created company-wide inertia, especially in response to threats from powerful competitors.[45] Such fear, said the study's authors, was "grounded in a culture of temperamental leaders and frightened middle managers, scared of telling the truth."[46]

The truth was that beginning in the first decades of the twenty-first century, the mobile phone industry had become increasingly competitive. Having staked its claim on the featurephone, Nokia was unwilling or unable to recognize the potential of the complex and expensive-to-develop software platform that became today's smartphone. In contrast Apple and Google, following the Canadian company RIM's introduction of the Blackberry, spent billions developing the proprietary platforms IOS and Android, both of which overshadowed Nokia's Symbian platform and effectively launched the smartphone revolution. In other words, Nokia found itself in a rapidly changing, knowledge-intensive industry, where collaboration, innovation, and communication were quickly becoming vital to future success.

Lacking a psychologically safe climate where candor was expected, Nokia's top managers and middle managers engaged in a subtle dance of mutual fear. When middle managers asked critical questions about the company's direction, they were told to "focus on implementation."[47] People who could not comply with top managers' unreasonable requests were "labeled a loser" or "put their reputations on the line."[48] One executive president was said to have "pounded the table so hard that pieces of fruit went flying."[49] Olli-Pekka Kallasvuo, former chairman and CEO of Nokia, was described as "extremely temperamental."[50] Managers reported that they regularly saw him "shouting at people at the top of his lungs" and "it was very difficult to tell him things he didn't want to hear."[51]

For their part, executives, fearful of the external market threats the company was facing, particularly from software developers at Apple and Google, did not communicate the severity of those threats to middle managers. One top manager, confessing to the fear that higher ups felt and the way that influenced management practice, said, "it was clear that we feared the iPhone. So we told the middle managers that they had to deliver touch-phones quickly."[52] Middle managers, afraid to deliver bad news, led their superiors to develop an overly optimistic perception of Nokia's technological capabilities in featurephones and to neglect long-term investments in developing more complex innovation. As one manager put it, "In Nokia's R&D, the culture was such that they wanted to please the upper levels. They wanted to give them good news . . . not a reality check."[53]

A reality check would have required that managers (both the temperamental and the frightened) put aside their fears and speak candidly to one another. Yet such candor seemed impossible, and the window for innovation and redirection passed. In 2007, as the industry became ever more software-reliant, the Finnish telecom company sank still lower. More and more mobile phone companies turned to Google's open source Android operating system. By 2008, when Apple launched the iPhone 3G and the App Store, it was too late to catch up. Although Nokia continued to develop software and launch new products, it would underperform and undersell compared to its more agile competitors.

Clearly, it is not possible to say that psychological safety would have ensured Nokia's success in an increasingly competitive industry.

Success required constant innovation, fueled by expertise, ingenuity, and teamwork. But without psychological safety, it is difficult for expertise and ingenuity to be put to good use. And with Nokia's senior executives in the dark about where the company and its technology really stood, the company simply could not learn fast enough to survive. A decade later, Nokia was able to make a comeback. As you will learn in Chapter 7, members of senior management would later realize that they had to change how they spoke and interacted to develop a better strategy.

Who Regulates the Regulators?

In the Nokia, Wells Fargo, and VW cases, we saw the pernicious effects of a culture of fear inside companies with ambitious dreams. What about when one company provides services to, or reviews the activities of, another? When relationships *between* companies are hampered by a culture of fear, the risks intensify, both for the organizations and for society.

Following the 2008–2009 global financial crisis, the Federal Reserve Bank of New York (FRBNY) received ample condemnation and criticism from the American public and Congress for its failure to effectively regulate the excessive financial risk-taking of several of the big US banks.[54] In response, the FRBNY commissioned a report to study itself. Bill Dudley, President of FRBNY, asked Columbia Business School Professor David Beim to investigate and assess the FRBNY's "organization and practices, with a particular focus on Bank Supervision."[55] The intention was to reveal lessons learned that could be used to improve the Feds' ability to supervise banks and monitor systemic risk going forward.

Beim and a small team interviewed approximately two dozen people who worked at the FRBNY, mostly senior officers, about things the Fed did well and didn't do well leading up to the crisis. The result of the examination was the *2009 Report of Systemic Risk and Bank Supervision*. The report allocated considerable attention to the FRBNY's culture and communication. In it, Beim described a workplace suffused with low psychological safety in which regulatory officers tasked with monitoring individual banks like Goldman Sachs felt "intimidated and passive," and thus were not "effective in communicating with other areas, forming their own views and signaling when something important seems to be wrong." As a result, the regulators "just followed orders."[56]

As part of their jobs, regulatory supervisors were involved in discussions about individual bank processes and policies, often focusing on specific and large-scale transactions a bank had made or was considering making. Every large bank was assigned a FRBNY regulatory team, tasked with the job of deciding whether a particular transaction was kosher. Here, Beim found that real decision-making was stymied by groupthink or "striving for consensus" – issues were discussed at length without moving to constructive action. The discussions were notably devoid of frank debate and cooperation, where people spoke up about problems and offered solutions, as warranted in any organization where highly complex processes are constantly unfolding at a furious pace. The report emphasized fear of speaking up as a frequent theme that characterized FRBNY meetings and employee experiences in all aspects of their job. It presented stark quotes from interviewees, such as "grow up in this culture and you'll find that small mistakes are not tolerated," and "[you] don't want to be too far outside where management is thinking."[57]

The relationship between the regulators and the bank managers was singled out as especially fraught. For one, an information asymmetry existed between the two groups that put the regulators at a disadvantage. Because the regulators had to request information from the banks, the banks could act as gatekeepers, in turn making the regulators feel dependent on the bank's willingness and good grace for timely and useful information. This led, as Beim argued, regulators to adopt a nonconfrontational and often overly deferential style to smooth their attempts to obtain information.[58] Most critically, Beim reported that within three weeks of his investigation he saw signs of *regulatory capture*, a phenomenon that journalist Ira Glass later described as like "a watchdog who licks the face of an intruder and plays catch with the intruder instead of barking at him."[59] The regulators were, in a sense, disabled from effectively carrying out their regulatory duties by a culture of fear and deference.

What makes this dynamic especially frustrating is that the banks were required by law to hand over whatever information the Feds asked for. Carmen Segarra, who worked as a regulator after the Beim investigation, said, "The Fed has both the power to get the information and the power to punish a bank if it chooses to withhold it." When asked why she thought the regulators chose deference even though they possessed this power, her answer was succinct: "they are coming from a place of fear."[60]

Could the colossal collapse of a financial system the likes of which the world had not seen since the 1930s have been prevented had the banks and regulators worked in a climate of psychological safety? That may be a stretch. Lax regulations, greed, and faulty incentives were certainly important contributing factors. However, we can say that the culture of fear silenced or inhibited anyone who wanted to ask questions or criticize, thereby squandering many opportunities to catch and correct excessive risk-taking and other sources of economic failure.

Avoiding Avoidable Failure

Volkswagen, Wells Fargo, Nokia, and the New York Federal Reserve serve as vivid examples of organizations that boasted deep reservoirs of expertise, driven, intelligent leaders, and clearly articulated goals. None lacked capable employees in any of the relevant fields required for the organization to succeed in its industry. In short, they had the talent. What they lacked was the leadership needed to ensure that a climate of psychological safety permeated the workplace, allowing people to speak truth to power inside the company – and, in the case of the Fed, to their industry partners. Chapter 7 will focus on what leaders need to do to create and recover psychological safety; here, I simply note that the kinds of large-scale business failures described in this chapter are preventable.

None of these failures occurred overnight or out of the blue. Quite the opposite. The seeds of failure were taking root for months or years while senior management remained blissfully unaware. In many organizations, like those discussed in this chapter, countless small problems routinely occur, presenting early warning signs that the company's strategy may be falling short and needs to be revisited. Yet these signals are often squandered. Preventing avoidable failure thus starts with encouraging people throughout a company to push back, share data, and actively report on what is really happening in the lab or in the market so as to create a continuous loop of learning and agile execution.

Each of the stories in this chapter can be seen as a case of strategic failure. What started as small gaps in execution spiraled into dramatic, headline-making failures when new information created by actual experience – whether of engineers or salespeople – was not captured and put to good use in rethinking and redirecting company efforts.[61] For instance, Wells Fargo's cross-selling strategy bumped up against customers' real spending power, planting a seed of strategic failure. But what cemented the failure was the salespeople's belief that senior managers would not tolerate underperformance. That they found it easier to fabricate false accounts than to report what they were learning in the field is as powerful a signal of low psychological safety as you can find.

In focusing our attention on psychological safety, I do not mean to dismiss the ethical dimensions of any of these cases. Wells Fargo, for instance. Yet to view the customer-accounts fraud as the result of individually-corrupt salespeople does not square with the widespread nature of the behavior in the company, which points to a system set up to fail. Set up to fail by the pernicious combination of a top-down strategy and insufficient psychological safety to encourage sharing bad news up the hierarchy. A similar point can be made about the VW and Fed cases. As argued earlier in this chapter, any explanation that looks only for a corrupt or foolish individual or individuals will be incomplete, given the complex dynamics at play. What is interesting to consider, however, is the extent to which having information about shortcomings come to light earlier rather than later can nearly always mitigate the size and impact of failures and sometimes prevent them altogether.

Adopting an Agile Approach to Strategy

Taken together, these four cases suggest the necessity of adopting alternate perspectives on strategy that are more in tune with the nature of value creation in today's VUCA world. Solvay Business School Professor Paul Verdin and I developed a perspective that frames an organization's strategy as a hypothesis rather than a plan.[62] Like all hypotheses, it starts with situation assessment and analysis – strategy's classic tools. Also, like all hypotheses, it must be *tested* through action. When strategy is seen as a hypothesis to be continually tested, encounters with customers provide valuable data of ongoing interest to senior executives. Imagine if Wells Fargo had adopted an agile approach to strategy: the company's top management would then have taken repeated instances of missed targets or false accounts as useful data to help it assess the efficacy of the original cross-selling strategy. This learning would then have triggered much-needed strategic adaptation.

Of course, sometimes, poor performance is simply poor performance. People underperforming. Not trying hard enough. Sometimes, companies do in fact need to find ways to better motivate and manage employees to help them reach desired performance standards. However, in a VUCA world, this is not the only explanation for missing a desired target; it is not even the most likely explanation. Early signs of gaps between results and plans must be viewed *first* as data – triggering analysis – before concluding that the gaps are clear and obvious evidence of employee underperformance.

Cheating and covering up are natural by-products of a top-down culture that does not accept "no" or "it can't be done" for an answer. But combining this culture with a belief that a brilliant strategy formulated in the past will hold indefinitely into the future becomes a certain recipe for failure. At both VW and Wells Fargo, signs that corners were being cut were repeatedly ignored. Thus, the illusion that the top-down strategies were working persisted – for a while. Particularly poignant is that disconfirming data were available for a surprisingly long time, but they were not put to good use.

Success in a VUCA world requires senior executives to engage thoughtfully and frequently with company operations across all levels and departments. The people on the front line who create and deliver products and services are privy to the most important strategic data the company has available. They know what customers want, what competitors are doing, and what the latest technology allows. Organizational learning – championed by company leaders but enacted by everyone – requires actively seeking deviations that challenge the assumptions underpinning a current strategy. Then, of course, these deviations must be welcomed because of their informative value for adapting the original strategy. Ironically, pushing harder on "execution" in response to early signals of underperformance may only aggravate the problem if shortcomings reveal that prior market intelligence or assumptions about the business model were flawed.

Finally, as unfortunate as the business failures in this chapter may have been, in many ways they pale in comparison to the human costs of low psychological safety explored in Chapter 4. Here we will see the even more vital role of speaking up to avoid preventable harm.

Chapter 3 Takeaways

- Leaders who welcome only good news create fear that blocks them from hearing the truth.
- Many managers confuse setting high standards with good management.
- A lack of psychological safety can create an illusion of success that eventually turns into serious business failures.
- Early information about shortcomings can nearly always mitigate the size and impact of future, large-scale failure.

Endnotes

1. Vlasic, B. "Volkswagen Official Gets 7-Year Term in Diesel-Emissions Cheating." *The New York Times*. December 6, 2017. https://www.nytimes.com/2017/12/06/business/oliver-schmidt-volkswagen.html Accessed June 13, 2018.

2. Kwak, J. "How Not to Regulate." *The Atlantic*. September 30, 2014. https://www.theatlantic.com/business/archive/2014/09/how-not-to-regulate/380919/ Accessed June 13, 2018.

3. The Volkswagen story in this chapter draws from new sources cited individually and from the following academic case studies:

    - Giolito, V., Verdin, P., Hamwi, M., & Oualadj, Y. Volkswagen: A Global Champion in the Making? Case Study. Solvay Brussels School Economics & Management, 2017; Lynch, L.J., Cutro, C., & Bird, E.

    - The Volkswagen Emissions Scandal. Case Study. UVA No. 7245. Charlottesville, VA. University of Virginia, Darden Business Publishing, 2016; and

    - Schuetz, M. Dieselgate – Heavy Fumes Exhausting the Volkswagen Group. Case Study. HK No. 1089. Hong Kong. The University of Hong Kong Asia Case Research Center, 2016.

4. Ewing, J. "Volkswagen C.E.O. Martin Winterkorn Resigns Amid Emissions Scandal." *The New York Times*. September 23, 2015. https://www.nytimes.com/2015/09/24/business/international/volkswagen-chief-martin-winterkorn-resigns-amid-emissions-scandal.html Accessed June 13, 2018.

5. Parloff, R. "How VW Paid $25 Billion for 'Dieselgate' – and Got Off Easy." *Fortune Magazine*. February 6, 2018. http://fortune.com/2018/02/06/volkswagen-vw-emissions-scandal-penalties/ Accessed June 13, 2018.

6. *Ibid.*

7. Sorokanich, B. "Report: Bosch Warned VW About Diesel Emissions Cheating in 2007." *Car and Driver*. September 28, 2015. https://blog.caranddriver.com/report-bosch-warned-vw-about-diesel-emissions-cheating-in-2007/ Accessed June 13, 2018.

8. Hakim, D., Kessler A.M., & Ewing, J. "As Volkswagen Pushed to Be No. 1, Ambitions Fueled a Scandal." *The New York Times*, September 26, 2015. https://www.nytimes.com/2015/09/27/business/as-vw-pushed-to-be-no-1-ambitions-fueled-a-scandal.html Accessed June 13, 2018.

9. Ewing, J. 2015, op cit.
10. Cremer, A. & Bergin, T. "Fear and Respect: VW's culture under Winterkorn." *Reuters*. October 10, 2015. https://www.reuters.com/article/us-volkswagen-emissions-culture/fear-and-respect-vws-culture-under-winterkorn-idUSKCN0S40MT20151010 Accessed June 13, 2018.
11. https://www.youtube.com/watch?v=YpPNVSQmR5c
12. Lutz, B. "One Man Established the Culture that Led to VW's Emission Scandal." *Road and Track*. November 4, 2015. https://www.roadandtrack.com/car-culture/a27197/bob-lutz-vw-diesel-fiasco/ Accessed June 13, 2018.
13. *Ibid.*
14. Kiley, D. *Getting the Bugs Out: The Rise, Fall, and Comeback of Volkswagen in America.* John Wiley & Sons, 2002. 38–49. Print.
15. https://www.youtube.com/watch?v=DfGs2Y5WJ14.
16. Cremer, A. & Bergin, T, 2015, op cit.
17. *Ibid.*
18. *Ibid.*
19. *Ibid.*
20. Details on the Wells Fargo story come from Lynch, L.J., Coleman, A.R., & Cutro, C. The Wells Fargo Banking Scandal. Case Study. UVA No. 7267. Charlottesville, VA. University of Virginia, Darden Business Publishing, 2017.
21. Wells Fargo, 2015 annual report
22. Wells Fargo, 2010 annual report
23. Wells Fargo, 2015 annual report
24. Gonzales, R. "Wells Fargo CEO John Stumpf Resigns Amid Scandal." *NPR*, October 12, 2016. https://www.npr.org/sections/thetwo-way/2016/10/12/497729371/wells-fargo-ceo-john-stumpf-resigns-amid-scandal Accessed June 13, 2018.
25. Reckard, E.S. "Wells Fargo's Pressure-Cooker Sales Culture Comes at a Cost." *The Los Angeles Times*, December 21, 2013. http://www.latimes.com/business/la-fi-wells-fargo-sale-pressure-20131222-story.html Accessed June 13, 2018.
26. Keller, L.J., Campbell, D., & Mehrotra, K. "While 5,000 Wells Fargo Employees Got Fired, Their Bosses Thrived." *Bloomberg*. November 3, 2016. https://www.bloomberg.com/news/articles/2016-11-03/wells-fargo-s-stars-climbed-while-abuses-flourished-beneath-them Accessed June 13, 2018.
27. Cao, A. "Lawsuit Alleges Exactly How Wells Fargo Pushed Employees to Abuse Customers." *TIME*. September 29, 2016. http://time.com/

money/4510482/wells-fargo-fake-accounts-class-action-lawsuit/ Accessed June 13, 2018.

28. Mehrotra, K. "Wells Fargo Ex-Managers' Suit Puts Scandal Blame Higher Up Chain." *Bloomberg.* December 8, 2016. https://www .bloomberg.com/news/articles/2016-12-08/wells-fargo-ex-managers-suit-puts-scandal-blame-higher-up-chain Accessed June 13, 2018.

29. Reckard, E.S. December 21, 2013, op cit.

30. Cowley, S. "Voices From Wells Fargo: 'I Thought I Was Having a Heart Attack.'" *The New York Times.* October 20, 2016. https://www .nytimes.com/2016/10/21/business/dealbook/voices-from-wells-fargo-i-thought-i-was-having-a-heart-attack.html Accessed June 13, 2018.

31. Cao, A. September 29, 2016, op cit.

32. Cowley, S. October 20, 2016, op cit.

33. Glazer, E. & Rexrode, C. "Wells Fargo CEO Defends Bank Culture, Lays Blame With Bad Employees." *The Wall Street Journal.* September 13, 2016. https://www.wsj.com/articles/wells-fargo-ceo-defends-bank-culture-lays-blame-with-bad-employees-1473784452 Accessed June 13, 2018.

34. Egan, M. September 8, 2016, op cit.

35. Freed, D. & Reckhard, E.S. "Wells Fargo Faces Costly Overhaul of Bankrupt Sales Culture." *Reuters,* October 12, 2016.

36. Corkery, M. & Cowley, S. "Wells Fargo Warned Workers Against Sham Accounts, but 'They Needed a Paycheck.'" *The New York Times,* September 16, 2016. https://www.nytimes.com/2016/09/ 17/business/dealbook/wells-fargo-warned-workers-against-fake-accounts-but-they-needed-a-paycheck.html Accessed June 13, 2018.

37. *Ibid.*

38. Consumer Financial Protection Bureau press release. "Consumer Financial Protection Bureau Fines Wells Fargo $100 Million for Widespread Illegal Practice of Secretly Opening Unauthorized Accounts." *ConsumerFinance.gov,* September 8, 2016. https://www .consumerfinance.gov/about-us/newsroom/consumer-financial-protection-bureau-fines-wells-fargo-100-million-widespread-illegal-practice-secretly-opening-unauthorized-accounts/ Accessed June 13, 2018.

39. Egan, M. "Wells Fargo Admits to Signs of Worker Retaliation." *CNN Money.* January 23, 2017. http://money.cnn.com/2017/01/23/ investing/wells-fargo-retaliation-ethics-line/index.html Accessed June 13, 2018.

40. Edmondson, A.C. & Verdin, P.J. "Your Strategy Should Be a Hypothesis You Constantly Adjust." *Harvard Business Review*. November 9, 2017. https://hbr.org/2017/11/your-strategy-should-be-a-hypothesis-you-constantly-adjust Accessed June 13, 2018.

41. "Our History." Nokia. https://www.nokia.com/en_int/about-us/who-we-are/our-history Accessed June 7, 2018.

42. Nokia Corporation, 1998 annual report.

43. Huy, Q. & Vuori, T. "Who Killed Nokia? Nokia Did." *INSEAD Knowledge*. September 22, 2015. https://knowledge.insead.edu/strategy/who-killed-nokia-nokia-did-4268 Accessed June 13, 2018.

44. Bass, D., Heiskanen, V., & Fickling, D. "Microsoft to Buy Nokia's Devices Unit for $7.2 Billion." *Bloomberg*. September 3, 2013. https://www.bloomberg.com/news/articles/2013-09-03/microsoft-to-buy-nokia-s-devices-business-for-5-44-billion-euros Accessed June 13, 2018.

45. Huy, Q. & Vuori, T. September 22, 2015, op cit.

46. *Ibid.*

47. Vuori, T. & Huy, Q. "Distributed Attention and Shared Emotions in the Innovation Process: How Nokia Lost the Smartphone Battle." *Administrative Science Quarterly* 61.1 (2016): 23.

48. *Ibid.*

49. *Ibid.*

50. *Ibid.*

51. *Ibid.*

52. Vuori, T. & Huy, Q. (2016): 30.

53. Vuori, T. & Huy, Q. (2016): 32.

54. Protess, B. & Craig, S. "Harsh Words for Regulators in Crisis Commission Report." *The New York Times*. January 27, 2011. https://dealbook.nytimes.com/2011/01/27/harsh-words-for-regulators-in-crisis-commission-report/?mtrref=www.google.com&gwh=54322022775D2A4C1766CE843F23C604&gwt=pay Accessed June 13, 2018.

55. Beim, D. & McCurdy, C. "Report on Systemic Risk and Bank Supervision" *Federal Reserve Bank of New York Report*. 2009. 1. https://info.publicintelligence.net/FRBNY-BankSupervisionReport.pdf. Accessed June 1, 2018.

56. Beim, D. & McCurdy, C. 2009: 9.

57. *Ibid.*

58. Beim, D. & McCurdy, C. 2009: 19.

59. "The Secret Recordings of Carmen Segarra." *This American Life.*
    September 26, 2014. https://www.thisamericanlife.org/536/the-
    secret-recordings-of-carmen-segarra. Accessed June 1, 2018.
60. *Ibid.*
61. Edmondson, A.C. & Verdin, P.J. "The strategic imperative of psycho-
    logical safety and organizational error management." *How could this hap-
    pen? Managing errors in organizations.* Ed. J. Hagen. Palgrave/MacMillan:
    in press.
62. Edmondson, A.C. & Verdin, P.J. November 9, 2017, op cit.

4 | Dangerous Silence

"Regret for the things we did can be tempered by time; it is regret for the things we did not do that is inconsolable."

—Sydney Harris[1]

More than just business failure is at stake when psychological safety is low. In many workplaces, people see something physically unsafe or wrong and fear reporting it. Or they feel bullied and intimidated by someone but don't mention it to supervisors or counselors. This reticence unfortunately can lead to widespread frustration, anxiety, depression, and even physical harm. In short, we live and work in communities, cultures, and organizations in which *not* speaking up can be hazardous to human health.

This chapter explores how silence at work leads to harm that could have been prevented. You will read stories that come predominantly, but not exclusively, from high-risk industries. In these cases, employees find themselves unable to speak up; the ensuing silence then creates conditions for physical and emotional harm. Although never easy, in some workplaces, as we will see in Chapter 5 and Chapter 6, people do feel both safe and compelled to speak up. This gives everyone the chance to develop constructive solutions and avoid harmful outcomes.

We'll start with stories of silence that gave rise to major accidents in high-risk settings where risk and routine often exist in an uneasy balance. The first two accidents take place in the air. From there, we'll move to a hospital bed, tsunami waves, and finally the volatile setting of public opinion.

Failing to Speak Up

On February 1, 2003, NASA's Space Shuttle *Columbia* experienced a catastrophic reentry into the Earth's atmosphere.[2] All seven astronauts perished. Although space travel is obviously risky and fatal accidents seem part of the territory, this particular accident did not come "out of the blue." Two weeks earlier, a NASA engineer named Rodney Rocha had watched launch-day video footage, a day after what had seemed to be a picture-perfect launch on a sunny Florida morning. But something seemed amiss. Rocha played the tape over and over. He thought a chunk of insulating foam might have fallen off the shuttle's external tank and struck the left wing of the craft. The video images were grainy, shot from a great distance, and it was impossible to really tell whether or not the foam had caused damage, but Rocha could not help worrying about the size and position of that grainy moving dot he saw on the screen. To resolve the ambiguity, Rocha wanted to get satellite photos of the Shuttle's wing. But this would require NASA higher ups to ask the Department of Defense for help.

Rocha emailed his boss to see if he could get help authorizing a request for satellite images. His boss thought it unnecessary and said so. Discouraged, Rocha sent an emotional email to his fellow engineers, later explaining that "engineers were . . . not to send messages much higher than their own rung in the ladder."[3] Working with an *ad hoc* team of engineers to assess the damage, he was unable to resolve his concern about possible damage without obtaining images. A week later, when the foam strike possibility was briefly discussed by senior managers in the formal mission management team meeting, Rocha, sitting on the periphery, observed silently.

A formal investigation by experts would later conclude that a large hole in the shuttle wing occurred when a briefcase-sized piece of foam hit the leading edge of the wing, causing the accident.[4] They also identified two, albeit difficult and highly-uncertain, rescue options that might have prevented the tragic deaths. Reporting on the investigation, ABC News anchor Charlie Gibson asked Rocha why he hadn't spoken up in the meeting. The engineer replied, "I just couldn't do it. I'm too low down [in the organization] . . . and she [meaning Mission Management Team Leader Linda Ham] is way up here," gesturing with his hand held above his head.[5]

Rocha's statement captures a subtle but crucial aspect of the psychology of speaking up at work. Consider his words carefully. He did not say, "I chose not to speak," or "I felt it was not right to speak." He said that he "couldn't" speak. Oddly, this description is apt. The psychological experience of having something to say yet feeling literally unable to do so is painfully real for many employees and very common in organizational hierarchies, like that of NASA in 2003. We can all recognize this phenomenon. We understand why his hands spontaneously depicted that poignant vertical ladder. When probed, as Rocha was by Gibson, many people report a similar experience of feeling un*able* to speak up when hierarchy is made salient. Meanwhile, the higher ups in a position to listen and learn are often blind to the silencing effects of their presence.

What Was Not Said

Twenty-six years earlier, workplace silence played a major role in the collision of two Boeing 747 jets on an island runway in the Canary Islands in March 1977.[6] The crash ignited two jumbo jets into flames, and 583 people died. Subsequent investigations into what has been called the Tenerife disaster, still considered the worst accident in the history of civil aviation, were among the first to study the roles played by human factors in airline fatalities. The resulting changes made to aviation procedures and cockpit training laid the groundwork for some of today's most crucial psychological safety measures.

Let's look at what went wrong on that afternoon in late March at the small Los Rodeos Airport on the island of Tenerife. The runway was covered in heavy fog and the airport was small, which made it difficult for the pilots of both aircrafts to see the runway and one another. An unexpected landing at Tenerife due to a bomb scare earlier that day at nearby Las Palamas airport put extra stress on the crew, intent on keeping to their scheduled flight arrival times. Air control personnel may have been watching a sports game, distracting their attention. However, these relatively common, if unfavorable, conditions need not have resulted in tragedy. If we look more closely into what was said in the aircraft cockpit – and more importantly, *what was not said, and why not* – we can better understand the outsized role played by psychological safety.

Captain Jacob Veldhuyzen van Zanten, one of the company's most senior pilots, chief flight trainer of most of the company's 747 pilots, and head of flight safety for Royal Dutch Airlines (KLM), piloted the flight.[7] Nicknamed "Mr. KLM," van Zanten held the power to issue pilots' licenses and oversaw pilots' six-month flight checks to determine whether licenses would be extended. His photograph, which had just appeared in a KLM advertising spread, depicted a smiling and confident man in a white shirt sitting in front of a control panel. He looked like a man who was comfortable being in charge.

Flying with van Zanten that day were two other top-notch and highly-experienced pilots: First Officer Klaas Meurs, age 32, and Flight Engineer Willem Schreuder, age 48. Importantly, two months earlier, van Zanten had been Meur's "check pilot," testing his ability to fly the Boeing 747.

The crucial moments came as the KLM and the Pan Am flights were preparing for takeoff. Immediately after lining up on the runway, Captain van Zanten impatiently advanced the throttles and the aircraft started to move forward. First Officer Meurs, implying that van Zanten was moving too soon, then advised that air traffic control (ATC) had not yet given them clearance.

Van Zanten, sounding irritated, responded: "No, I know that. Go ahead, ask."[8]

Following his captain's request, Meurs then radioed the tower that they were "ready for takeoff" and "waiting for our ATC clearance." The ATC then specified the route that the aircraft was to follow after takeoff. Although the ATC used the word "takeoff," their communication did not include an explicit statement that KLM was cleared for takeoff. Meurs began reading the flight clearance back to the controller, but van Zanten interrupted with an imperative: "We're going."

Given the captain's authority, it was in this moment that Meurs apparently did not feel safe enough to speak up. Meurs, in that split second, did *not* open his mouth to say, "wait for clearance!"

Meanwhile, after the KLM plane had started its takeoff roll, the tower instructed the Pan Am crew to "report when runway clear." To which the Pan Am crew replied, "OK, will report when we're clear." On hearing this, Flight Engineer Schreuder expressed his concern that Pan Am was not clear of the runway by asking, "is he not clear, that Pan American?"

Van Zanten emphatically replied, "oh, yes," and continued with the takeoff.

And in this moment Schreuder did not say a thing. Although he had correctly surmised that the Pan Am jet might be blocking their way, Schreuder did not challenge Van Zanten's confident retort. He did not ask ATC to clarify or confirm by asking, for example, "is Pan American on the runway?" His reticence indicates a lack of the psychological safety that would make such a query all but second nature.

By then it was too late. The KLM Boeing was going too fast to stop when van Zanten, Meurs, and Schreuder finally could see the Pan Am jet blocking their way. The KLM's left-side engines, lower fuselage, and main landing gear struck the upper right side of the Pan Am's fuselage, ripping apart the center. The KLM plane remained briefly airborne before going into a stall, rolling sharply, hitting the ground, and igniting into a fireball.

Such is the inexorably psychological pull of hierarchy that even when their own lives were at risk, not to mention the lives of others, the first officer and the flight engineer did not push back on their captain's authority. In those moments where speaking up might make sense, we all go through an implicit decision-making process, weighing the benefits and costs of speaking up. The problem, as explained in Chapter 2, is that the benefits are often unclear and delayed (e.g. avoiding a possible collision) while the costs are tangible and immediate (van Zanten's irritation and potential anger). As a result, we consistently underweight the benefits and overweight the costs. In the case of Tenerife, this biased process led to disastrous outcomes.

Many who analyze events leading up to tragic accidents such as this one-which could have been avoided had the junior officer spoken up-cannot help pointing out that people should demonstrate a bit more backbone. Courage. It is impossible to disagree with this assertion. Nonetheless, agreeing doesn't make it effective. Exhorting people to speak up because it's the right thing to do relies on an ethical argument but is not a strategy for ensuring good outcomes. Insisting on acts of courage puts the onus on individuals without creating the conditions where the expectation is likely to be met.

For speaking up to become routine, psychological safety – and expectations about speaking up – must become institutionalized and systematized. After Tenerife, cockpit training was changed to place more emphasis on crew decision-making, encourage pilots to assert their opinion when they believed something was wrong, and help captains listen to concerns from co-pilots and crews.[9] These measures were a precursor to the official crew resource management (CRM) training that all pilots must now undergo.

Excessive Confidence in Authority

Medicine, like commercial aviation, is another profession where authority is well understood and tightly linked to one's place in a strict hierarchy. A direct line of command, where everyone knows his or her place, has its benefits. However, deference to others, especially in the face of ambiguity, can become the default mode of operation, leading everyone to believe that the person-on-top always knows best. In some cases, an implicit belief that the person with the highest place on the hierarchy must also be the authority can lead to fatal consequences. In other cases, an implicit belief in the authority of the medical system itself can be fatal.

On December 3, 1994, Betsy Lehman, a 39-year-old mother of two and a healthcare columnist at *The Boston Globe*, died at the Dana-Farber Cancer Institute while undergoing a third round of high-dose chemotherapy for breast cancer.[10] In part because of her profession as a journalist, Lehman's death was well publicized in the media, especially once it was linked to a medical error.[11]

The Dana-Farber Cancer Institute where Lehman sought treatment was renowned for its cancer research and its success in treating complex and difficult cases. With only 57 inpatient beds, its patient care was a kind of boutique unit that enabled informal information sharing among physicians, nurses, and pharmacy staff rather than the formal communications mechanisms that exist in a traditional hospital setting. As Senior Oncologist Stephen Sallan noted, "our confidence was based on the assumption that if we were all wonderful then our pharmacy safety would be wonderful."[12] Unfortunately, this assumption did not leave much room for questioning or routine checking. The absence of a Director of Nursing at the time of Lehman's admittance, a post that had been vacant for over a year, also signals that the medical and clinical teams did not adequately appreciate the interdependence and complexity of their work.

Lehman was admitted to the Dana-Farber for the planned chemotherapy on November 14, 1994. Although the chemotherapy agent was the commonly used cyclophosphamide, the dose was especially high because Lehman's treatment plan involved a cutting-edge stem-cell transplant. The protocol called for the chemotherapy to be infused over four days, with the amount given during each 24-hour period to be "barely shy of lethal."[13] As part of the clinical trial, Lehman was also given another drug, cimetidine, which was supposed to boost the effect of the first drug.[14]

In routine cancer treatments, courses of chemotherapy doses are typically standardized; however, in a research trial such as Lehman was undergoing, upper limits could be ambiguous. At Dana-Farber, where 30% of patients might be enrolled in a clinical trial at any one time, staff members who administered chemotherapy were accustomed to seeing unusual drug combinations and dosages.[15] That may partly explain why no alarm bells went off even though the prescription – written by a clinical research fellow in oncology, copied into Lehman's records by a nurse, and filled by three different pharmacists – had mistakenly ordered the entire four-day dosage for each day, providing Lehman with four times the dosage she was supposed to receive.

The treatment was expected to produce severe nausea and vomiting. However, over the next three weeks in the hospital, Lehman's symptoms were extraordinary. She had not been as sick during the first two high-dose treatments. Now she was "grossly swollen" and had abnormal blood and EKG tests.[16] High-dose cyclophosphamide was known to be toxic to the heart. Lehman's husband reported that she was "vomiting sheets of tissue. [The doctors] said this was the worst they had ever seen. But the doctors said this was all normal with bone marrow transplant."[17] At one point, Lehman asked a nurse, "Am I going to die from vomiting?"[18] Meanwhile, another patient, admitted shortly before Lehman, given the same incorrect chemotherapy dose, had suddenly collapsed and was rushed to the intensive care unit.

The day before Lehman's discharge, her symptoms seemed to be abating. And there were signs that the experimental stem cell transplant was proceeding successfully. An EKG, however, was abnormal. On December 3, the day of her discharge and the day she died of heart failure, the last people she spoke to – a friend, a social worker, and a nurse – confirmed that she was very upset, frightened, and felt that something "was wrong."[19] We do not know whether or not she had voiced this concern as distinctly or coherently in the previous weeks. Surely, she must have wondered. Of course, an extremely ill patient is usually not in a position to assertively question her treatment plan, especially one that is experimental.

The medical error was not discovered until three months later – by a routine data check rather than by a clinical inquiry. As part of its corrective actions, Dana-Farber instituted automated medication checks into its chemotherapy procedures. Ultimately, Lehman's death became a catalyst for hospital and healthcare institutions in the US to craft policy to help reduce medical errors, including more systemic checking of routine procedures throughout a patient's treatment process and more reporting provisions for caregivers, regardless of their professional status.

From the perspective of psychological safety, however, the bigger question that remains is why, given Lehman's extreme physical distress, did no one deeply and persistently question whether something had gone profoundly wrong? Did Lehman and her husband place too much trust in the highly regarded medical institution? Similarly, why did pharmacists not question the extraordinary fourfold dosage of the already high-dose chemotherapy agent? The same can be asked about the nurses. Perhaps their implicit trust in the expertise of the physician-researchers left them incurious. Or, they may have been reluctant to speak up to inquire into rationale for the treatment plan only to be put down by their higher-status colleagues. We don't know whether the nurses and physicians who observed Lehman's symptoms assigned too little significance to the type of side effects the high-dose chemotherapy was supposed to induce. No one involved seemed to accurately assess the gravity of her condition. Ultimately, Betsy Lehman's mother, Mildred K. Lehman, was the one who concisely summed up the problem: "Betsy's life might have been saved if staff had stepped forward to attend to the multiple signs that her treatment was far off course."[20]

What is important to take away from this story, and what most hospitals today work hard to avoid, is that a climate in which people err on the side of silence – implicitly favoring self-protection and embarrassment avoidance over the possibility that one's input may be desperately needed in that moment – is a serious risk factor. It is clearly far better for people to ask questions or raise concerns and be wrong than it is for them to hold back, but most people don't consciously recognize that fact. Raising concerns that turn out to be unfounded presents a learning opportunity for the person speaking up and for those listening who thereby glean crucial information about what others understand or don't understand about the situation or the task.

A Culture of Silence

Cassandra, one of the most tragic characters in classical Greek mythology, was given the gift of prophecy along with the curse that she would never be believed. Low levels of psychological safety can create a culture of silence. They can also create a Cassandra culture – an environment in which speaking up is belittled and warnings go unheeded. Especially when speaking up entails drawing attention to unpleasant outcomes, as was the case for Cassandra in her prediction of war, it's easy for others not to listen or believe. A culture of silence is thus not only one that inhibits speaking up but one in which people fail to listen thoughtfully to those who do speak up – especially when they are bringing unpleasant news.

Consider the *Challenger* shuttle explosion back in 1986. Unlike Rodney Rocha's silence in a crucial workplace moment, Roger Boisjoly, an engineer at NASA contractor Morton-Thiokol, did speak up. The night before the disastrous launch, Boisjoly raised his concern that unusually cold temperatures might cause the O-rings that connected segments of the shuttle to malfunction. His data were incomplete and his argument vague, but the assembled group could have readily resolved the ambiguity with some simple analyses and experiments had they listened intensely and respectfully. In short, for voice to be effective requires a culture of listening.

Let's take a look at a more recent example of what can happen when the listening culture is weak.

Dismissing Warnings

On March 11, 2011, a 9.0 magnitude earthquake occurred off the northeastern coast of Japan. The quake, later dubbed the "Great East Japanese Earthquake," created tsunami waves up to 45 feet high that struck the Fukushima Daiichi Nuclear Power Plant.[21] Waves of mythic proportions leapt easily over the plant's undersized sea walls, flooding the site and completely destroying emergency generators, seawater cooling pumps, and the electric wiring system. Without power to cool down the nuclear reactors, three of the reactors overheated, resulting in multiple explosions that injured workers on the ground. Most alarmingly, nuclear fuel was released into the ocean, and radionuclides were released from the plant into the atmosphere. As a result of the nuclear meltdown, hundreds of thousands of Japanese were forced to flee their homes to avoid radiation exposure. Most will be unlikely to ever return home, as it's estimated the cleanup will take between 30 and 40 years.[22]

Although the earthquake itself, the most powerful ever recorded in Japan's history, wreaked unpreventable catastrophic damage that killed an estimated 15,000 people,[23] it's now universally accepted that the corollary disaster at the nuclear power plant was in fact preventable. By the summer of 2012, an independent investigation, released after having conducted 900 hours of hearings, interviews with over a thousand people, 9 plant tours, 19 committee meetings, and 3 town halls, concluded that "the accident was clearly man-made" and the "direct causes of the accident were all foreseeable."[24] Examining the evidence, it becomes clear that in the years leading up to the disaster at the Daiichi Nuclear Power Plant, more than one Cassandra-like figure spoke up more than once to warn of such an accident. Recommendations were made for reasonable safety measures that would likely have prevented or mitigated the plant's destruction. But each time, the warnings were dismissed or not believed. The question is, why?

In 2006, Katsuhiko Ishibashi, a professor at the Research Center for Urban Safety and Security at Kobe University, was appointed to a Japanese subcommittee tasked with revising the national guidelines on the earthquake-resistance of the country's nuclear power plants. Ishibashi proposed that the group review the standards for surveying active fault lines and criticized the government's record of allowing the construction of power plants, like Fukushima Daiichi, in areas with the potential for such high seismic activity. But the rest of the committee, the majority of which consisted of advisors with ties to the power companies, rejected his proposal and downplayed his concerns.[25]

The following year, Ishibashi spoke up again, publishing a prescient article titled *Why Worry? Japan's Nuclear Plants at Grave Risk from Quake Damage,* with the claim that Japan had been lulled into a false sense of confidence after many years of relatively quiet seismic activity. An expert on seismicity and plate tectonics in and around the Japanese islands, he believed that tectonic plates followed regular schedules and that the area in question was overdue for an earthquake. His warning was explicit: "unless radical steps are taken now to reduce the vulnerability of nuclear power plants to earthquakes, Japan could experience a true nuclear catastrophe in the near future," including one caused by tsunamis.[26] Unfortunately, others dismissed Ishibashi's warnings. For instance, Haruki Madarame, a nuclear regulator and chairman of Japan's Nuclear Safety Commission during the Fukushima disaster, told the Japanese legislature not to worry, as Ishibashi was a "nobody."[27]

If Madarame was harsh in his condemnation of Ishibashi as a "nobody," it's true that, as an academic rather than an industry or government official, he was an outsider. He was, perhaps, not as tightly bound to the dominant post–World War II push for Japan to become independent from its historical dependence on energy imports. Since the mid-fifties, the island, which has few fossil fuels in the ground, had invested heavily in nuclear energy to diversify its energy supply from oil and achieve greater energy security.[28] For the next 40 years, following the 1970s "oil shocks," and despite the highly publicized 1979 Three Mile Island and 1986 Chernobyl accidents, Japan had worked doggedly and ferociously to develop its own domestic nuclear power production capacity.[29] For instance, the government had provided subsidies and other incentives for rural towns to build plants. It even conducted public relations campaigns to convince citizens that nuclear power was safe.[30] Even so, public opinion surrounding nuclear power remained mixed to negative, with several anti-nuclear demonstrations and the abandonment of several plans to build more plants.[31] Given this political context, Ishibashi's safety concerns may have been perceived as unpatriotic or meddlesome.

A 2000 in-house study by Tokyo Electric Power Company (TEPCO), the country's biggest electric company and the owner of the Fukushima Daiichi plant, did acknowledge the possibility that Japan could experience a tsunami of as high as 50 feet. In fact, the report recommended that measures be taken to provide better protection from the risks of flooding. However, nothing was ever done because TEPCO thought the risk of such a low probability event was unrealistic.[32] Japanese regulators like the Nuclear and Industrial Safety Agency (NISA) also may have hesitated from policing the utilities because, by then, nuclear energy had become even more of a strategic priority for Japan, and increased nuclear power generation was required to reach the greenhouse gas emission goals laid out by the Kyoto protocol. A dozen new plants were slated to be built by 2011.[33] Prior to the Fukushima disaster, Japan was generating 30% of its electricity via nuclear reactors, and the government planned to increase that percentage to 40% in the years to come.[34]

Although safety issues were ostensibly part of the nuclear power expansion plans, retrospective investigations demonstrate that the government and industry culture had not given due credence or consideration to the gravity of existing threats. For example, in a

June 2009 meeting held by NISA specifically to discuss the readiness
of Fukushima Daiichi to withstand a natural disaster, tsunamis were
not even on the agenda. The agency simply did not see them as
likely enough in the Fukushima region to warrant consideration. In
creating safety guidelines for Fukushima, the panel thus used data
from the biggest earthquake on record in the area, a 1938 earthquake
that measured only 7.9 in magnitude and caused only a small
tsunami. Because the reactors at Fukushima Daiichi were located
near the sea, TEPCO constructed a seawall – one just tall enough to
stop a tsunami similar to the one in 1938 from hitting it. The panel
assumed that the wall was tall enough to stop any future tsunami and
thus focused mainly on preparing the plant for earthquakes.

Another Cassandra-like figure spoke up at that June meeting. Dr.
Yukinobi Okamura, the director of Japan's Active Fault and Earthquake Research Center, told the panel he disagreed with TEPCO's
decision.[35] He did not think the 1938 quake was big enough to serve
as the basis for the Daiichi guidelines and instead brought up a much
earlier example, the Jogan tsunami, which occurred in AD 869 after
a massive earthquake. TEPCO representatives, wishing to discredit
Okamura, minimize his concern, or both, claimed the Jogan earthquake "did not cause much damage." Okamura insisted otherwise.
The Jogan tsunami had destroyed castles and killed at least a thousand people. Historical writings compared the tsunami's fury to waves
that "raged like nightmares and immediately reached the city center."
Okamura told the panel that he was worried that a tsunami like Jogan
could overwhelm the Fukushima region and was confused that the
panel was not using all of the available data.

Instead of listening and taking Okamura's concerns seriously,
as might occur in a culture where psychological safety was high, a
TEPCO executive countered that it didn't make sense to base the
safety recommendations on a legendary earthquake that wasn't measured by contemporary tools and techniques. Besides, this meeting
was to discuss the risks from earthquakes, rather than tsunamis. The
meeting moved on, with TEPCO executives saying they would try
to learn more. The next meeting, Okamura again tried to convince

the panel of the severity of the threat. He described the predictive models his institute had created to show that the current seawall would not be high enough for anything above an 8.4 magnitude earthquake, and the detailed surveys they'd performed on the sand left behind by the Jogan tsunami. In the end, however, the panel did not listen.

Going Along to Get Along

A culture of silence can thus be understood as a culture in which the prevailing winds favor going along rather than offering one's concerns. It is based on the assumption that most people's voices do not offer value and thus will not be valued. Perhaps the most cogent indictment of how a culture of silence perpetuated a set of attitudes that enabled the Daiichi plant disaster was articulated by Kiyoshi Kurokawa, the Chairman of the NAIIC, who wrote at the beginning of the English version of the report that

> For all the extensive detail it provides, what this report cannot fully convey – especially to a global audience – is the mindset that supported the negligence behind this disaster. What must be admitted – very painfully – is that this was a disaster "Made in Japan." Its fundamental causes are to be found in the ingrained conventions of Japanese culture: our reflexive obedience; our reluctance to question authority; our devotion to "sticking with the program"; our groupism; and our insularity.[36]

Japanese culture does not have a monopoly on any of the ingrained conventions that Kurokawa lists. Each one is endemic of a culture with low levels of psychological safety where the internal reluctance to speak up or push back combines with a very strong desire to look good to the outside world. Concern with reputation can silence employees' voices internally as well as externally. Resistance to warnings about the safety about the Fukushima Daiichi plant – and what it would take to install better safety measures – were bound up in national aspirations for nuclear energy.

Similar to what we learned about the FRBNY in Chapter 3, where another powerful set of institutional bodies tacitly colluded to silence the few who dared to speak up, push back, or disagree, Japan's nuclear power industry suffered regulatory capture. According to Kurokawa, Japan's long-held policy goal to achieve national energy security via nuclear energy became "such a powerful mandate, [that] nuclear power became an unstoppable force, immune to scrutiny by civil society. Its regulation was entrusted to the same government bureaucracy responsible for its promotion."[37] This blinding need and ambition helped create a culture where "it became accepted practice to resist regulatory pressure and cover up small-scale accidents . . . that led to the disaster at the Fukushima Daiichi Nuclear Plant."[38]

In 2013, a Stanford study concluded that a mere $50 million could have financed a wall high enough to prevent the disaster.[39] Yet, the case shows how very challenging it can be to be heard – to have voice welcomed, explored, and sometimes acted upon – when the dominant culture does not want to hear the message.

Silence in the Noisy Age of Social Media

On October 15, 2017, actress Alyssa Milano tapped fewer than 140 characters into her personal device: "If you've been sexually harassed or assaulted write 'me too' as a reply to this tweet." Within 24 hours, the hashtag #MeToo had been tweeted nearly half a million times.[40] Although the MeToo movement had been created 10 years earlier by Tarana Burke,[41] Milano's tweet, posted in the context of a slew of recent and highly publicized sexual harassment accusations leveled against celebrities, ignited a social media activism campaign. The goal: the simple act of speaking up. Women and men from all walks of life who had suffered myriad types of unwanted sexual attention, often egregious and persistent, the majority afraid to tell even their closest relations, were emboldened to tweet, post, and message about their experiences in what became a public forum.

Milano's tweet was hardly the first act of speaking up. Nine months earlier, on February 19, 2017, the social media landscape was emblazoned by a 3000-word blog post written by a young software engineer.[42] Susan Fowler, who had recently left her job as a site-reliability engineer at the ride-sharing company Uber, was exercising her right to candor on her personal website. The specificity and honesty with which she described her experience, which she called "a strange, fascinating, and slightly horrifying story," reveals much about how mechanisms of power and silence can perpetuate a psychologically unsafe culture. Fowler's voice, echoed by some of her colleagues, amplified by social media, and made louder still by mainstream press, tells us how an unsafe culture can ultimately become unsustainable.

On her first day at the company, Fowler's manager sent her a series of inappropriate messages over the company's chat system. The manager told her "he was looking for women to have sex with." Fowler said, "It was clear that he was trying to get me to have sex with him . . ." She took screenshots of the messages and reported the manager to HR. But things didn't go as she expected. Both HR and upper management informed Fowler that it was "this man's first offense, and that they wouldn't feel comfortable giving him anything other than a warning and a stern talking-to" because he "was a high performer." Fowler was given the choice of either finding another team to work on or remaining on her present team with the understanding that her manager would "most likely give [her] a poor performance review when review time came around, and there was nothing they could do about that." Fowler tried to protest this "choice," but got nowhere, and ultimately ended up switching teams.

Over the next few months, Fowler met other women engineers who had similar experiences of sexual harassment at Uber. They had also reported these to HR and gotten nowhere. Some of the women even reported having similar interactions with the same manager as Fowler. All were told it was his first offense. In each case, nothing was done. Fowler and her colleagues, feeling unheard, fell silent – for a while.

Ironically, as reported in her blog post, Fowler had been initially excited about joining Uber back in November 2015, citing that she had "the rare opportunity to choose whichever team was working on something that I wanted to be part of."

Promoted and Protected

Uber Technologies, Inc., founded in 2009 by serial entrepreneurs and friends Garrett Camp and Travis Kalanick, had launched in San Francisco in 2011 with funding from prominent Silicon Valley venture capital firms.[43] As Uber grew, so did its reputation as an aggressive, fast-moving, in-your-face company, not inconsistent with its overt intention to disrupt the long-established taxicab industry, replacing it with a ride-sharing economy.[44] Top employees were "promoted and protected" – as long as they could hit or exceed their numbers, they were rewarded.[45] After Fowler's post broke, current and former employees came forward to describe Uber's culture as "unrestrained," a "Hobbesian environment . . . in which workers are sometimes pitted against one another and where a blind eye is turned to infractions from top performers."[46] Fowler's manager had merely been a case in point.

Fowler, like other new Uber hires, had been advised of the company's core values.[47] Several of those values were likely to have contributed to a psychologically unsafe environment. For example, "super-pumpedness," especially central to the company, involved a can-do attitude and doing whatever it took to move the company forward. This often meant working long hours, not in itself a hallmark of a psychologically unsafe environment; Fowler seems to have relished the intellectual challenges and makes a point to say that she is "proud" of the engineering work she and her team did. But super-pumpedness, with its allusions to the sports arena and male hormones, seems to have been a harbinger of the bad times to come.

Another core value was to "make bold bets," which was interpreted as asking for forgiveness rather than permission. In other words, it was better to cross a line, be found out wrong, and ask for forgiveness than it was to ask permission to transgress in the first place. Another value, "meritocracy and toe-stepping," meant that employees were incented to work autonomously, rather than in teams, and cause pain to others to get things done and move forward, even if it meant damaging some relationships along the way.[48]

You may ask, so what? The same company that silenced, hurt, and eventually lost hardworking and talented engineers such as Susan Fowler was still tremendously successful in getting millions of people to speak with a new vocabulary word – "to uber." The company's growth was exponential and as of early 2018 is valued at north of $70 billion.[49] Maybe a bit of super-pumpedness and a little toe-stepping is just what it takes today to get ahead?

One problem is that social media enables a new kind of speaking up that makes it that much harder for companies to actively and shamelessly advocate for a psychologically unsafe culture. Fowler's exposé sent reporters running to investigate. *The New York Times* interviewed over 30 current and former Uber employees and reported on numerous incidents of harassment, some as egregious as an Uber manager who "groped female co-workers' breasts at a company retreat in Las Vegas" and "a director [who] shouted a homophobic slur at a subordinate during a heated confrontation in a meeting."[50] According to Fowler, when she joined Uber, the engineering site reliability organization was over 25% women, but before she left it had dropped to 6%. In the aftermath and reckoning that followed Fowler's blog, multiple lawsuits ensued, massive numbers of employees at all levels were either fired or left of their own accord, and the company's valuation and reputation fell far and fast.[51] A second problem is that people suffer unnecessary harm.

On June 21, 2017, Travis Kalanick stepped down as Uber's CEO after five of its major shareholders demanded his resignation.[52]

Although Fowler petitioned the United States Supreme Court to consider her experience at Uber in its decision on whether employees can forfeit rights to collective litigation in their employment contracts, the proposal was later voted down.[53] That year, she was featured on the cover of *TIME Magazine* as one of its "Person(s) of the Year" as one of five "Silence Breakers" who spoke out about sexual harassment in 2017.[54] She was also named *The Financial Times* "Person of the Year 2017,"[55] one of Vanity Fair's "New Establishments,"[56] and No. 2 on Recode's Top 100, behind only Jeff Bezos.[57]

Susan Fowler at Uber is just one example of how social media has enabled the speaking of truth to power in the workplace. In 2017, thousands of women spoke up to say, "Me Too," to workplace harassment, and hundreds of men in high-profile positions suffered the consequences of behavior that had, in many cases, worked for awhile – decades, or even entire careers. Communication technology gave social media movements such as MeToo and Black Lives Matter the power to ignite and move with rapidity into mainstream media, public opinion, and in some cases, into the legal courts. Such movements raise the sense of urgency to create and maintain organizations where psychological safety supports people to do their best work.

When Uber's new CEO, Dara Khosrowshahi, first came on board in August 2017, one of his priorities was to meet with women engineers. Alert to the damage done to the company's culture, he began by laying the groundwork for a psychologically safe workplace. As Jessica Bryndza, Uber's Global Director of People Experience, commented, "He [Khosrowshahi] didn't come in guns blazing. He came in listening."[58]

The operative word here is "listening." In the Chapters 5 and 6, you will read about eight flourishing organizations where leaders have created the conditions to make listening and speaking up the norm, not the exception. In these fearless workplaces, it's far less likely that employees will refrain from sharing valuable information, insights, or questions and far more likely that leaders will listen to rather than dismiss bad news or early warnings.

Chapter 4 Takeaways

- When people fail to speak up with their concerns or questions, the physical safety of customers or employees is at risk, sometimes leading to tragic loss of life.

- Excessive confidence in authority is a risk factor in psychological and physical safety.

- A culture of silence is a dangerous culture.

Endnotes

1. Harris. S.J. "Syd Cannot Stand Christmas Neckties." *The Akron Beacon Journal*. January 5, 1951, pp. 6. https://www.newspapers.com/newspage/147433987/ Accessed July 23, 2018

2. Roberto, M.A, Edmondson, A.C., &. Bohmer, R.J., *Columbia's* Final Mission. Case Study. HBS No. 304-090. Boston, MA: Harvard Business School Publishing, 2004.

3. Whitcraft, D., Katz, D., & Day, T. (Producers). "Columbia: Final Mission," *ABC Primetime*. New York: ABC News, 2003.

4. National Aeronautics and Space Administration. *Columbia Accident Investigation Board: Report Volume 1*. Washington, D.C.: U.S. Government Printing Office, 2003.

5. Whitcraft, D. *et al.* 2003, op cit.

6. The story of the disaster on Tenerife in this chapter draws on a number of sources produced by Jan Hagen and his colleagues, including:

   - Schafer, U., Hagen, J., & Burger, C. Mr. KLM (A): Jacob Veldhuyzen. Case Study. ESMT No. 411-0117. Berlin, Germany: European School of Management and Technology, 2011.

   - Schafer, U., Hagen, J., & Burger, C. Mr. KLM (B): Captain van Zanten. Case Study. ESMT No. 411-0118. Berlin, Germany: European School of Management and Technology, 2011.

   - Schafer, U., Hagen, J., & Burger, C. Mr. KLM (C): Jaap. Case Study. ESMT No. 411-0119. Berlin, Germany: European School of Management and Technology, 2011.

   - Hagen, J.U. *Confronting Mistakes: Lessons From The Aviation Industry When Dealing with Error*. United Kingdom: Palgrave Macmillan UK, 2013. Print.

7. Royal Dutch Airlines is Koninklijke Luchtvaart Maatschappij in Dutch, abbreviated as KLM.

8. The dialogue reported in this story was captured by the cockpit voice recorders of both planes involved in the collision and reported in Appendix 6 of the following investigation report: Air Line Pilots Association. *Aircraft accident report: Human factors report on the Tenerife accident, Tenerife, Canary Islands, March 27, 1977.* Washington D.C.: Engineering and Air Safety, 1977.

9. For history and background on CRM, refer to Alan Diehl's book on air safety: Diehl, A.E. *Air Safety Investigators: Using Science to Save Lives – One Crash at a Time.* United States: XLIBRIS, 2013. Print.

10. The story of Betsy Lehman's death at the Dana-Farber Cancer Institute in this chapter draws on information from a case study by my colleague Richard Bohmer: Bohmer, R. & Winslow, A. The Dana-Farber Cancer Institute. Case Study. HBS Case No. 699-025. Boston, MA: Harvard Business School Publishing, 1999.

11. *The Boston Globe* broke the Lehman story and continued to follow it closely in the months and years that followed. Richard Knox, who was later sued for his coverage of the incident, wrote the first article about the error: Knox, R.A. "Doctor's Orders Killed Cancer Patient." *The Boston Globe*, March 23, 1995.

12. Bohmer, R. & Winslow, A. 1999: 8.

13. Gorman, C. & Mondi, L. "The disturbing case of the cure that killed the patient." *TIME Magazine.* April 3, 1995: 60. http://content .time.com/time/magazine/article/0,9171,982768,00.html Accessed June 14, 2018.

14. Bohmer, R. & Winslow, A. 1999, op cit.

15. *Ibid.*

16. Knox, March 23, 1995, op cit.

17. *Ibid.*

18. *Ibid.*

19. *Ibid.*

20. Knox, R.A. "Dana-Farber puts focus on mistakes in overdoses." *The Boston Globe.* October 31, 1995. https://www.highbeam.com/doc/ 1P2-8310418.html Accessed June 12, 2018.

21. Details on the disaster at Fukushima Daiichi come from multiple reports:

   ■ Fukushima Nuclear Accident Independent Investigation Commission (NAIIC). "Official Report of the Fukushima Nuclear Accident

Independent Investigation Commission: Executive Summary." *National Diet of Japan*. 2012. https://www.nirs.org/wp-content/uploads/fukushima/naiic_report.pdf Accessed June 12, 2018.

- Amano, Y. "The Fukushima Daiichi Accident: Report by the Director General." *International Atomic Energy Agency Report*. 2015. https://www-pub.iaea.org/MTCD/Publications/PDF/Pub1710-ReportByTheDG-Web.pdf Accessed June 12, 2018.

22. Amano, Y. 2015, op cit.
23. *Ibid*.
24. Fukushima NAIIC. 2012: 16.
25. Clenfield, J. & Sato, S. "Japan Nuclear Energy Drive Compromised by Conflicts of Interest." *Bloomberg*. December 12, 2007. http://www.bloomberg.com/apps/news?pid=newsarchive&sid=awR8KsLlAcSo Accessed June 12, 2018.
26. Ishibashi, K. "Why Worry? Japan's Nuclear Plants at Grave Risk From Quake Damage." *The Asia-Pacific Journal*. August 1, 2007. https://apjjf.org/-Ishibashi-Katsuhiko/2495/article.html Accessed June 12, 2018.
27. Clenfield, J. "Nuclear Regulator Dismissed Seismologist on Japan Quake Threat." *Bloomberg.com*. November 21, 2011. https://www.bloomberg.com/news/articles/2011-11-21/nuclear-regulator-dismissed-seismologist-on-japan-quake-threat Accessed June 12, 2018.
28. World Nuclear Association. "Nuclear Power in Japan." *World-Nuclear.org* www.world-nuclear.org/information-library/country-profiles/countries-g-n/japan-nuclear-power.aspx. Accessed June 4, 2018.
29. *Ibid*.
30. Aldrich, D.P. "With a Mighty Hand." *The New Republic*. March 19, 2011. https://newrepublic.com/article/85463/japan-nuclear-power-regulation Accessed June 11, 2018.
31. See, for instance: BBC News. "Japan cancels nuclear power plant." *BBC News*. February 22, 2000. http://news.bbc.co.uk/2/hi/asia-pacific/652169.stm Accessed June 10, 2018.
32. Tokyo Electric Power Company. "Fukushima Nuclear Accident Summary & Nuclear Safety Reform Plan" *Tokyo Electric Power Company, Inc*. March 29, 2013: 19. As the company wrote in this report after the Fukushima disaster: "in June and July of [2000], the cost of constructing flooding embankment to protect against tsunami and the impact on surrounding areas were evaluated. The reliability

of the computational result was also discussed." But they ultimately concluded that the "technological validity" of such a model could not be verified, and did nothing more.

33. World Nuclear Association. "Nuclear Power in Japan," op cit.

34. *Ibid.*

35. All information from the Okamura story is from Clarke, R. & Eddy, R.P. *Warnings: Finding Cassandras to Stop Catastrophes.* HarperCollins Publishing, 2017, Chapter 5, pp. 75-98.

36. Fukushima NAIIC. 2012: 9

37. *Ibid.*

38. *Ibid.*

39. Lipscy, P.Y., Kushida, K.E., & Incerti, T. "The Fukushima Disaster and Japan's Nuclear Plant Vulnerability in Comparative Perspective." *American Chemical Society: Environmental Science & Technology*, (2013): 47, 6082–6088.

40. Gilbert, S. "The Movement of #MeToo: How a Hashtag Got Its Power." *The Atlantic.* October 16, 2017. https://www.theatlantic .com/entertainment/archive/2017/10/the-movement-of-metoo/ 542979/ Accessed June 14, 2018.

41. Garcia, S.E. "The Woman Who Created #MeToo Long Before Hashtags." *The New York Times.* October 20, 2017. https://www .nytimes.com/2017/10/20/us/me-too-movement-tarana-burke.html Accessed June 13, 2018.

42. Fowler, S. "Reflecting on One Very, Very Strange Year at Uber." Susan Fowler personal site. February 19, 2017. https://www.susanjfowler .com/blog/2017/2/19/reflecting-on-one-very-strange-year-at-uber Accessed June 5, 2018

43. Several details on Uber were taken from a case written by my friend Jay Lorsch and colleagues: Srinivasan, S., Lorsch, J.W., & Pitcher, Q. Uber in 2017: One Bumpy Ride. Case Study. HBS No. 117-070. Boston, MA: Harvard Business School Publishing, 2017.

44. Isaac, M. "Inside Uber's Aggressive, Unrestrained Workplace Culture." *The New York Times.* February 22, 2017. https://www.nytimes.com/ 2017/02/22/technology/uber-workplace-culture.html Accessed June 13, 2018.

45. Isaac, M. "Uber's C.E.O. Plays With Fire." *The New York Times.* April 23, 2017. https://www.nytimes.com/2017/04/23/technology/travis-kalanick-pushes-uber-and-himself-to-the-precipice.html   Accessed June 13, 2018.

46. Isaac, M. February 22, 2017, op cit.

47. Quora. "What Are Uber's 14 Cultural Values?" *Quora*, https://www
.quora.com/What-are-Ubers-14-core-cultural-values

48. *Ibid.*

49. Schleifer, T. "Uber's latest valuation: $72 billion." *Recode*. February
9, 2018. https://www.recode.net/2018/2/9/16996834/uber-latest-
valuation-72-billion-waymo-lawsuit-settlement Accessed June 13,
2018.

50. Isaac, M. February 22, 2017, op cit.

51. Srinivasan, S., Lorsch, J.W., & Pitcher, Q. Uber in 2017: One Bumpy
Ride. Case Study. HBS No. 117-070. Boston, MA: Harvard Business
School Publishing, 2017.

52. Isaac, M. "Uber Founder Travis Kalanick Resigns as C.E.O." *The New
York Times*. June 21, 2017. https://www.nytimes.com/2017/06/21/
technology/uber-ceo-travis-kalanick.html Accessed June 13, 2018.

53. Blumberg, P. "Ex-Uber Engineer Asks Supreme Court to Learn From
Her Ordeal." *Bloomberg.Com*. August 24, 2017; Hurley, L. "Companies
win big at U.S. top court on worker class-action curbs." *Reuters*. May
21, 2018.

54. Kim, L. "Two Bay Area Women on Time Cover for 'Person of the
Year.'" *ABC7 San Francisco*. December 7, 2017.

55. Hook, L. "FT Person of the Year: Susan Fowler." *Financial Times*.
December 12, 2017.

56. Morse, B. "Elon Musk, Susan Fowler, and Mark Zuckerberg Join Tech's
Biggest Names in 'New Establishment' List." *Inc.com*. October 2, 2017.
https://www.inc.com/brittany-morse/elon-musk-susan-fowler-and-
markzerberg-join-big-tech-names-in-new-establishment-list.html
Accessed June 8, 2018.

57. Bhuiyan, J. "With Just Her Words, Susan Fowler Brought Uber to Its
Knees." *Recode*, December 6, 2017. https://www.recode.net/2017/
12/6/16680602/susan-fowler-uber-engineer-recode-100-diversity-
sexual-harassment Accessed June 12, 2018.

58. Kerr, D. "Uber's U-Turn: How the New CEO Is Cleaning House after
Scandals and Lawsuits." *C-NET*. April 27, 2018. https://www.cnet
.com/news/ubers-u-turn-how-ceo-dara-khosrowshahi-is-cleaning-
up-after-scandals-and-lawsuits/ Accessed June 14, 2018.

5 | The Fearless Workplace

The only thing we have to fear is fear itself.

—Franklin D. Roosevelt[1]

Perhaps the truly fearless workplace is an impossibility. People are naturally averse to losing their standing in the eyes of peers and bosses. Nonetheless, a growing number of organizations are making the fearless workplace an aspiration. Leaders of these organizations recognize that psychological safety is mission critical when knowledge is a crucial source of value. In that sense, the fearless organization is something to continually strive toward rather than to achieve once and for all. It's a never-ending and dynamic journey.

In this chapter I describe the practices and culture that a handful of successful companies have worked hard to create - to show how psychological safety works. When people speak up, ask questions, debate vigorously, and commit themselves to continuous learning and improvement, good things happen. It's not that it's easy, or always enjoyable, but as you will see in the pages ahead, investing the effort and living with the challenges pays off. Workplaces where employees know that their input is valued create new possibilities for authentic engagement and stellar performance.

The organizations profiled in this chapter thus provide a glimpse into what psychologically safe workplaces look like; they show what happens – for the quality of the product, for customers, and for share-holders – when employees are freed up to express their ideas, ques-tions, and concerns. Fewer in number than their more fearful coun-terparts, these organizations boast a hidden source of competitive advantage, which plays out in a variety of ways, depending on the industry, the company leaders, and the nature of the work.

As we will see, there is more than one way in which psycholog-ical safety manifests in the workplace. When a team, department, or organization gets psychological safety right, it can seem remarkably straightforward, especially when compared to the stories of people navigating the interpersonal and conversational complexities created by fear and distrust. For this reason, you may notice the relative sim-plicity of these "good news" stories. You'll hear more from leaders, in their own words, in this chapter, about their visions and philosophies about effective workplaces in a fast-paced world. This is because the individuals you'll meet in the pages ahead tended to have thought deeply to inform conscious decisions about creating workplaces to bring out the best in people.

The companies profiled in this chapter range from the creative fields of film and fashion to high-tech computing and finance to machine manufacturing. Yet, for all the striking differences, each of the companies profiled relies on employee learning, ingenuity and engagement for its success.

Making Candor Real

If you were over the age of three in 1995, chances are you were aware – or would soon become aware – of a movie called *Toy Story,* the first computer animated feature film released by a company named

Pixar. That year, *Toy Story* would become the highest grossing film and Pixar the largest initial public offering.[2] The rest, as they say, is history. Pixar Animation Studios has since produced 19 feature films, all of which have been commercial and critical triumphs. This is a remarkable statement in an industry where hits are prized but rare, and a series of hits without fail from a single company is all but unheard of. How do they do it? Through leadership that creates the conditions where both creativity and criticism can flourish. Pixar may be in the business of creating and animating stories, but the way the company works offers lessons about psychological safety that, much like their movies, are universal.

Pixar co-founder Ed Catmull credits the studio's success, in part, to candor. His definition of candor as forthrightness or frankness[3] and his insight that we associate the word "candor" with truth-telling and a lack of reserve support psychological safety's tenets. When candor is part of a workplace culture, people don't feel silenced. They don't keep their thoughts to themselves. They say what's on their minds and share ideas, opinions, and criticisms. Ideally, they laugh together and speak noisily. Catmull encourages candor by looking for ways to institutionalize it in the organization – most notably, in what Pixar calls its "Braintrust."

A small group that meets every few months or so to assess a movie in process, provide candid feedback to the director, and help solve creative problems, the Braintrust was launched in 1999, when Pixar was rushing to save *Toy Story 2,* which had gone off the rails. The Braintrust's recipe is fairly simple: a group of directors and storytellers watches an early run of the movie together, eats lunch together, and then provides feedback to the director about what they think worked and what did not. But the recipe's key ingredient is candor. And candor, though simple, is never easy.

Embracing the bad on the journey to good

As Catmull candidly admits, " . . . early on, *all* of our movies suck."[4] In other words, it would have been easy to make *Toy Story* a movie about the secret life of toys that was sappy and boring. But the creative process, innately iterative, relies on feedback that is truly honest. If the people in the Braintrust room had murmured words of polite praise for early screenings rather than feeling safe enough to candidly say what they felt was wrong, missing, or unclear or made no sense, chances are that *Toy Story* and *Toy Story 2* would not have soared into the cinematic stratosphere.

Pixar's Braintrust has rules. First, feedback must be constructive – and about the project, not the person. Similarly, the filmmaker cannot be defensive or take criticism personally and must be ready to hear the truth. Second, the comments are suggestions, not prescriptions. There are no mandates, top-down or otherwise; the director is ultimately the one responsible for the movie and can take or leave solutions offered. Third, candid feedback is not a "gotcha" but must come from a place of empathy. It helps that the directors have often already gone through the process themselves. Praise and appreciation, especially for the director's vision and ambition, are doled out in heaping measures. Catmull, again: "The Braintrust is benevolent. It wants to help. And it has no selfish agenda."[5] The Braintrust, seen as a neutral and free-floating "it" rather than as a fearsome "them," is perceived as more than the sum of its individual members. When people feel psychologically safe enough to contribute insight, opinion, or suggestion, the knowledge in the room thereby increases exponentially. This is because individual observations and suggestions build on each other, taking new shape and creating new value, especially compared to what happens when individual feedback is collected separately.

Braintrusts – groups of people with a shared agenda who offer candid feedback to their peers – are subject to individual personalities and chemistries. In other words, they can easily go off the rails if the process isn't well led. To be effective, managers have to monitor dynamics continually over time. It helps enormously if people respect each other's expertise and trust each other's opinions. Pixar director Andrew Stanton offers advice for how to choose people for an effective feedback group. They must, he says, "make you think smarter and put lots of solutions on the table in a short amount of time."[6] Stanton's point about having people around who make us "think smarter" gets to the heart of why psychological safety is essential to innovation and progress. We can only think smarter if others in the room speak their minds.

Sadly, a caveat is necessary here. In late 2017, Ed Catmull's co-founder and Pixar's chief creative officer, John Lasseter, stepped down for behavioral misconduct and apologized in an email to "anyone who has ever been on the receiving end of an unwanted hug or any other gesture they felt crossed the line in any way, shape or form."[7] Complaints by individual Pixar employees about Lasseter's harassment soon followed. Lasseter's behavior and consequent outing, part of the MeToo movement, which I will discuss in Chapter 6, underscores the fragile and temporal nature of psychological safety. Unwanted physical attention easily undermines hard-earned trust.

The Braintrust resembles what the academic community calls peer review – a process by which other experts in the field read and offer constructive criticism on a colleague's article draft or book in-progress. This can be invaluable input for improvement, and it's almost always the case that a published article is vastly better than the original submitted manuscript. However, academic peer review also can be competitive and unfriendly – especially when anonymous – and these are attributes that the Braintrust, at its best, defiantly lacks. Pixar's method also resembles "art crits" (critiques), in which a group of art students, usually led by a professor or professional artist, offers candid critical comments on one another's work. Although art crits – like any group process – can veer into a domain of low psychological safety when the honesty becomes destructive and is not accompanied by empathic support,[8] this is not necessarily The case; peer feedback is valuable enough for young artists to self-organize.[9] Imagine if the ill-fated Volkswagen diesel engine had been subject to a braintrust of engineers who could have offered candid feedback on its feasibility rather than a secretive group who worked in fear of failure. Things might have turned out quite differently.

Freedom to Fail

Failure is another ingredient Catmull cites as crucial to Pixar's exponential numbers at the box office. That might sound odd, in that the last thing Pixar wants is a box office flop. But avoiding that outcome is understood to be dependent on embracing failure earlier in the creative journey. The Braintrust views risk and failure as a necessary part of the creative process. In its early stages a film will "suck" according to Catmull. Stanton compares the process of moviemaking to that of learning to ride a bicycle; no one learns how to pedal gracefully without falling over a few times.[10] Catmull believes that without the freedom to fail people "will seek instead to repeat something safe that's been good enough in the past. Their work will be derivative, not innovative."[11] As in so many other contexts, experimentation and its inevitable trial-and-error process are necessary to innovation.

Catmull is honest and human in acknowledging that failure hurts. Embracing failure is far easier to say than to actually put into practice! "To disentangle the good and bad parts of failure," he says, "we have to recognize both the reality of the pain and the benefit of the resulting growth."[12] He points out that it's not enough to simply accept failure when it happens and move on, more or less hoping to avoid it going forward. We need to understand failure not as something to fear or try to avoid, but as a natural part of learning and exploration. Just as learning to ride a bike entails the physical discomfort of skinned knees or bruised elbows, creating a stunningly original movie requires the psychological pain of failure. Moreover, trying to avoid the pain of failure in learning will lead to far worse pain. Catmull: "for leaders especially, this strategy – trying to avoid failure by outthinking it – dooms you to fail."[13]

Failure can, of course, be costly, and Pixar is strategic in seeking to have failures occur early in the process by, for example, allowing directors to spend years in the development phase, which involves expenditures of salaries but limits excess production costs. How do you know when failure isn't productive? When is it better to cut losses and give up? According to Catmull, when a project isn't working out, the only reason Pixar will fire a director is if the director has clearly lost the confidence of his or her team or has received constructive feedback in a Braintrust meeting and refused to act on it for a prolonged period. In this way, Pixar tries to institutionalize what Catmull calls "uncouple[ing] fear and failure"[14] by creating an environment where psychological safety is high enough that a "making mistakes doesn't strike terror into employees' hearts." Of course, Pixar is not alone in embracing candor and failure. In fact, it's likely that any successful creative endeavor does this, either implicitly or explicitly. The enormously successful (and controversial) Ray Dalio of Bridgewater Associates, one of the world's largest hedge funds, provides another example.

Extreme Candor

In 1975, a twentysomething Ray Dalio founded Bridgewater Associates in his two-bedroom New York City apartment. Since then, the firm has grown to over 1500 employees, earned consistently high returns (even during the 2008–2009 financial crisis), and been the recipient of dozens of industry awards. Dalio has been on the *Forbes* 400 list and *TIME* Magazine's 100 most influential people. He attributes Bridgewater's success to its culture of "valuing meaningful work and meaningful relationships," which has been achieved through "radical truth and transparency."[15] In 2011–2012, as part of a plan to preserve the firm's culture, Dalio created a document titled *Principles* to record the tried-and-true ideas, methods, and processes that he'd developed.[16] Now a best-selling book,[17] *Principles* provides a detailed and extensive guide to one way – by no means the only way – that psychological safety can work to promote learning, innovation, and growth.

Dalio's extreme candor begins with his principle that leaders must "create an environment in which . . . no one has the right to hold a critical opinion without speaking up about it."[18] Note the use of the word "right." The framing here is an ethical one. At Bridgewater, if you think it, you must say it. No holding back. In Dalio's view, candor is always in service to the truth, no matter how painful, because only by facing the truth can you take effective action to produce good outcomes. By way of example, he points out that if a person has a terminal illness, it's better to know the truth, no matter how frightening, because only then can one figure out what to do.[19] In framing silence as an unethical choice, Dalio is taking a more extreme stance than I have adopted. But it's worth reflecting on this idea, which to me implies that you owe your colleagues the expression of your opinion or ideas; in a sense, those ideas belong to the collective enterprise, and you therefore don't have the right to hoard them.

Candid feedback at Bridgewater is thus constant and detailed. Every employee is required to keep an Issue Log, which records individual mistakes, strengths and weaknesses, and a "pain button," which records the employee's reaction to specific criticisms as well as their changes in behavior to remedy weaknesses, and whether those changes were effective.

Transparency Libraries

Radical transparency and extreme candor go hand in hand at Bridge-water. There's even a prohibition on talking about people who are not present and thus cannot learn from what's being said. Managers are not supposed to talk about their supervisees if the person is not in the room. In Dalio's words, "If you talk behind people's backs at Bridgewater you are called a slimy weasel."[20] A tally of ongoing assessment statistics for each employee are kept on "baseball cards," publicly available to everyone in the firm, and used by managers for making decisions around compensation, incentives, promotions, and firing. No one at the firm, including Dalio, can hide behind opacity. A "transparency library" containing videos of every executive meeting, is available for viewing in case employees want to see how policies or initiatives were discussed.

Dalio's views on the need for error and smart failures as a part of the learning process are consistent with what we know about how growth and innovation occur. He believes that "our society's 'mistakephobia' is crippling"[21] because, beginning in elementary school, we are taught to seek the right answer instead of learning to learn from mistakes as a pathway to innovative and independent thinking. Early on, he says he "learned that everyone makes mistakes and has weaknesses and that one of the most important things that differentiates people is their approach to handling them." For that reason, at Bridgewater, "it is okay to makes mistakes, but unacceptable not to identify, analyze, and learn from them."[22]

Productive Conflict

Candor, transparency, and learning from error – a psychological safety triad – are emphasized in Dalio's *Principles* as scaffolding for both his life and his company. To that list we can add conflict resolution, an important input to innovation and good decision-making for which psychological safety is sorely needed. Conflict, in the Bridgewater culture, is conducted in the service of finding "what is true and what to do about it."[23] It involves having task-based conversations about who will do what, as well as exchanging alternate points of view and overcoming differences or misunderstandings. Recognizing the innate human tendency to treat a conflict as a contest, Dalio offers up advice, such as, "don't try to 'win' the argument. Finding out that you are wrong is even more valuable than being right, because you are learning."[24] It's important to know when to move on from a disagreement and not spend too much time on trivial details. He concedes that "open-minded disagreements" are frequent at Bridgewater, and, naturally, people sometimes do get angry. (Not surprisingly, new employees at Bridgewater have a high attrition rate; the culture is not for everybody). Managers are advised to "enforce the logic of conversations" when people's emotions get too hot to handle; this is best done by remaining "calm and analytical in listening to others' points of view."[25]

Dalio distinguishes between three categories of conversation – debate, discussion, and teaching – and advises that managers evaluate explicitly which method of discourse is most appropriate for the issue at hand. Discussion, according to Dalio, is an open exploration of ideas and possibilities and involves people with varying levels of experience and authority in the organization. In a discussion, everyone is encouraged to ask questions, offer opinions, and make suggestions. All views are welcomed and considered. Debate, however, takes place between "approximate equals," and teaching takes place between people with "different levels of understanding." While the boundaries between debate, discussion, and teaching may often be fluid in a fearless organization – communications may combine all three categories – these three categories offer useful ways of thinking about and structuring how to speak to one another in a psychologically safe environment.

We see here that explicit hierarchy and psychological safety are not mutually exclusive in a fearless organization. While the Bridgewater environment is clearly one where people must get used to speaking up often and openly, speaking up coexists with a hierarchy that is based in part on individual track records. But decision-making is not by consensus. Like Pixar's Brainstrusts, open debate's purpose is to provide the lead decision-maker with alternative perspectives to help him or her figure out the best outcome. And in a culture that likely preselects for opinionated, self-assured personalities, Dalio warns against arrogance. "Ask yourself whether you have earned the right to have an opinion," he says.[26] Such a right is earned through successful track records and proven responsibility. Dalio compares this to skiing down a difficult slope; if you can't successfully manage such a feat, you shouldn't tell others how to do it.[27] For their part, managers must distinguish between opinions that have the most merit – because they draw on a person's experience – and those that are merely conjecture.

Although a leader nearing the end of a successful career, Dalio tempers the dangers of over-confidence by including among his own most valued principles "the power of knowing how to deal with not knowing."[28] He attributes his success in part to having recognized and adhered to this principle, because its power has enabled him to ask questions, seek advice, and find the best answers to difficult questions. Surprisingly, this hard-driving financier shares a belief in not knowing with a soft-spoken designer of women's fashion, Eileen Fisher, who otherwise bears very little resemblance to Dalio.

Be a Don't Knower

Eileen Fisher is among those leaders who calls herself a "don't knower."[29] She began her now-celebrated clothing brand in 1984, at the age of 34, when she did not know how to sew and knew little about either fashion or business. Today, as a leader, Fisher models vulnerability and humility, which unsurprisingly helps to create psychological safety in the workplace, as we will explore further in Chapter 7. She speaks honestly about her struggles and fears. Painfully shy when she was younger, she was afraid to go into Bloomingdale's with her first clothing designs because she was afraid of being rejected. Inspired by the kimonos she'd seen while working as a graphic designer in Japan and with access to one friend's booth at the Boutique Show – a kind of arts and crafts fair – and another friend's skill with a sewing machine, Fisher launched her company by designing first four and then eight pieces of clothing for the borrowed booth. On the first go-around she received orders from buyers for $3000, and for the second show, she was surprised to find buyers lining up to orders totaling $40 000.[30]

Today, Eileen Fisher, the company, operates nearly 70 retail stores, which generated between $400 and $500 million in revenue in 2016.[31] It's a supplier to many other clothing retailers and has consistently been recognized as one of the best companies to work for. Unlike the businesses featured in Chapter 3 that faced enormous failures, the company has enjoyed continuous growth and thoughtful, productive change, unblemished by financial, legal, or safety failures.

Its management practices and governance structures have created a showcase for psychological safety.

Humble Listening

Fisher calls herself a natural listener, which helps to make "not know-ing" a positive trait. When first setting up her company, she found the combination of these two traits to be an advantage. As she says, "when you don't know and you're really listening intently, people want to help you. They want to share."[32] Evidently, she's managed to maintain the vulnerability and receptivity of her original "I don't know," even as she's become a seasoned leader of an enduring brand in the fashion industry. One of the outcomes of managing by not knowing is, as Fisher says, that "people feel safe to explore their own ideas instead of feeling like they just need to do what you tell them to do."[33]

Eileen Fisher clothing is structured along simple lines and fluid designs. The same could be said for the way the company conducts its meetings. People sit in a circle, with the intention of de-emphasizing hierarchies and instead encouraging what's called "a leader in every chair."[34] To create the mindfulness and focus conducive to an environment where everyone collaborates and contributes, meetings begin with a minute of silence. Sometimes an object, such as a gourd, is passed from person to person; the idea is the person is allowed and expected to speak when the object is in hand.[35] The point is that Fisher, like the other leaders discussed in this chapter, has institutionalized very specific processes that help create psychological safety.

Among the things that Fisher does know is what it's like to feel unsafe to speak up. In school she felt that speaking up meant risking criticism, humiliation, and embarrassment; consequently, it was, she felt, "safer to say nothing than to figure out what you think and what you want to say."[36] Perhaps that's partly why she's so consciously and carefully created an environment where employees feel safe speaking their minds. Fisher, again: "My inclination is to ask questions, to get the right people in the conversation and let everyone have a voice. The collective and collaborative process produces a lot of energy – it's the source of creativity and innovation."[37] Interestingly, Fisher, as a clothing designer, is not looking for "right answers" but for the multiplicity of voices that produce a collaborative process and creative energy. She's framing success as a certain kind of energy rather than an immediate result.

Permission to Care

When Fisher describes how projects and initiatives come about in her organization, she emphasizes encouraging employees to be passionate and giving them "permission to care."[38] For example, an assistant, Amy Hall, rose in the company to become Director of Social Consciousness by following her passion for how the company was running its factories and treating its factory workers, eventually becoming involved in setting standards for how factories operate worldwide. In 2013, at a four-day off-site company sustainability conference, the staff made a commitment to produce only environmentally sustainable clothing by the year 2020. Although the idea had not originally come from Fisher, she wanted to lend her support and realized the importance of simply saying, "yes." Although she doesn't call herself a CEO, she realized that "saying yes gives people permission" to go forward.[39]

Like any company, Eileen Fisher has had to change and grow. Fisher rejected offers to become a public company, as well as an offer to sell to Liz Claiborne, a larger women's clothing company, because she didn't feel that they were passionate enough about her company's clothing and vision. Instead, in 2005, Fisher decided to pass part of the company ownership to her employees. In 2009, the brand underwent a major change in its marketing and product lines to appeal to younger women in addition to the loyal customer base that had aged along with Fisher. More recently, Fisher sees empowering women and girls as part of the company mission, and to that end she has founded the Eileen Fisher Leadership Institute. The company also gives grants to women entrepreneurs and to nonprofits that foster leadership in women and girls.[40]

As it turns out, Fisher does know. As she says, "I've learned over time that I actually have a lot to say, particularly around issues like sustainability and business as a movement. My voice matters."[41] It may be that Fisher herself is the last to know the strength of her own voice. For as the president of Macy's North, Frank Gazetta, said about the seasonal product lines with which he stocks his stores, "the voice of Eileen is always there."[42]

Ultimately, Eileen's voice has been widely heard (and seen) in the fashion industry because she was willing to take risks, willing to fail. In any creative industry, failure is a fact of life. Most design ideas never come to fruition. Similarly, most film footage hits the cutting room floor, and many financial bets will fail before you hit a winner. Indeed, more and more people in leading companies around the world are embracing the notion of failing well to succeed sooner. But as appealing and logical as the idea of learning from failure may be, the truth is no one really wants to fail.

When Failure Works

A team of smart, motivated people in Palo Alto had worked for two full years on an innovation project. The goal was to develop a process to turn seawater into an affordable fuel. You might think achieving such a goal would be impossible. But, scientists had already figured out the necessary technology to make it work in very small quantities. The challenge for Project Foghorn, as the endeavor was called, was to assess if the process could be commercially viable on a massive scale. After two years of hard work, however, the team reluctantly admitted that it could not get production costs low enough to produce an economically competitive fuel, especially since by then the price of oil had fallen. They decided to terminate the project.

Was the team fired? Humiliated? Did team members hang their heads for weeks? Far from it. Every member of the Foghorn team received a bonus from the company.[43]

Make It Safe to Fail

The company was Google X, an invention and innovation lab that operates as an independent entity within Google's parent company, Alphabet. The mission of X, as it's come to be called, is to launch "moonshot" technologies that will make the world a better place.[44] The explicit goal is to develop and commercialize radical, world-changing solutions to big problems, to produce the kind of breakthroughs that could eventually become as big as the *next* Google.[45] Intelligent failure is especially integral to success at X, and for this reason we can learn a lot about what makes it work and the mindsets that leaders encourage to make failure acceptable in their organizations.

Although the idea of rewarding people for failing may seem to create a problematic incentive, if we look closely enough we can see its business logic, especially for a research organization that pursues big, audacious ideas. Astro Teller, CEO at X – or "Captain of Moonshots," to be precise – believes that it's a superior economic strategy to reward people for killing unpromising projects than it is to let unworkable ideas languish in purgatory for years and soak up resources.[46] In other words, you have to fail at many attempts before coming up with a success. X considers over 100 ideas for moonshots each year, in areas ranging from clean energy to sustainable farming to artificial intelligence. However, only a handful of these ideas become projects with full-time staff working on them.[47]

Teller explained in his 2016 TED talk why and how X "make[s] it safe to fail."

You cannot yell at people and force them to fail fast. People resist. They worry. "What will happen to me if I fail? Will people laugh at me?

Will I be fired? . . . The only way to get people to work on big, risky things — audacious ideas — and have them run at all the hardest parts of the problem first is if you make that the path of least resistance for them. We work hard at X to make it safe to fail. Teams kill their ideas as soon as the evidence is on the table because they're rewarded for it. They get applause from their peers. Hugs and high fives from their manager, me in particular. They get promoted for it. We have bonused every single person on teams that ended their projects, from teams as small as two to teams of more than 30.[48]

Teller highlights how unpleasant it feels for us to fail, especially at work. It's natural to worry what other people will think and about losing our job. That's why, unless a leader expressly and actively makes it psychologically safe to do so, people will seek to avoid failure.

Rapid Evaluation

Just as vital as creating a psychologically safe environment for smart failure is constructing a specific process for handling failure. Teller and X pursue the mission through a process of disciplined experimentation. Just as scientists seek to find evidence that rejects their hypotheses, the company seeks to find evidence that its most optimistic and idealistic ideas will *not* work so it can kill off these ideas sooner rather than later and move onto other ones.[49] Project proposals can come from anyone inside or outside the company. To make sure that X only works on the most promising ideas, the company has a "Rapid Evaluation" team that processes proposals, vets ideas, and promotes only those that seem achievable. This team, which consists of a combination of senior managers and inventors, first runs a pre-mortem, trying to come up with as many reasons as possible why the idea could fail.[50] "Rapid Eval," as the team is known, considers the problem's scale, feasibility, and technological risks. During this iterative stage, issues are questioned, changed, and refined by engaging in candid conversation that's not unlike Pixar's Braintrust.

Very few ideas make it past this Rapid Eval stage.[51] If an idea is deemed promising, its team must develop a crude prototype, ideally in a few days. X has a "Design Kitchen" in one of its buildings equipped with tools and materials to create such physical prototypes.[52] If Rapid Eval is convinced by the prototype, it runs the idea by a second business group called "Foundry," which asks, "*Should* this solution exist? Is there a business case to be made for the proposed solution? If we can build it, will people actually use it?"

The company honors smart failures in other ways, too. Prototypes that never made it past the Foundry stage, and thus were dropped, are showcased in the Palo Alto office.[53] Since November 2016, X has held an annual celebration to hear testimonials about failed projects. (Failed relationships and personal tragedies are also welcomed.) Failed prototypes are placed on a small altar, and people say a few words about what the project meant to them. Employees feel that this ritual helps remove some of the emotional baggage they still carry from investing themselves into something that never came to be.[54]

Failing to Fail Is the Real Failure

For X, then, failing is not taboo. In fact, as Teller told BBC News in 2014, "real failure is trying something, learning it doesn't work, then continuing to do it anyway."[55] Real failure is defined as not learning, or not taking enough risks to fall flat on your face. Teller and X embrace failure so much that they don't talk about succeeding on their projects at all; instead, they speak of "failing to fail."[56] Successful failure is an art. It helps if you can fail at the right time and for the right reasons. In Chapter 7, we'll see other ways organizations make use of and institutionalize failure.

Caring for Employees

The power of psychological safety is not reserved for creative industries such as film, fashion, and cutting-edge technology. The global equipment and engineering company Barry-Wehmiller demonstrates that psychological safety brings immense rewards in a manufacturing setting. These rewards come in both economic and human development forms.[57]

Founded in St. Louis in the mid-1880s as a machine manufacturer for the brewing industry, Barry-Wehmiller today is a $3 billion organization that employs 12 000 people at 100-plus locations in 28 countries.[58] In 2015, CEO Bob Chapman and co-author Raj Sisodia published *Everybody Matters: The Extraordinary Power of Caring for Your People Like Family,* a book whose title concisely declares the company's mission to "measure success by the way we touch the lives of people." Caring for employees – "team members" in Barry-Wehmiller-speak – using tangible measures of employee well-being has proved to be a sure recipe for establishing a psychologically safe workplace where learning and growth thrive.

The Great Recession of 2007–2009 presented a dramatic opportunity for Barry-Wehmiller to make good on its promise to care for people like family. When new equipment orders declined considerably and layoffs seemed inevitable, Chapman instead initiated a program of shared sacrifice. Following his principle that in a caring family "all the family members would absorb some pain so that no member of the family had to experience a dramatic loss,"[59] there were no layoffs. Instead, all employees, no matter their position, took a mandatory unpaid furlough of four weeks at the time of their choosing. Cost-cutting in the form of shared sacrifice manifested in other ways as well. Chapman reduced his salary to $10 500, suspended executive bonuses, halted contributions to retirement accounts, and reduced travel expenses. What was the result? Unions supported the program. Team members created a market to help each other; those who could afford to take more than a month off voluntarily traded with those who could not. Barry-Wehmiller rallied from the economic downturn relatively easily and by 2010 reported record financial results. In other words, by continuing to make its team members feel safe and cared for during a crisis, the company created a win–win situation for everyone.

Barry-Wehmiller has developed a rigorous and well-documented approach to systematizing its values and methods, which create psychological safety as a by-product. That may be because the company has flourished by acquiring poorly performing companies and turning them profitable since the mid-1980s. The majority were companies that provided equipment and services to industries such as packaging or paper manufacturing. Each acquisition – as of this writing, there are over 100 – has been another opportunity to articulate and develop Barry-Wehmiller's culture and vision.[60]

Its internal "Guiding Principles of Leadership" document, formulated with employee input, is meant to, among other things, create an environment of trust, meaning, and pride that celebrates and brings out the best in each person.[61] Shortly after the document was drafted, Chapman traveled to various units and sat down with small groups of people to listen to their feelings about the Principles. He learned that trust – employees feeling trusted by management – was key, and that time clocks, break bells, and locking inventory in cages inhibited that trust. Chapman describes immediately getting rid of what he calls "trust-destroying and demeaning practices"[62] inappropriate for responsible adults. Listening sessions, as they are called, have since become institutionalized times where team members are asked to speak their minds.

Barry-Wehmiller University was founded in 2008 to impart the company's distinct leadership practices and vision. Instructors are mostly recruited and trained from within the organization, are encouraged to impart insight rather than information, and make use of storytelling to share experiences and emotions. Chapman says the company's practice is to "Treat people superbly and compensate them fairly."[63] For example, when the company instituted healthcare policies that included checks into employee well-being and habits, which contributed to a 5% reduction in healthcare costs for Barry-Wehmiller, team members were given a free month on paying their premiums.

Because most of their work involves the repetitive but intricate process-laden work that's germane to assembly factories – see

Chapter 7 for more about the implications of different types of work for psychological safety and learning – process improvements or their opposite (stuck processes) have enormous consequences for performance. No one wants to institute changes to workplace processes that make a job more difficult and create employee resentment, but too often memos handed down from the top do just that. Far more reasonable is to have the people who are actually doing the work design and redesign the process. In the fearless organization, suggestions for improvement *(kaizen)* are actively recruited and instituted when apt.

Asking for Input

Bob Chapman tells the story of setting up a machine shop in Green Bay, Wisconsin. Ten divisional presidents first spent a week on how to improve the process of getting spare parts orders entered, completed, and shipped to customers. Analyses were run and reports generated, only to realize that the plan wasn't going to work in practice. Another leadership team met, spent another week analyzing and projecting, this time also looking at how manufacturing space might be laid out. Still, no one felt confident enough to proceed. Finally, a third improvement event was held, this time with two senior leaders and ten people who were actually going to do the work: forklift drivers, assemblers, pickers, packers, and clerical staff. Now, suddenly, the way forward was clear. In Chapman's telling:

> They [the workers] took cardboard cutouts onto the floor of the factory and measured what they would need to bring different carts and forklifts through. They could see the different clearance issues and recognized that work from one area often flowed to another. Lighter parts would be easier to carry a farther distance. They looked at how many steps it took, how safe it was to have a forklift in an area, or whether it could come around the outside in a safer configuration.[64]

This is a prime example of asking people for input and of the benefits of doing so. Even better than to, for example, open an online portal to invite employee suggestions is to invite the responsible parties to the meeting! In Dalio's terms, it's the forklift operators themselves who have earned the "right to have an opinion" on whether or not there's enough clearance for their trucks to pass through an area. Contrast Barry-Wehmiller's approach with the factory fellow from Chapter 2 who had an idea for improvement and could point to no good reason for not offering it up. Had he been given a seat at the table, chances are that management could have benefitted from his idea.

Chapman reports that the solution the assembly workers devised was still in place five years later. They were, he says, "able to share to improve the process and create a meaningful, lasting, and more human process for everybody in that organization."[65] What's important to note is just how much it can take on the part of everyone involved to create a fearless organization. Top management had to spend considerable time and have the good sense to recognize that its ideas would not succeed. Factory workers had to be explicitly involved in the process of designing process. I don't mean to imply that working in a fearless organization takes more effort or a tremendously difficult undertaking. It doesn't. But initially, when we've been entrenched in fear and its attendant mental frameworks, it's not always obvious. Barry-Wehmiller leaders are superb practitioners of an essential psychological safety building practice I call Inviting Participation, to be discussed in Chapter 7.

Learning from Psychologically Safe Work Environments

Barry Wehmiller, Google X, Eileen Fisher, Bridgewater, and Pixar have little in common on the surface. Yet they have managed to create work environments characterized by unusual levels of candor, engagement, collaboration, and risk-taking, all of which have contributed to the creation of successful businesses – in strikingly varied ways. Chapter 6 highlights a few other unusual organizations and leaders. But this time our focus will be on efforts to promote or improve human health, dignity, or safety.

Chapter 5 Takeaways

- Workplaces characterized by candor can offer immense benefits for creativity, learning, and innovation.

- Leaders who are willing to say "I don't know" play a surprisingly powerful role in engaging the hearts and minds of employees.

- Creating an environment that values employees yields benefits in engagement, problem solving, and performance.

Endnotes

1. Franklin Delano Roosevelt. Presidential Inaugural Address. *History*. March 4, 1933. https://www.history.com/speeches/franklin-d-roosevelts-first-inaugural-address Accessed June 7, 2018
2. "Our Story." Pixar Animation Studios, https://www.pixar.com/our-story-1#our-story Accessed June 7, 2018.
3. Catmull, E. & Wallace, A. *Creativity, Inc.: Overcoming the Unseen Forces That Stand in the Way of True Inspiration*. New York: Random House, 2013. Print.
4. Catmull, E. & Wallace, A. 2013: 90.
5. Catmull, E. & Wallace, A. 2013: 95.
6. Catmull, E. & Wallace, A. 2013: 105.
7. Barnes, B. "John Lasseter, a Pixar Founder, Takes Leave After 'Missteps.'" *The New York Times*, January 20, 2018. https://www.nytimes.com/2017/11/21/business/media/john-lasseter-pixar-disney-leave.html Accessed July 25, 2018.
8. Finkel, J. "Tales From the Crit: For Art Students, May Is the Cruelest Month." *The New York Times*. April 30, 2006. https://www.nytimes

.com/2006/04/30/arts/design/tales-from-the-crit-for-art-students-may-is-the-cruelest-month.html Accessed June 13, 2018.

9. For more on art crits, see http://bushwickartcritgroup.com/.

10. Catmull, E. & Wallace, A. 2013. 109

11. Catmull, E. & Wallace, A. 2013: 111.

12. Catmull, E. & Wallace, A. 2013: 108–109.

13. Catmull, E. & Wallace, A. 2013: 109.

14. Catmull, E. & Wallace, A. 2013: 123.

15. Dalio, R. "How to Build a Company Where the Best Ideas Win." *TED*. 2017. https://www.ted.com/talks/ray_dalio_how_to_build_a_ company_where_the_best_ideas_win Accessed June 12, 2018.

16. Dalio, R. "Principles." Ray Dalio. 2011. https://docs.google.com/ viewer?a=v&pid=sites&srcid=ZGVmYXVsdGRvbWFpbnxlYm9va3dubG9hZG5vZIwMTZ8Z3g6MjY3NGU2Njk5N2QxNjViMg Accessed June 13, 2018.

17. Dalio, R. *Principles, Vol. 1: Life & Work*. New York: Simon & Schuster, 2017. Print.

18. Dalio, R. 2011: 88.

19. *Ibid.*

20. Dalio, R. 2011: 89.

21. Dalio, R. 2011: 17.

22. Dalio, R. 2011: 88.

23. Dalio, R. 2011: 19.

24. Dalio, R. 2011: 96.

25. Dalio, R. 2011: 105.

26. Dalio, R. 2011: 102.

27. Dalio, R. 2011: 190.

28. Dalio, R. 2011: 189.

29. Tenney, M. "Be a Don't Knower: One of Eileen Fisher's Secrets to Success." *The Huffington Post*. May 15, 2015. https://www .huffingtonpost.com/matt-tenney/be-a-dont-knower-one-of-e_b_ 7242468.html Accessed June 12, 2018.

30. Malcolm, J. "Nobody's Looking At You: Eileen Fisher and the art of understatement." *The New Yorker*. September 23, 2013. https:// www.newyorker.com/magazine/2013/09/23/nobodys-looking-at-you Accessed June 12, 2018.

31. Fernandez, C. "Eileen Fisher Makes Strides Towards Circularity With 'Tiny Factory.'" *The Business of Fashion*. December 6, 2017. https://www.businessoffashion.com/articles/intelligence/eileen-fisher-makes-strides-towards-circularity-with-tiny-factory Accessed June 8, 2018.

32. Tenney, M. May 15, 2015, op cit.

33. *Ibid.*

34. According to Janet Malcolm, Fisher subscribes to the philosophy articulated in a 2010 book called *The Circle Way: A Leader in Every Chair* by Ann Linnea and Christina Baldwin (published by Barret-Koehler) which posits circle leadership as both a paradigm shift for group collaboration and a practice that draws upon the circle "lineage" derived from cultures, such as Native American and Aboriginal.

35. Malcolm, J. September 23, 2013, op cit.

36. *Ibid.*

37. Dunbar, M.F. "Designer Eileen Fisher on how Finding Purpose Changed Her Company. *Conscious Company Media.* July 4, 2015. https://consciouscompanymedia.com/sustainable-business/designer-eileen-fisher-on-how-finding-purpose-changed-her-company/ Accessed June 8, 2018.

38. *Ibid.*

39. *Ibid.*

40. "Business as a Movement." Eileen Fisher. https://www.eileenfisher .com/business-as-a-movement/business-as-a-movement   Accessed June 8, 2018.

41. "Eileen Fisher, No Excuses." *A Green Beauty.* December 7, 2016. https://agreenbeauty.com/fashion/eileen-fisher-no-excuses Accessed June 8, 2018.

42. Beckett, W. "Eileen Fisher: A Pocket of Prosperity." *Women's Wear Daily.* October 17, 2007.

43. Thompson, D. "Google X and the Science of Radical Creativity." *The Atlantic.* November 2017. https://www.theatlantic.com/magazine/ archive/2017/11/x-google-moonshot-factory/540648/ Accessed June 8, 2018.

44. "What We Do." X. https://x.company/about/ Accessed June 8, 2018.

45. Thompson, D. November, 2017, op cit.

46. *Ibid.*

47. *Ibid.*

48. Teller, A. "The Unexpected Benefit of Celebrating Failure." *TED.* 2016. https://www.ted.com/talks/astro_teller_the_unexpected_benefit_ of_celebrating_failure Accessed June 8, 2018.

49. "Celebrating Failure Fuels Moonshots." *Stanford ECorner*, April 20, 2016. https://ecorner.stanford.edu/podcast/celebrating-failure-fuels-moonshots/ Accessed June 8, 2018.

50. Thompson, D. November 2017, op cit.

51. Gertner, J. "The Truth About Google X: An Exclusive Look Behind The Secretive Lab's Closed Doors." *Fast Company*. April 15, 2014. https://www.fastcompany.com/3028156/the-google-x-factor Accessed June 13, 2018.
52. *Ibid.*
53. Thompson, D. November 2017, op cit.
54. *Ibid.*
55. Wakefield, D. "Google boss on why it is OK to fail." *BBC News*. February 16, 2016. http://www.bbc.com/news/technology-35589220 Accessed June 14, 2018.
56. Dougherty, C. "They Promised Us Jet Packs. They Promised the Bosses Profit." *The New York Times*. July 23, 2016. https://www.nytimes.com/2016/07/24/technology/they-promised-us-jet-packs-they-promised-the-bosses-profit.html Accessed June 14, 2018.
57. Information on Bob Chapman and Barry-Wehmiller comes from Chapman's book *Everybody Matters* and a case study conducted by my HBS colleague Jan Rivkin:

    - Chapman, B. & Sisodia, R. *Everybody Matters: The Extraordinary Power of Caring for Your People Like Family*. US: Penguin-Random House, 2015. Print.

    - Minor, D. & Rivkin, J. Truly Human Leadership at Barry-Wehmiller. Case Study. HBS No. 717-420. Boston, MA: Harvard Business School Publishing, 2016.

58. "Surpassing 100 acquisitions, Barry-Wehmiller looks to the future." Barry-Wehmiller. February 6, 2016. https://www.barrywehmiller.com/docs/default-source/pressroom-library/pr_bw_100acquisitions_020618_final.pdf?sfvrsn=2 Accessed June 8, 2018.
59. Chapman, B. & Sisodia, R. 2015: 101.
60. "Surpassing 100 acquisitions, Barry-Wehmiller looks to the future." February 6, 2016, op cit.
61. Chapman, B. & Sisodia, R. 2015: 53.
62. Chapman, B. & Sisodia, R. 2015: 59.
63. Chapman, B. & Sisodia, R. 2015: 53.
64. Chapman, B. & Sisodia, R. 2015: 170
65. *Ibid.*

6 | Safe and Sound

"It is not death that a man should fear, but he should fear never beginning to live."
—Marcus Aurelius[1]

"Birds," said Captain Chesley "Sully" Sullenberger III.

"Whoa," said First Officer Jeffrey Skiles.

The two pilots, side by side nearly three thousand feet above Manhattan on a cold, clear day in January 2009, both knew that this deceptively simple word – birds – could spell disaster. Sullenberger, age 57, and Skiles, age 49, had met for the first time just hours earlier. Both were highly-experienced pilots, well-versed in the clipped verbal exchanges of cockpit communications.[2] For the next few seconds they watched as Canadian geese filled the windscreen, heard a loud thudding as the large birds were ingested into the Airbus' engines, and then smelled burning feathers and flesh. The lives of 150 passengers and five crew, including their own, would depend on how the two pilots, the crew, and the air traffic controller handled the next three minutes. What would become a miraculous, zero-fatality

129

landing on the Hudson River drew on aviation training, navigation skills, old-fashioned luck, and that extra, less tangible quality that knowledge workers today must acquire: the ability to team by communicating fearlessly. Fearless communication is vital input into making complex decisions, often quickly, that have no precedent and bring serious consequences.

Use Your Words

We have many examples of how even brief verbal exchanges can be thwarted by a lack of psychological safety. The nurse who hesitates to speak up to a surgeon about a possible procedural error because past exchanges led her to think this would bother him; the new engineer on a project who doesn't ask a question because she fears looking stupid; and the boss who doesn't listen to ideas from employees because he thinks it will make him appear weak. We have fewer examples of the nuanced exchanges that occur in situations of high psychological safety, especially those with high stress, and of the positive outcomes that ensue. But those excruciating few minutes of cockpit conversation, recorded that January afternoon, are worth deconstructing. Each of the small team of key participants felt safe enough with one another to become heroes together.

The bird strike took place about 90 seconds after Flight 1549's takeoff from New York City's LaGuardia airport. The immediate problem: dual engine failure. The next problem: dual engine failure was classified as a "non-normal situation," and was not included in the automated systems that warn pilots of system failures and display instructions on the monitor for handling the failure.[3] In short, dual engine failure from bird strikes was exceedingly rare – bordering on unheard of. Airline policy asked captains "to use common sense and good judgment, especially in those situations not specifically covered."[4] In other words, they were on their own.

Immediately, Sullenberger, or "Sully" as he has been immortalized in the eponymous Hollywood film, who had been serving as copilot, took over the controls from Skiles. "My aircraft," said Sullenberger, using aviation coded shorthand, as he put his hands on the controls.

Although almost instinctive, the decision was driven by good reasoning: Sully had logged far more hours flying the A320 than had Skiles. Perhaps most important, from where he sat, Sullenberger could see the cityscape and George Washington Bridge out his left viewing window, while Skiles could not. Also relevant: Skiles was the pilot who was more familiar with emergency procedures and could thus better manage the landing equipment.

"Your aircraft," replied Skiles.

That was all it took. There was no hesitancy, fear, apology, or disagreement from either man.

Sullenberger had long played a major role in training other pilots in Cockpit Resource Management (CRM) at US Airways.[5] Passionately committed to the program, which emphasizes interpersonal communication, leadership, and decision-making under pressure, it's hard to imagine any pilot with a better understanding of the need for crew members to feel able to speak up than Sully. Both he and Skiles felt they were operating in a psychologically safe environment. But the cockpit pilots were not the only members of that intensely high-performing team that day.

Next, Sullenberger informed Patrick Harten, the air traffic controller who worked out of the large Long Island center that controls arrivals and departures out of the greater New York area, that they'd hit birds and were turning back to LaGuardia. "Mayday, mayday, mayday," said Sullenberger, citing the universal message for life-threatening distress. Harten took the necessary measures, which included calling the LaGuardia control tower to tell them to prepare for an emergency landing.

A Virtual Team in the Learning Zone

Meanwhile, Skiles was unsuccessful in his attempts to restart the engines, in part because the plane was not moving fast enough.

"We don't have that," he told Sullenberger, referring to the plane's speed. Sullenberger agreed, and then was silent. He was mentally calculating whether they'd have a better chance trying to make it to an airport runway or to land on the river below. Although Harten tried several times to direct the Airbus toward a nearby airport from the control tower, each time Sullenberger replied that he was "unable." He then reported he would be taking the riskiest but, to him, most feasible option: landing in the Hudson River. It was also the option that would minimize chances of harming bystanders on the ground in the densely populated city below. Harten, dumbfounded and believing landing in the water would almost certainly result in the pilots' deaths, asked Sullenberger to repeat his intention. This was as much a trained reflex as a conscious request. As we saw in the 1977 Tenerife disaster when a Royal Dutch Airlines (KLM) captain misunderstood the instructions of an air traffic controller – who said he was *not* cleared for takeoff – and proceeded to speed down a foggy runway and collide with another plane, the tiniest break in clarity can result in hundreds of needless deaths. Harten was well trained.

Soon – no more than a minute later – it was time for the cockpit to alert the rest of the flight crew and the passengers. Again, Sullenberger communicated deliberately and carefully in the way he thought most likely to achieve a good outcome. Afraid of how hard the plane might hit the water, he chose not to tell the flight crew to prepare for a water landing – in which case he knew they would instruct passengers to don life jackets, consuming valuable time. Instead, he broadcast, "This is the captain. Brace for impact." The three flight attendants then shouted at the passengers to put their heads down and grab their legs, as directed by emergency landing protocol. Sullenberger steered the airplane to a perfect, if unavoidably violent, landing, while Skiles called out altitude and speed. Some passengers suffered injuries, most relatively minor, but not a single life was lost in this almost miraculous outcome. Soon, nearby boats swarmed to area and rescued passengers before anyone suffered hypothermia.

Using Time Well

Let's look more closely at what was accomplished here with very few, very precise words. Although clearly an extreme case, the human interactions in this extraordinary situation provide a compelling demonstration that clarity and candor do not necessarily mean getting bogged down in endless discussions. Psychological safety does not imply excessive talking and over-processing. Psychologically safe meetings do not have to take longer. Conversely, I've studied management team meetings where low psychological safety gave rise to indirectness of argument that consumed far more time than necessary. Worse, key decisions were often postponed due to evident conflict that was not effectively discussed, making the discussions and the total decision time (in months) take far more time than necessary.[6]

Learning from Other Industries

What we can learn from this extreme case, as well as from many cases of normal business conversation, is that psychological safety must be paired with discipline to achieve optimal results efficiently. Consider that, for his part, Harten asked only essential questions; also, he kept the phone lines open as he spoke to the other air controllers, so that Sullenberger could hear those conversations at the same time, again saving valuable time because Harten did not have to repeat them. Sullenberger later wrote about Harten, "his words let me know that he understood that these hard choices were mine to make, and it wasn't going to help if he tried to dictate a plan to me."[7] And then there was what was *not* said. For many of those crucial seconds, Sullenberger and Skiles silently concentrated on their respective tasks and kept an eye on each other for the visual clues that kept them working as a coordinated team.

Flight 1549's experienced flight crew was well trained in standard aviation equipment protocols and procedures. Equally important, they were trained in threat and error management (TEM) and CRM (also sometimes called Crew Resource Management). Both programs teach ways of thinking and decision-making. CRM – a program that, among other skills, instructs aviation crews to speak up to their captain when they feel something is wrong and likewise instructs captains to listen to crew concerns – is especially well suited to creating environments of psychological safety. CRM training, now required for all pilots, was first begun in response to Tenerife and other similarly tragic accidents, such as the 1982 Air Florida fatal landing in the Potomac in which a copilot could not bring himself to insist that the captain turn back in the face of freezing rain and incomplete de-icing, and the 2013 Asiana Airlines crash at the San Francisco airport, when a copilot was afraid to warn his captain about a low-speed landing.[8]

Training modeled after CRM has also spread to medical environments. The goal has been to increase patient safety by promoting better communication and teamwork.[9] In one study, a CRM-like training in communication and teamwork was shown to produce better outcomes in the delivery room for both mothers and babies. The program also led to greater patient and staff satisfaction.[10]

It can be tempting to discount the value of the Hudson Miracle in demonstrating psychological safety and teaming in action because of the role played by emergency protocols in shaping the response. However, as we have seen far too often in aviation, as well as in other highly-protocolized settings like the operating room, the *existence* of procedures does not ensure their use. Without psychological safety, micro-assessments of interpersonal risk tend to crowd out proper responses. We simply fail to recognize the implications of our hesitation or silence in the moments in which we could have spoken up. Psychological safety can thus be seen as a precondition for the effective use of emergency protocols. But, as we will see in the next case, emergencies are not the only context where a psychologically safe work environment can foster human health and safety.

One for All and All for One

What does a leading provider of kidney dialysis services for 200 000 patients around the world have in common with a nineteenth century historical novel?[11] Answer: a swashbuckling hero who brandishes a sword and lives by the motto "one for all and all for one."

At DaVita Kidney Care, the swashbuckler is CEO and Chairman Kent Thiry.[12] Thiry is known to leap about the stage brandishing a sword while wearing full musketeer regalia in front of hundreds of frontline employees – patient care technicians, nurses, and social workers – in attendance for the regularly offered two-day DaVita Academy program, one of the foundational seminars for new employees put on by the DaVita University. Thiry's unusual choice of persona and costume, along with frequent high-fives and other high-intensity interactions, seem to reflect his comfort bringing his whole self to the workplace, so as to signal to others that they can do so too. The program offers many team-building and socializing activities for attendees that include songs, skits, games, storytelling, refreshments, music, and dancing and is intended to introduce employees to the DaVita culture. Thiry also leads a town hall question and answer session, where he is willing to be vulnerable (often admitting, for example, that he doesn't know the answer to a question) and open, entertaining direct questions about wages and promotions. The "One for All and All for One" slogan conveys a company core value – the idea of shared obligations and responsibility. All Davita workers are called upon to contribute their best to the company; likewise, the company is responsible for helping individuals develop and succeed. Attendance at the Academy program is voluntary, but the company's data shows that people who do attend have a turnover rate of about 12% compared to the 28% who do not attend.[13]

Hired in 1999 to rescue the company from the brink of ruin, Thiry is credited with having turned it around by building a set of values and a culture that combine to create a high level of psychological safety. Much like Bob Chapman at Barry-Wehmiller, discussed in Chapter 5, Thiry believes in fostering a community where people on every level of the organization have a voice and are developed as leaders. As part of giving people a voice, Thiry decided to involve them in creating a list of core values, which were then voted on by 600 of the company's clinician-managers. Employees (called team-mates) were asked to vote to find the new name, DaVita, when Thiry wanted to rename the company, previously called Total Renal Care. To help prepare frontline employees for their responsibilities as team-mates, and to support them in taking on administrative roles, DaVita University provides many leadership development programs, with an emphasis on management and team skills, along with programs on quality improvement.

Thiry refers to himself as the "mayor" of DaVita "village" and emphasizes that "building a successful company is a means to the end of building a healthy community."[14] Also in support of a healthy community, the DaVita Village Network fund exists to help teammates who may encounter unexpected medical expenses or have other financial difficulties. This is part of the "all for one" philosophy. The company matches donations teammates make into the fund. Although the majority of teammates are low-skilled, hourly workers, DaVita offers comprehensive health and welfare benefits, including provisions for healthcare, retirement, tuition reimburse-ments, and, most surprisingly, stock options and profit sharing. These incentives help support Thiry's demand that teammates come to work "intending not only to do a solid day's work, but also to strive to make DaVita a special place."[15]

Kidney dialysis patients, the majority of whom are suffering from end-stage renal condition, are especially in need of the combined efforts of a medical team that is "all for one." Patients typically visit a local clinic three to four times per week and are hooked up to the dialysis machine for about four hours at a time – for the rest of what they know is likely to be a shortened life. They must endure the poke of needles and sit quietly while the machine draws out and cleans the blood that their failed kidneys can no longer process. They must adhere to a strict diet and often suffer from other chronic conditions, such as diabetes and heart disease.

Unsurprisingly, some become depressed, or worse, stop coming to the clinic for treatments, which leads soon to death. It's emotionally difficult to care for dialysis patients. Up to 25% will die each year. Given these morale-lowering conditions, the excessively upbeat tone of the DaVita Academy sessions begins to make more sense.

Most importantly, DaVita consistently delivers top clinical outcomes in its industry. That's because good clinical outcomes in large part depend on the quality of care delivered by the staff at the outpatient dialysis clinics where most patients are treated. Although a technician's job is ostensibly practical – to connect and disconnect the patient to the machine and monitor the ongoing treatment – much can also depend on the relationships technicians establish with both the patient and other caregivers. Patients who feel comfortable and trusting – psychologically safe – with the clinic staff are more likely to comply with a rigorous treatment plan. To encourage these positive feelings, DaVita centers are often decorated with photographs of patients and their families, as well as by drawings made by them, their children, and their grandchildren. As one DaVita administrator said, "it's important that the teammates like their jobs and smile and relate in a compassionate way to patients, because that makes the patients feel better about being here."[16] In other words, clinic staff who themselves feel supported by high levels of psychological safety are able to support and bond with patients, which contributes to positive clinical outcomes.

As we have seen in other healthcare settings, speaking up and feeling psychologically safe enough to communicate across boundaries and well-established medical hierarchies also contributes to positive clinical outcomes. In 2017, DaVita successfully participated in a pilot program run by the Centers for Medicare and Medicaid Services (CMS) to institute integrated care for dialysis patients – specifically for nurses, social workers, and technicians to communicate regularly with nephrologists about individual patients. As Roy Marcus, a medical director and participating nephrologist put it, "DaVita's integrated care team regularly communicates with nephrologists to better address gaps in care that extend beyond dialysis. This frequent communication means I have the time and details I need to provide better, more holistic care to my patients."[17]

Kidney dialysis treatment is especially well suited to follow the Institute for Healthcare Improvement's triple aim for healthcare: improving patient experience, improving population health, and reducing cost per patient.[18] Here, as in other industries, making dramatic, systemic change happen is highly-dependent on building the psychological safety that allows employees to speak up with their concerns and ideas for improvement, as well as to experiment in small ways to figure out what works best.

Speaking Up for Worker Safety

By now you're well aware that speaking up is easier said than done. There's no switch to flip that will instantaneously turn an organization accustomed to silence and fear into one where people speak candidly. Instead, creating a psychologically safe workplace, as we'll explore in depth in Chapter 7, requires a lot of effort to alter systems, structures, and processes. Ultimately, it means that deep-seated entrenched organizational norms and attitudes must change. And it begins with what I call "stage setting." Let's look at how Anglo American, one of the world's largest mines, headquartered in South Africa, prepared for and then institutionalized speaking up.

When Cynthia Carroll was appointed in 2007, with much fanfare, as the first female CEO of an international mining company, she was appalled by the number of worker fatalities been occurring in the company – nearly 200 in the 5 years prior to her arrival.[19] Realizing that she was "in an unprecedented position to influence change" as both an American/outsider in a foreign country and as a woman where "until very recently women hadn't been allowed to visit underground at mines in South Africa, let alone work there,"[20] she immediately used her position to speak up and demand a policy of zero fatalities or serious injuries.

At first, others in the company, especially members of the old guard who saw themselves as upholding tradition, refused to take Carroll seriously. At least one executive responded by saying that zero harm "will never happen in our lifetime."[21] Likewise, when Carroll visited individual mines, the local managers tried to make her understand that while safety was important, her demands were unrealistic. Serious injuries and deaths were considered an inevitable hazard, part of mining's dangerous physical demands. Furthermore it was not uncommon to blame errors on the workers themselves. The prevailing attitude in South Africa, according to Anglo American's chairman, Sir Mark Moody-Stuart, who was instrumental in hiring Carroll, was that workers who suffered injuries "took shortcuts, did not always follow the rules; they were stupid."[22]

Carroll's response to the resistance could not have been more unambiguous. She shut down one of the most problematic and dangerous mines. Rustenburg, located about 60 miles from Johannesburg, was the world's foremost supplier of platinum and generated about $8 million in revenue per day. Shutting down the mine was both bold and unprecedented. It immediately got everyone's attention. Even more shocking, Carroll insisted that before the mine could restart, she wanted to find out what the workers were thinking, and she intended to get input from every single worker about how to improve safety. This, she knew, was a direct challenge to Anglo American's strict hierarchical culture and rigid, top-down management style, which had begun with the mine's founding in 1917 and was further strengthened by South Africa's apartheid history.

Here's where things get interesting. After shutting down the mine, Anglo American executives gathered 3000 to 4000 workers at a time in a stadium and spoke about the importance of safety. Because the workers spoke a range of languages and literacy rates were low, the company used visuals to illustrate safety and hired a theater group to role-play safety interactions between workers and supervisors. Employees were then divided into groups of 40 to 50 and asked to speak up about their safety concerns and opinions. Understandably, the workers were reluctant to do so, having historically had no say.

As Carroll observed, "I wondered how much authority someone who is underground for hours on end, with a shift supervisor right behind him, really has. I questioned whether a line worker had the power to put up his hand and say, 'I'm not going to do this, because it is unsafe.'"[23] In other words, the workers had to feel psychologically safe in order to speak up about their physical safety.

Psychological safety had to be created in the mines by finding a culturally appropriate approach. With help from the unions, Anglo American leadership adopted a traditional South African method of conducting village assemblies, called *lekgotla*. As you will see, *lekgotla* seems to echo tenets and practices of psychological safety. Traditionally, in these assemblies (somewhat like meetings at Eileen Fisher), everyone sits in a circle and has a chance to speak without being interrupted or criticized; conversation continues for as long as it takes to reach consensus on whatever issue is at stake.[24]

During Anglo American's *lekgotla,* senior managers reframed the initial question. Instead of asking workers to give their opinions directly about safety issues, they asked, "what do we need to do to create a work environment of care and respect?" That was when workers started to feel safe enough to speak up about specific concerns. One group said that they'd like hot water at their work site to clean up and make tea. (Management complied with this request.) The dialogue continued until each group had developed a contract stating what specific actions were needed to maximize safety. In a powerful symbolic gesture of shared commitment, workers and Anglo American executives both signed the contract. As Judy Ndlovu, an Anglo American executive said about this process, "the real change was listening to the workers . . . Cynthia challenged management to understand what the employees were thinking, what they felt when they went into the mine each day."[25] Previously, for an individual miner to speak up would have taken courage but might very well have been a foolish act if not well received by management. Once psychological safety started to take root in the culture, miners could then speak up to help insure physical safety.

When the mines reopened, more than 30,000 workers were retrained to comply with the newly agreed-upon safety protocols. Top leadership met with managers to discuss compliance with the new rules and to emphasize that employees now had the right to stop work if safety standards were not being met. New policies were instituted to insure regular review of safety procedures and to schedule times when management and executives continued to solicit input from workers regarding safety operations. Guiding values were established. Executive meetings were now required to begin with lengthy updates and discussions on safety. Although fatalities fell considerably – from 44 in 2006 to 17 in 2011, a reduction of 62%[26] – they did not reach zero. The company honored any worker who died with memorial services and by posting their photographs in all buildings. The supervisor of the deceased visited the worker's family and village to convey respect and sympathy. All these measures helped to institutionalize not only the safety protocols but also a psychologically safe culture built by care and respect.

A year after the shutdown, Carroll chose to speak up yet again, this time to people outside the organization – the National Union of Mineworkers and the Minister of Mines – to ask for their help in working together to achieve zero harm. Again, she was rebuffed. However, in April 2008, a Safety Summit was held in Johannesburg between Anglo American, the South African Department of Minerals and Energy, and the National Union of Mineworkers. It was the first time the three major stakeholders had come together. As with the mineworkers, it took time for representatives from the three governing entities to build trust and respect. The catalyst for working together was the shared goal of dramatically improving physical safety in the mines. And process was instrumental. By visiting different mines together and continuing to convene, the three groups developed a growing sense of respect and trust for one another. The stakeholder partnerships that eventually developed helped spread of the passion for safety ignited at Anglo American into the rest of South Africa's mining industry.

Although production and revenues fell in the year following the mine shutdown, in both 2008 and 2011, during Carroll's tenure, the company achieved the highest operating profits in its history. Share price rose commensurably. Carroll realized that increasing physical safety in the mines was as much about transforming old attitudes about worker safety and changing the culture to make it safe to speak up as it was about technical or process improvements.

In previous chapters we saw how people up and down and across an organization can contribute to creating a climate of silence and fear. Similarly, people up and down and across the organization can contribute to creating a climate of voice and safety. A leader can be the driving force and catalyst for others to speak up; but ultimately, the practice must be co-created – and continuously nurtured – by multiple stakeholders. As we have seen, commitment to doing this is particularly vital for preventing or managing a crisis.

Transparency by Whiteboard

When people think of leadership in a crisis, all too often they think of someone like General George Patton, issuing decisive orders to his soldiers and commandeering them to victory with toughness. But that isn't always the case, especially when the enemy is technology or natural forces, or both.

Let's look at a less obvious example of heroic leadership in a crisis: Naohiro Masuda, the plant superintendent of the second Fukushima nuclear plant when the giant earthquake struck in March 2011. Like Patton, he inspired life-saving teamwork from his followers. However, Masuda did so by adhering to key principles that build psychological safety: honesty, vulnerability, communication, and information sharing. And his key weapon was a whiteboard.

Fukushima Daini, less than five miles down the coast from its sister plant, Daiichi, also suffered severe damage from the earthquake and tsunami waves.[27] In stark contrast to Daiichi, however, Masuda and his 400 employees managed to safely shut down all 4 of the plant's reactors, thereby averting the ultimate disaster of releasing nuclear material into the air and sea. They managed to lay 5.5 miles of extremely heavy cable in 24 hours – a job that under normal circumstances would take a team of 20, with machinery, at least a month. And they worked for over 48 hours without sleep, in a state of tremendous uncertainty, with fear for their lives and those of their families.

How did Masuda motivate his men to stay under such tough conditions? From the beginning, Masuda chose to issue information rather than orders. After evacuating his workers to the Emergency Response Center (ERC), and having heard from operators in the control rooms that three of the plant's four reactors had lost all operative cooling systems (the operators had bravely weathered the tsunami from their posts), Masuda knew the situation was "extremely serious."[28] If the reactors could not be cooled, they would overheat, resulting in a nuclear breach.

Masuda and his team unfortunately lacked information about the physical condition of the plant. They didn't know what was broken or what resources they might have. To find that out, workers would need to venture outside to assess the damage and figure out what could be done to restore power to the reactors and stabilize the plant. And, for Masuda, that meant helping the workers – already shaken by earthquake and flood – feel psychologically safe enough to act.

Instead of grabbing a megaphone or commanding his men into action, Masuda began writing things down on a whiteboard: the magnitude and frequency of the earthquake's aftershocks, calculations, and a rough chart that demonstrated the decreasing danger of the quakes over time. In other words, he armed his men with data. "I was not sure if my team would go to the field if I asked, and if it was even safe to dispatch people there," Masuda later reflected.[29] Indeed, he allowed the men to make their own decisions about whether they wanted to assist in what might be a dangerous mission. At 10 p.m., when Masuda finally asked the men to pick 4 groups of 10 workers to go out and survey the damage at each of the 4 reactors, not a single one refused.

Having begun his career at Daini in 1982, when it was still under construction, Masuda was intimately acquainted with the plant. That knowledge allowed him to give each group detailed instructions about where to go and what to do. Concerned that fear might interfere with workers' ability to remember his instructions, he made the groups repeat the instructions back to him before they left. The point was not to command action but to assist them in acting quickly should the situation change, and their safety be compromised.

By 2 a.m. on March 12, all 40 workers had safely returned to the ERC with information. One of the reconnaissance teams reported a crucial break of good luck: there was still power inside the radiation waste building behind Reactor 1. That meant the men could potentially get power to the cooling systems. But they would need to lay heavy-duty cables – and a lot of them.

By dawn, Masuda and his team had drawn up a route to run cables from the building down to the reactor units by the water. However, team leaders calculated that they lacked sufficient supplies to do the job. Masuda, in turn, quickly contacted TEPCO headquarters and the Japanese government to request additional supplies and the calculated 50 spools of cables.

While the men waited for the cables to arrive – which would not be until the morning of March 13 – they learned about the explosion at Daiichi. Some were in disbelief. Many were afraid. Could the same thing happen at Daini? Might they be endangering themselves by sticking around? Masuda addressed the 500–600 people in the room: "Please, trust me," he said. "I definitely won't do anything to harm you, but Fukushima Daini is still in trouble, and I need you to do your best."[30]

When the cables finally arrived, the men immediately got to work laying them from the waste building to the reactor units down by the water. They began with Reactor 2, because it was at greatest risk of overheating. To power the three disabled reactors, the men would need to lay almost 9 kilometers (5.5 miles) of cable. Each piece of cable was 200 meters long and weighed about a ton. The operators calculated they had only about 24 hours to perform a job that under normal circumstances would take a month or more. And so, 200 workers began frantically laying cables. Working in shifts, they made agonizingly slow progress. It took about 100 workers to move each piece.

As the men raced against the clock, Masuda slowly came to an unwelcome realization: his plan was untenable. Even at the superhuman pace the men were working, they would not have enough time to hook up all three reactors. The waste building was just too far away.

Masuda's strength as a leader was demonstrated by the immediate admission of his mistake. In keeping with Ray Dalio's Principles, Masuda succeeded by virtue of extreme candor – by telling people the worst news, which he believed would increase the chances they could figure out how to handle the situation. Despite its unwelcome nature, the admission increased the psychological safety in the team and bonded the group more tightly. Consulting with his team leaders, Masuda concluded that they had no choice but to gamble by utilizing some of the power from the generator of the lone functioning reactor unit. On the whiteboard, Masuda added in adjustments to the original plan.

The men continued to work tirelessly throughout the day. Yet, as night approached, some engineers noticed that the pressure in Unit 1 was now climbing faster than that of Unit 2. Fortunately, they spoke up to inform Masuda that they now believed Unit 1 to be most vulnerable and suggested to him that the workers refocus their energy. Equally important, Masuda listened closely to his engineers and took their suggestions seriously.

Having seen his team push onward, without having slept in almost two days, Masuda was understandably reluctant to tell them, "redo it! Shift from Unit 2 to Unit 1!" Still, he broke the news. Though some were upset, a climate of psychological safety and a recognition of what was at stake helped them to commit to the new course of action.

Just before midnight, ecstatic applause broke out when the workers finished laying the last of the cable. At 1:24 a.m., they were notified that the cooling function had been restored to Unit 1 – with about two hours to spare. On the morning of March 15, Masuda and his team were notified that all reactors were finally in cold shutdown. Finally, they could rest.

Masuda influenced the workers to act, even as the ground shook beneath their feet. Through his calmness, openness, and willingness to admit his own fallibility as a leader, Masuda created the conditions for the team to make sense of their surroundings, overcome fear, and solve problems on the fly. Although their physical safety was in constant danger, they felt psychologically safe, and this allowed them to come together, try things, fail, and regroup. In the many moments of fear for their lives over the course of those days, interpersonal fear within the group was nearly nil. Masuda's words and actions set the tone and reassured workers that they could – and must – save the plant.

Unleashing Talent

Reflecting on the more than 20 cases included in Part II of this book helps us understand both how challenging and how important it is to build psychological safety to ensure that the talent in an organization is able to be put to good use to learn, innovate, and grow. Speaking up is not a natural act in hierarchies. It must be nurtured. When it's not, the results can be catastrophic – for people and for the bottom line. But when it is nurtured, you can be certain that it is the product of deliberate, thoughtful effort.

Creating a psychologically safe workplace takes leadership. Leadership can be seen as a force that helps people and organizations engage in unnatural acts like speaking up, taking smart risks, embracing diverse views, and solving remarkably challenging problems. And so the chapters that lie ahead in Part III are focused on what leaders can and must do to create psychological safety. They invite you to consider, and perhaps try out, a variety of practices that can contribute to creating a fearless organization.

Chapter 6 Takeaways

- Clear, direct, candid communication is an important aspect of reducing accidents.

- A compelling company purpose combined with caring leadership motivates people to go the extra mile to do what's needed to ensure safe work practices and employee dignity.

- Worker safety starts with encouraging and reinforcing employees' speaking up about hazards and other concerns.

Endnotes

1. This quote is the popular version of a line written by the Stoic philosopher Marcus Aurelius in Book XII of his *The Meditations:* "... *if thou shalt be afraid not because thou must some time cease to live, but if thou shalt fear never to have begun to live according to nature- then thou wilt be a man worthy of the universe which has produced thee.*" You can find Book XII of *The Meditations*, translated by George Long, for free here: http://classics.mit.edu/Antoninus/meditations.12.twelve.html. Accessed July 27, 2018.

2. Key details in the story of US Airways Flight 1549 described in this chapter come from the National Transportation Safety Board's accident report, and from a series of published case studies:

   - National Transportation Safety Board. "Loss of Thrust in Both Engines After Encountering a Flock of Birds and Subsequent Ditching on the Hudson River, US Airways Flight 1549, Airbus A320-214, N106US, Weehawken, New Jersey, January 15, 2009."

   - *Aircraft Accident Report NTSB/AAR-10/03*. Washington, D.C., 2010;

   - Howitt, A.M., Leonard, H.B., & Weeks, J. Miracle on the Hudson (A): Landing U.S. Airways Flight 1549. Case Study. HKS No. 1966. Cambridge, MA: HKS Case Program, 2012;

   - Howitt, A.M., Leonard, H.B., & Weeks, J. Miracle on the Hudson (B): Rescuing Passengers and Raising the Plane. Case Study. HKS No. 1967. Cambridge, MA: HKS Case Program, 2012;

- Howitt, A.M., Leonard, H.B., & Weeks, J. Miracle on the Hudson (C): Epilogue. Case Study. HKS No. 1967.1. Cambridge, MA: HKS Case Program, 2012.

3. "Statement of Captain Marc Parisis, Vice President, Flight Operations and Services, Airbus." National Transportation Safety hearing. June 9, 2009. Washington, DC. 80–82.
4. U.S. Airways FOM 1.3.4, Captains Authority, online at National Transportation Safety Board, Operations/Human Performance Group Chairmen, Exhibit No. 2-Q.
5. Sullenberger III, C. & Zaslow, Z. *Highest Duty: My Search for What Really Matters.* New York, NY: William Morrow, 2009.
6. Edmondson, A.C. "The Local and Variegated Nature of Learning in Organizations: A Group-Level Perspective." *Organization Science,* 13.2 (2002): 128–46.
7. Sullenberger III, C. & Zaslow, Z. 2009: 229.
8. Wheeler, M. "Asiana Airlines: 'Sorry Captain, You're Wrong.'" *LinkedIn Pulse.* 2014. https://www.linkedin.com/pulse/20140217220032-266437464-asiana-airlines-sorry-captain-you-re-wrong/ Accessed June 12, 2018.
9. See, for instance, Oriol, M.D. "Crew resource management: applications in healthcare organizations." *Nursing Administration* 36.9 (2006): 402–6; McConaughey E. "Crew resource management in healthcare: the evolution of teamwork training and MedTeams." *Journal of Perinatal Neonatal Nursing,* 22.2 (2008): 96–104.
10. Shea-Lewis, A. "Teamwork: crew resource management in a community hospital." *Journal of Healthcare Quality.* 31.5 (2009): 14–18.
11. *The Three Musketeers,* written in 1844 by French author Alexandre Dumas and set in 1625 France, has achieved popularity via its many adaptations into film, video, and television.
12. Key details about DaVita and its CEO/lead musketeer Kent Thiry come from a series of case studies:

   - Pfeffer, J. Kent Thiry and DaVita: Leadership Challenges in Building and Growing a Great Company. Case Study. Stanford GSB No. 0B-54. Palo Alto, CA: Stanford Graduate School of Business, 2006.

   - O'Reilly, C. Pfeffer, J., Hoyt, D., & Drabkin, D. DaVita: A Community First, A Company Second. Case Study. Stanford GSB No. OB-89. Palo Alto, CA: Stanford Graduate School of Business, 2014.

- George, B., & Kindred, N. Kent Thiry: "Mayor" of DaVita. Case Study. HBS Case No. 410-065. Boston, MA: Harvard Business School Publishing, 2010.

13. Pfeffer, J. Kent Thiry and DaVita: Leadership Challenges in Building and Growing a Great Company. 2006: 19.

14. Pfeffer, J. Kent Thiry and DaVita: Leadership Challenges in Building and Growing a Great Company. 2006: 2.

15. Kent Thiry, presentation at the Stanford Graduate School of Business. November 17, 2011.

16. O'Reilly, C. *et al.* DaVita: A Community First, A Company Second. 2014: 7.

17. "Integrated Care Enhances Clinical Outcomes for Dialysis Patients." News-Medical.net. October 31, 2017. https://www.news-medical .net/news/20171031/Integrated-care-enhances-clinical-outcomes-for-dialysis-patients.aspx Accessed June 8, 2018.

18. Berwick, D.M., Nolan, T.W., & Whittington, J. "The Triple Aim: Care, Health, and Cost." *Health Affairs*. 27.3 (2008): 759–69.

19. Key details describing the safety initiative at Anglo American under Cynthia Carroll in this chapter come from a series of case studies by HBS Professor Gautam Mukunda and colleagues:

  - Mukunda, G., Mazzanti, L., & Sesia, A. Cynthia Carroll at Anglo American (A). Case Study. HBS No. 414-019. Boston, MA: Harvard Business School Publishing, 2013.

  - Mukunda, G., Mazzanti, L., & Sesia, A. Cynthia Carroll at Anglo American (B). Case Study. HBS No. 414-020. Boston, MA: Harvard Business School Publishing, 2013.

  - Mukunda, G., Mazzanti, L., & Sesia, A. Cynthia Carroll at Anglo American (C). Case Study. HBS No. 414-021. Boston, MA: Harvard Business School Publishing, 2013.

20. Carroll, C. "The CEO of Anglo American on Getting Serious about Safety" *Harvard Business Review*. 2012. https://hbr.org/2012/06/the-ceo-of-anglo-american-on-getting-serious-about-safety Accessed June 14, 2018.

21. Mukunda, G. *et al.* Cynthia Carroll at Anglo American (A). 2013: 7.

22. *Ibid*.

23. Carroll, C. 2012, op cit.

24. De Liefde, W. *Lekgotla: The Art of Leadership Through Dialogue*. Houghton, South Africa: Jacana Media, 2005.

25. Mukunda, G. *et al.* Cynthia Carroll at Anglo American (B). 2013: 2.

26. Carroll, C. 2012, op cit.

27. Key details on the close call at Fukushima Daini in this chapter come from a spectacular episode of PBS's *NOVA* from 2015, as well as a *Harvard Business Review* piece by my colleague Ranjay Gulati, which documented Masuda's leadership style:

- O'Brien, M. (producer). "*NOVA:* Nuclear Meltdown Disaster." *PBS*, aired July 29, 2015. http://www.pbs.org/wgbh/nova/tech/nuclear-disaster.html Accessed June 15, 2018.

- Gulati, R., Casto, C., & Krontiris, C. "How the Other Fukushima Plant Survived." *Harvard Business Review*, 2015. https://hbr.org/2014/07/how-the-other-fukushima-plant-survived Accessed June 13, 2018.

28. O'Brien, M. (producer). July 29, 2015, op cit.

29. Gulati, R. *et al.* 2015, op cit.

30. *Ibid.*

PART III

Creating a Fearless Organization

7

Making it Happen

You can tell whether a man is clever by his answers. You can tell whether a man is wise by his questions.

—Naguib Mahfouz[1]

When Julie Morath came on board as chief operating officer at Children's Hospital and Clinics in Minneapolis, Minnesota, her goal was simple: 100% patient safety for the hospitalized children under her care.[2] The goal may have been simple. How to accomplish it was not. This was late 1999, and few people were talking about patient safety. It's not that most clinicians thought patients were completely safe from mistakes and harm; it's just that they tended to think that when things went wrong, someone was to blame. This made it hard to talk about the problem. Nurses and doctors, Morath knew, first had to become willing to speak up to report errors if was going to be possible to reduce the incidence of harm. In short, she needed the

153

data on what was happening, when, and where. Only then could the hospital find new ways to enhance the safety of all of the vulnerable young patients at their six medical facilities in the Twin Cities.

The Leader's Tool Kit

In previous chapters, we saw how a lack of psychological safety stopped a NICU nurse from speaking up about a possible medication error for fear of annoying the physician. We saw how well-trained clinicians at a cutting-edge medical facility failed to question a fatal chemotherapy dosing regimen over a period of several days. These situations both took place in settings where a lot was going on.

Tertiary care hospitals, like Children's, are complex. It's challenging to get every single task done perfectly every single time. To begin with, every patient is different. No two care episodes are identical. Upping the ante, the highly-interdependent work of patient care must be seamlessly coordinated among narrow specialists with complementary knowledge and skills – who may not even know each other's names. Multiple, interdependent departments – pharmacy, laboratory, physicians, and nursing – who have conflicting priorities about what service to provide at what time must coordinate their actions for safe care to be consistently delivered. And so the organization had long accepted that things would occasionally go wrong. A certain number of slip-ups and crossed wires was just the way things were. It wasn't discussed much, and there was an unfortunate tendency to blame individuals (rather than system complexity) for errors that slipped through the cracks and led to patient harm.

Morath felt that this attitude had to change if progress was to be made. She needed a leadership tool kit to get this done. In retrospect, what happened to profoundly shift attitudes and behaviors at Children's can be divided into three categories: setting the stage, inviting participation, and responding productively.

Setting the Stage

As soon as she took the job, Morath began speaking to large and small groups in the hospital to explain that healthcare delivery, by its nature, was a complex system prone to breakdowns. She presented new research and statistics on medical adverse events to educate everyone about their prevalence. She introduced new terminology ("words to work by") that altered the meaning of events and actions in important ways; for instance, instead of an "investigation" into an adverse event, the hospital would use the term "study;" instead of "error" she suggested people use "accident" or "failure." In subtle but important ways, Morath was trying to help people think differently about the work – and especially about what it means when things go wrong. These leadership actions comprise what I refer to as framing the work.

Frames consist of assumptions or beliefs that we layer onto reality.[3] All of us frame objects and situations automatically. Our focus is on the situation itself, and we are typically blind to the effects of our frames. Our prior experiences affect how we think and feel about what's presently around us in subtle ways. We believe we're seeing reality – seeing what is *there*. For instance, if we frame medical accidents as indications that someone screwed up, we will ignore or suppress them for fear of being blamed or of pointing the finger at a colleague. However, we can shift our automatic frames and create a shared frame that more accurately represents reality. More information about framing the work is provided later in this chapter. But when Morath began to give presentations that called attention to hospital care as a complex, error-prone system, what she was doing was framing the work – or, more accurately, *re*framing it. Her goal was to help people shift from a belief that incompetence (rather than system complexity) was to blame. This shift in perspective would prove essential to helping people feel safe speaking up about the problems, mistakes, and risks they saw.[4]

In setting the stage for open discussion of error, Morath also communicated urgency about the goal of 100% patient safety.

I consider this an important stage-setting act because it helped people reconnect with the reasons they went into healthcare in the first place: to save lives. This reminder helped motivate people to do the hard work of reporting, analyzing, and finding ways to prevent harm. In short, with an emphasis on the complex and error-prone nature of the work, and a reminder of what was at stake (children's lives), Morath had set the stage for candor. But that was not enough to make it happen.

Inviting Participation

As you may imagine, hardworking neonatal nurses and experienced pediatric surgeons did not immediately flock to Morath's office to confess to having made or seen mistakes. People found it easier to believe that medical errors happened elsewhere rather than in their own esteemed institution. Even if they understood, deep down, that things can and do go wrong, it was not front of mind, and they genuinely believed they were providing great care.

Morath, hearing silence from the staff, stopped to consider. I'm sure it crossed her mind to try again – to re-explain the complex, error-prone nature of tertiary care hospital operations so as to correct the staff's implicit response that nothing was going wrong. If so, she resisted the temptation to lecture. Instead, she did something that was as simple as it was powerful. She asked a question. "Was everything as safe as you would like it to have been this week with your patients?"[5]

The question – genuine, curious, direct – was respectful and concrete: "this week," "your patients." Its very wording conveys genuine interest. Curiosity. It makes you think. Interestingly, she did *not* ask, "did you see lots of mistakes or harm?" Rather, she invited people to think in aspirational terms: "Was everything as safe as you would like it to be?" Sure enough, psychological safety started to take hold. People began to bring up incidents that they had seen and even contributed to.

Morath enhanced her invitation to participate with several structural interventions. First, she set up a core team called the Patient Safety Steering Committee (PSSC) to lead the change initiative. The PSSC was designed as a cross-functional, multilevel group to ensure that voices from all over the hospital would be heard. Each member was invited with a personal explanation for why his or her perspective was sought. Second, Morath and the PSSC introduced a new policy called "blameless reporting" – a system inviting confidential reports about risks and failures people observed. Third, as people began to feel safe enough to speak up, Morath led as many as 18 focus groups to make it easy for people throughout the organization to share concerns and experiences.

These simple structures made speaking up easier. When you join a focus group, your input is explicitly requested. It feels more awkward to remain silent than to offer your thoughts. In this way, the voice asymmetry described in Chapter 2, in which silence dominates because of the inherent risks of voice, is mitigated.

Responding Productively

Speaking up is only the first step. The true test is how leaders respond when people actually do speak up. Stage setting and inviting participation indeed build psychological safety. But if a boss responds with anger or disdain as soon as someone steps forward to speak up about a problem, the safety will quickly evaporate. A productive response must be appreciative, respectful, and offer a path forward.

Consider the "focused event analysis" (FEA), a cross-disciplinary meeting that Morath instituted at Children's to bring people together after a failure. The FEA represents a disciplined exploration of what happened from multiple perspectives – like the proverbial blind men around the elephant. In this setting, however, the goal is not to fight about who was right, as the blind men did, but rather to identify contributing factors with the goal of improving the system to prevent similar failures in the future.[6] The FEA is thus a prime example of responding productively.

Equally important, the blameless reporting policy enabled productive responses to messengers who brought bad news about an error or mishap. Instead of expecting blame or punishment, the healthcare personnel at Children's began to expect – and experience – appreciation for their effort in bringing valuable information forward.

This goal of this chapter is to provide further examples of specific ways leaders build psychological safety in their organizations by setting the stage, inviting participation, and responding productively. With some practice and reflection, this tool kit is available to any leader wishing to create psychological safety. Table 7.1 summarizes the framework. To develop these behavioral tools, I drew from both research and my years of experience studying and consulting with organizations around the world.

How to Set the Stage for Psychological Safety

Whenever you are trying to get people on the same page, with common goals and a shared appreciation for what they're up against, you're setting the stage for psychological safety. The most important skill to master is that of framing the work. If near-perfection is what is needed to satisfy demanding car customers, leaders must know to frame the work by alerting workers to catch and correct tiny deviations before the car proceeds down the assembly line. If zero worker fatalities in a dangerous platinum mine is the goal, then leaders must frame physical safety as a worthy and challenging but attainable goal. If discovering new cures is the goal, leaders know to motivate researchers to generate smart hypotheses for experiments and to feel okay about being wrong far more often than right. In this section, I'll first explaining how and why framing the work includes reframing failure and clarifying the need for voice. From there I'll move on to another stage-setting tool in the leader's tool kit: motivating effort.

Table 7.1 The Leader's Tool Kit for Building Psychological Safety.

Category	Setting the Stage	Inviting Participation	Responding Productively
Leadership tasks	**Frame the Work** ■ Set expectations about failure, uncertainty, and interdependence to clarify the need for voice **Emphasize Purpose** ■ Identify what's at stake, why it matters, and for whom	**Demonstrate Situational Humility** ■ Acknowledge gaps **Practice Inquiry** ■ Ask good questions ■ Model intense listening **Set up Structures and Processes** ■ Create forums for input ■ Provide guidelines for discussion	**Express Appreciation** ■ Listen ■ Acknowledge and thank **Destigmatize Failure** ■ Look forward ■ Offer help ■ Discuss, consider, and brainstorm next steps **Sanction Clear Violations**
Accomplishes	Shared expectations and meaning	Confidence that voice is welcome	Orientation toward continuous learning

Framing the Work

Reframing Failure

Because fear of (reporting) failure is such a key indicator of an environment with low levels of psychological safety, how leaders present the role of failure is essential. Recall Astro Teller's observation at Google X that "the only way to get people to work on big, risky things . . . is if you make that the path of least resistance for them [and] make it safe to fail."[7] In other words, unless a leader expressly and actively makes it psychologically safe to do so, people will automatically seek to avoid failure. So how did Teller reframe failure to make it okay? By saying, believing, and convincing others that "I'm not pro failure, I'm pro learning."[8]

Failure is a source of valuable data, but leaders must understand and communicate that learning only happens when there's enough psychological safety to dig into failure's lessons carefully. In his book *The Game-Changer,* published while he was still CEO of Proctor and Gamble, A.G. Lafley celebrates his 11 most expensive product failures, describing why each was valuable and what the company learned from each.[9] Recall, also, Ed Catmull's assurance to Pixar animators, that movies always start out bad, to help them "uncouple fear and failure."[10] Here, Catmull is making a leadership framing statement. He is making sure that people know this is the kind of work for which stunning success occurs only if you're willing to confront the "bad" along the way to the "good." Similarly, OpenTable CEO Christa Quarles tells employees, "early, often, ugly. It's O.K. It doesn't have to be perfect because then I can course-correct much, much faster."[11] This too is a framing statement. It says that success in the online restaurant-reservation business occurs through course correction – not through magically getting it right the first time. Quarles is framing early, ugly versions as vital information to make good decisions that lead to later, beautiful versions.

Learning to learn from failure has become so important that Smith College (along with other schools around the country) is creating courses and initiatives to help students better deal with failures, challenges, and setbacks. "What we're trying to teach is that failure is not a bug of learning, it's a feature,"[12] said Rachel Simmons, a leadership development specialist in Smith's Wurtele Center for Work and Life and the unofficial "failure czar" on campus. "It's not something that should be locked out of the learning experience. For many of our students – those who have had to be almost perfect to get accepted into a school like Smith – failure can be an unfamiliar experience. So when it happens, it can be crippling."[13] With workshops on impostor syndrome, discussions on perfectionism and a campaign to remind students that 64% of their peers will get (gasp) a B-minus or lower, the program is part of a campus-wide effort to foster student resilience.

Note that failure plays a varying role in different kinds of work.[14] At one end of the spectrum is high-volume repetitive work, such as in an assembly plant, a fast-food restaurant, or even a kidney dialysis center. Failing to correctly plug a patient into a dialysis machine or install an automobile airbag in precisely the right manner can have disastrous consequences. So in this kind of work it's vital that people eagerly catch and correct deviations from best practice. Here, celebrating failure is a matter of viewing such deviations as "good catch" events and appreciating those who noticed tiny mistakes as observant contributors to the mission.

At the other end of the spectrum lies innovation and research, where little is known about how to obtain a desired result. Creating a movie, a line of original clothing, or a technology that can convert seawater to fuel are all examples. In this context, dramatic failures must be courted and celebrated because they are and integral part of the journey to success. In the middle of the spectrum, where much of the work done today falls, are complex operations, such as hospitals or financial institutions. Here, vigilance and teamwork are both vital to preventing avoidable failures and celebrating intelligent ones.

Reframing failure starts with understanding a basic typology of failure types. As I have written in more detail elsewhere, failure archetypes include preventable failures (never good news), complex failures (still not good news), and intelligent failures (not fun, but must be considered good news because of the value they bring).[15] Preventable failures are deviations from recommended procedures that produce bad outcomes. If someone fails to don safety glasses in a factory and suffers an eye injury, this is a preventable failure. Complex failures occur in familiar contexts when a confluence of factors come together in a way that may never have occurred before; consider the severe flooding of the Wall Street subway station in New York City during Superstorm Sandy in 2012. With vigilance, complex failures can sometimes, but not always, be avoided. Neither preventable nor complex failures are worthy of celebration.

In contrast, intelligent failures, as the term implies, must be celebrated so as to encourage more of them. Intelligent failures, like the preventable and complex, are still results no one wanted. But, unlike the other two categories, they are the result of a thoughtful foray into new territory. Table 7.2 presents definitions and contexts to clarify these distinctions. An important part of framing is making sure people understand that failures will happen. Some failures are genuinely good news; some are not, but no matter what type they are, our primary goal is to learn from them.

Clarifying the Need for Voice

Framing the work also involves calling attention to other ways, beyond failure's prevalence, in which tasks and environments differ. Three especially important dimensions are uncertainty, interdependence, and what's at stake – all of which also have implications for failure (e.g. expectations about its frequency, its value, and its consequences). Emphasizing uncertainty reminds people that they need to be curious and alert to pick up early indicators of change in, say, customer preferences in a new market, a patient's reaction to a drug, or new technologies on the horizon.

Emphasizing interdependence lets people know that they're responsible for understanding how their tasks interact with other

Table 7.2 Failure Archetypes – Definitions and Implications.[16]

	Preventable	Complex	Intelligent
Definition	Deviations from known processes that produce unwanted outcomes	Unique and novel combinations of events and actions that give rise to unwanted outcomes	Novel forays into new territory that lead to unwanted outcomes
Common Causes	Behavior, skill, and attention deficiencies	Complexity, variability, and novel factors imposed on familiar situations	Uncertainty, experimentation, and risk taking
Descriptive Term	Process deviation	System breakdown	Unsuccessful trial
Contexts Where Each Is Most Salient	Production line manufacturing Fast-food services Basic utilities and services	Hospital care NASA shuttle program Aircraft carrier Nuclear power plant	Drug development New product design

people's tasks. Interdependence encourages frequent conversations to figure out the impact their work is having on others and to convey in turn the impact others' work has on them. Interdependent work requires communication. In other words, when leaders frame the work they are emphasizing the need for taking interpersonal risks like sharing ideas and concerns.

Finally, clarifying the stakes is important whether the stakes are high or low. Reminding people that human life is on the line – say, in a hospital, a mine, or at NASA – helps put interpersonal risk in perspective. People are more likely to speak up – thereby overcoming the inherent asymmetry of voice and silence – if leaders frame its importance. Similarly, reminding people that the only thing that is at stake is a bruised ego when a lab experiment doesn't go as hoped is a good way to get them to be willing to go for it – offer possibly crazy ideas and figure out which ones to test first!

Finally, how most people see bosses presents a crucial area for reframing. Table 7.3 compares a set of default frames to a deliberate reframe for how we might think about bosses and others at work. As a default, bosses are viewed as having answers, being able to give orders, and being positioned to assess whether the orders are well executed. With this frame, others are merely subordinates expected to do as they are told. CEO Martin Winterkorn at VW is a prime example of an executive governed by the default frame. Notice that the default set of frames makes interpersonal fear sensible.

Table 7.3   Framing the Role of the Boss.

	Default Frames	**Reframe**
The Boss	Has answers	Sets direction
	Gives orders	Invites input to clarify and improve
	Assesses others' performance	Creates conditions for continued learning to achieve excellence
Others	Subordinates who must do what they're told	Contributors with crucial knowledge and insight

In a world in which bosses have the answers and absolute authority over how your work is judged, it makes sense to fear the boss and to think very carefully about what you reveal. The reframe, in contrast, spells out logic that clarifies the necessity for a psychologically safe environment. This logic applies to the successful execution of work in most organizations today.

The reframe shows that leaders must establish and cultivate psychological safety to succeed in most work environments today. The leader is obliged to set direction for the work, to invite relevant input to clarify and improve on the general direction that has been set, and to create conditions for continued learning to achieve excellence. Cynthia Carroll reframed the work at Anglo American by actively inviting the miners' input to draw up new physical safety practices. Naohiro Masuda, the plant superintendent for Fukushima Daini, reframed the work when he set up a whiteboard to lead his team successfully through a tsunami's onslaught. He gave the team as much ongoing information as he had available in a quickly changing environment. The more creativity and innovation are required to achieve a particular goal, the more this stance is needed. The problem with Winterkorn's stance at VW wasn't that it was wrong in a moral sense; rather, it was wrong in a practical sense; it was wrong for achieving a goal that called for innovation. Making the company the largest automaker in the world by leveraging diesel engine technology was somewhat of a "moonshot" goal such as those pursued at Google X. The diesel engine technology was not yet able to perform in ways consistent with regulatory requirements; no amount of giving orders could overcome that basic truth about the situation. A psychologically safe environment, such as we saw at Google X, could have productively absorbed this innovation failure, allowing the senior executives to rethink their strategy.

In the reframe, those who are not the boss are seen as valued contributors – that is, as people with crucial knowledge and insight. When Julie Morath asks people to speak up about patient error or when Eileen Fisher orchestrates staff meetings to give everyone a chance to speak, they do so because it will improve decision-making and execution – not because they want to be nice. Leaders in a volatile, uncertain, complex, and ambiguous (VUCA) world, who understand that today's work requires continuous learning to figure out when and how to change course, must consciously reframe how they think, from the default frames that we all bring to work unconsciously to a more productive reframe.

Framing the work is not something that leaders do once, and then it's done. Framing is ongoing. Frequently calling attention to levels of uncertainty or interdependence helps people remember that they must be alert and candid to perform well. Had NASA leaders emphasized these essential features of the work, the invitation to engineers to share tentative concerns would have been far more visible to them.

Motivating Effort

Emphasizing a sense of purpose is another key element of setting the stage for psychological safety. Motivating people by articulating a compelling purpose is a well-established leadership task. Leaders who remind people of why what they do matters – for customers, for the world – help create the energy that carries them through challenging moments. Kent Thiry's "one for all and all for one" motto motivates staff at DaVita to care for patients with kidney disease. In this motto, he at once reminds people of patients' vulnerability and reminds them that the team is all in it together. Note that even when it seems obvious (for instance, taking care of vulnerable patients) that the work is meaningful, leaders still must take the time to emphasize the purpose the organization serves. This is because anyone can get tired, distracted, and frustrated and lose sight of the larger picture – of what's at stake. Carroll brought her passion for zero harm to the South African government and larger mining institutional bodies. Once stakeholders from previously disconnected groups began working together for the shared goal of safety in the mines they were able to develop trust for one another. It's the leader's job to bring people back to a psychological place where they are in touch with how much their work matters. This also helps the overcome the interpersonal risks they face at work.

Meaning can be defined and framed in other ways, too. Ray Dalio at Bridgewater Associates emphasizes to his hedge fund employees that personal growth is as important as profit. That each employee is becoming a better person matters to Dalio, and he hopes to them as well. Bob Chapman's belief that the company measures success by how well it touches the lives of employees motivates all to bring their best selves to the job.

Most leaders would be well served by stopping to reflect on the purpose that motivates them and makes the organization's work meaningful to the broader community. Having done so, they should ask themselves how often and how vigorously they are conveying this compelling rationale for the work to others. Our primal need to feel purpose and meaning in our lives, including at work, has been demonstrated by numerous studies in psychology.[17]

How to Invite Participation So People Respond

The second essential activity in the leaders' tool kit is inviting participation in a way that people find compelling and genuine. The goal is to lower what is usually a too-high bar for what's considered appropriate participation. Realizing that self-protection is natural, the invitation to participate must be crystal clear if people are going to choose to engage rather than to play it safe. Two essential behaviors that signal an invitation is genuine are adopting a mindset of situational humility and engaging in proactive inquiry. Designing structures for input, another powerful tool I discuss in this section, also serves as an invitation for voice.

Situational Humility

The bottom line is that no one wants to take the interpersonal risk of imposing ideas when the boss appears to think he or she knows everything. A learning mindset, which blends humility and curiosity, mitigates this risk. A learning mindset recognizes that there is always more to learn.

Frankly, adopting a humble mindset when faced with the complex, dynamic, uncertain world in which we all work today is simply realism. The term situational humility captures this concept well (the need for humility lies in the situation) and may make it easier for leaders, especially those with abundant self-confidence, to recognize the validity, and the power, of a humble mindset. MIT Professor Ed Schein calls this "Here-and-Now Humility."[18] Keep in mind that confidence and humility are not opposites. Confidence in one's abilities and knowledge, when warranted, is far preferable to false modesty. But humility is not modesty, false or otherwise. Humility is the simple recognition that you don't have all the answers, and you certainly don't have a crystal ball. Research shows that when leaders express humility, teams engage in more learning behavior.[19]

Demonstrating situational humility includes acknowledging your errors and shortcomings. Anne Mulcahy, Chairperson and CEO of Xerox, who led the company through a successful transformation out of bankruptcy in the 2000s, said that she was known to many in the company as the "Master of I Don't Know" because rather than offer an uninformed opinion she would so often reply, "I don't know," to questions.[20] Although reminiscent of Eileen Fisher's "Be a Don't Knower," Mulcahy adopts this stance as the newly promoted chief executive of a global corporation rather than as a founder of her own company. Speaking to executives in the Advanced Management Program at Harvard Business School, Mulcahy commented that her willingness to be vulnerable with others and admit her own shortcomings turned out to be a huge asset. "Instead of people losing confidence, they actually gain confidence [in you] when you admit you don't know something," she said.[21] This created the space for others at Xerox to step up, offer their expertise, and engage in the process of turning the company around. Although this may seem downright obvious, such humility can be strangely rare in many organizations.

London Business School Professor Dan Cable sheds light on why. In a recent article in *Harvard Business Review*, he writes, "Power... can cause leaders to become overly obsessed with outcomes and control," inadvertently ramping up "people's fear – fear of not hitting targets, fear of losing bonuses, fear of failing – and as a consequence... their drive to experiment and learn is stifled."[22] Being overly certain or just plain arrogant can have similar effects – increasing fear, reducing motivation, and inhibiting interpersonal risk taking.

Recall that in our study of neonatal intensive care units mentioned in Chapter 2, Ingrid Nembhard, Anita Tucker, and I found that NICUs with high psychological safety had substantially better results from their quality improvement work than those with low psychological safety.[23] A factor we called leadership inclusiveness made the difference. To illustrate, inclusive Medical Directors (physicians in charge of the intensive care organization) said things like, "I may miss something; I need to hear from you." Others perhaps took it for granted that people knew to speak up. Our survey measure rated three behavioral attributes of leadership inclusiveness: one, leaders were approachable and accessible; two, leaders acknowledged their fallibility; and three, leaders proactively invited input from other staff, physicians, and nurses. The concept of leadership inclusiveness thus captures situational humility coupled with proactive inquiry (discussed in the next section).

Building on this work, Israeli researchers Reuven Hirak and Abraham Carmeli and two of their colleagues surveyed employees from clinical units in a large hospital in Israel on leader inclusiveness, psychological safety, units' ability to learn from failures, and unit performance. They found that units in which leaders were perceived as more inclusive had higher psychological safety, which led to increased learning from failure and better unit performance.[24] In sum, leaders who are approachable and accessible, acknowledge their fallibility, and proactively invite input from others can do much to establish and enhance psychological safety in their organizations. Powerful tools, indeed.

Proactive Inquiry

The second tool for inviting participation is inquiry. Inquiry is purposeful probing to learn more about an issue, situation, or person. The foundational skill lies in cultivating genuine interest in others' responses. Why is this hard? Because all adults, especially high-achieving ones, are subject to a cognitive bias called naive realism that gives us the experience of "knowing" what's going on.[25] As noted in the previous section, we believe we are seeing "reality" – rather than a subjective view of reality. As a result, we often fail to wonder what others are seeing. We fail to be curious. Worse, many leaders, even when they are motivated to ask a question, worry that it will make them look uninformed or weak. Further exacerbating the challenge, some companies sport "a culture of telling," as a senior executive in a global pharmaceutical company put it in a recent conversation we had about his company. In a culture of telling, *asking* gets short shrift.

Yet when leaders overcome these biases to ask genuine questions, it fosters psychological safety. Recall Morath at Children's Hospital: Was everything as safe as you would like it to have been this week with your patients? Or Carroll's question to the mineworkers: What do we need to create a work environment of care and respect? Genuine questions convey respect for the other person – a vital aspect of psychological safety. Contrary to what many may believe, asking questions tends to make the leader seem not weak but thoughtful and wise.

The leaders' tool kit contains a few rules of thumb for asking a good question: one, you don't know the answer; two, you ask questions that do not limit response options to Yes or No, and three, you phrase the question in a way that helps others share their thinking in a focused way. Consistent with these basic principles, the World Café organization, which is dedicated to fostering conversations that focus on finding new ways to accomplish important organizational or social goals, identifies attributes of "powerful questions" – those that provoke, inspire, and shift people's thinking – as shown in the sidebar.

Attributes of a Powerful Question[26]

- Generates curiosity in the listener
- Stimulates reflective conversation
- Is thought-provoking
- Surfaces underlying assumptions
- Invites creativity and new possibilities
- Generates energy and forward movement
- Channels attention and focuses inquiry
- Stays with participants
- Touches a deep meaning
- Evokes more questions

All of us can benefit from introducing more inquiry into our work. The essential skill of inquiry involves picking the right type of question for a situation. For instance, questions can go broad or deep. To broaden understanding of a situation or expand an option set, ask, "what might we be missing?", "what other ideas could we generate?", or "who has a different perspective?"[27] Such questions ensure that more comprehensive information is considered and that a larger set of options is generated related to a problem or decision. Other questions are designed to deepen understanding. Ask, "what leads you to think so?" or "can you give me an example?" Such questions are crucial to helping people learn about each other's expertise and goals. Moreover, when asked thoughtfully, a good question indicates to others that their voices are desired – instantly making that moment psychologically safe for offering a response.

Bob Pittman, founder of MTV, offers an example of inquiry to push for depth of analysis and diversity of perspective at the same time. In an interview with former *New York Times* "Corner Office" writer Adam Bryant, Pittman recounts,

Often in meetings, I will ask people when we're discussing an idea, "What did the dissenter say?" The first time you do that, somebody might say, "Well, everybody's on board." Then I'll say, "Well, you guys aren't listening very well, because there's always another point of view somewhere and you need to go back and find out what the dissenting point of view is."[28]

Here we can see that Pittman is practicing proactive inquiry and also modeling to his employees how to do it. Further, the idea that there's always another point of view is a subtle move to frame the work. In this small point, he is framing the work, implicitly reminding the team that creative programming work, such as practiced at MTV, benefits from a diversity of views. For more cases and detail on the power of inquiry as a fundamental leadership skill, I recommend Ed Schein's thoughtful book, *Humble Inquiry*.[29]

Designing Structures for Input

A third way to invite participation and reinforce psychological safety is to implement structures designed to elicit employee input. The focus groups and FEA meetings at Children's are examples of such structures. These were so successful in getting conversations on safety underway that hospital staff members began to design structures of their own to elicit their own colleagues' ideas and concerns. Notably, Casey Hooke, a clinical nurse specialist, came up with the idea for a safety action team in her unit. The cross-functional unit-based team met monthly to identify safety hazards in the oncology unit. Soon, two other units, inspired by Hooke's efforts, launched their own safety action teams. Eventually, the patient safety steering committee suggested that all hospital units implement such teams.

Another way to chip away at interpersonal fear is through employee-to-employee learning structures, as Google has done with its creation of the "g2g" (Googler-to-Googler) network, consisting of more than 6000 Google employees who volunteer time to helping their peers learn.[30] Participants in g2g do one-on-one mentoring, coach teams on psychological safety, and teach courses in professional skills ranging from leadership to Python coding. Google claims that g2g has helped develop the skills of countless employees. It is also helping to build a psychologically safe culture where everyone is both a learner and a teacher.

The global food company Groupe Danone created structured conference events called "knowledge marketplaces" to foster inquiry and knowledge sharing across country business units.[31] Although many good ideas and practices that improved operational performance came out of these workshops, which brought employees from different countries together, the executives who sponsored them saw the most important outcome as a shift in the organizational culture toward speaking up, asking for help, and sharing good ideas.

How to Respond Productively to Voice – No Matter Its Quality

To reinforce a climate of psychological safety, it's imperative that leaders – at all levels – respond productively to the risks people take. Productive responses are characterized by three elements: expressions of appreciation, destigmatizing failure, and sanctioning clear violations.

Express Appreciation

Imagine if Christina, the NICU nurse in Chapter 1, had spoken up to Dr. Drake. Her quiet fear was that he would have berated or belittled her. But what if he had said, "thank you so much for bringing that up"? Her feeling of psychological safety would have gone up a notch. This is an example of an appreciative response. It does not matter whether the doctor believes the nurse's suggestion or question is good or bad. Either way, his *initial* response must be one of appreciation. Then he can educate – that is, give feedback or explain clinical subtleties. But to ensure that staff keeps speaking up so as to keep patients safe from unexpected lapses in attention or judgment, the courage it takes to speak up must receive the mini-reward of thanks.

Stanford Professor Carol Dweck, whose celebrated research on mindset shows the power of a learning orientation for individual achievement and resilience in the face of challenge, notes the importance of praising people for efforts, regardless of the outcome.[32] When people believe their performance is an indication of their ability or intelligence, they are less likely to take risks – for fear of a result that would disconfirm their ability. But when people believe that performance reflects effort and good strategy, they are eager to try new things and willing to persevere despite adversity and failure.

Praising effort is especially important in uncertain environments, where good outcomes are not always the result of good process, and vice versa. Although many of the examples in this book present responses from CEOs, an equally important leadership responsibility for C-level executives is making sure that people throughout the organization respond productively to their colleagues. It helps if everyone understands the logic conveyed in Figure 7.1, which depicts the imperfect relationship between process and outcome. Clearly, good process can lead to good outcomes, and bad process can lead to bad outcomes (Figure 7.1a). But, as shown in Figure 7.1b, good process also can produce bad outcomes (especially facing high uncertainty or complexity, as in VUCA conditions), and bad process can produce a good outcome (when you get lucky), or the *illusion* of a good outcome (for a while, anyway, as in the cases of VW and Wells Fargo). The lack of simple cause–effect relationships in uncertain, ambiguous environments reinforces the importance of productive responses to outcomes of all kinds, but especially to bad news outcomes.

Productive responses often include expressions of appreciation, ranging from the small ("thank you so much for speaking up") to the elaborate – celebrations or bonuses in response to intelligent failure.

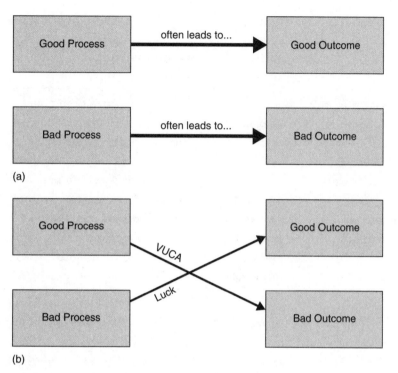

Figure 7.1 **The Imperfect Relationship between Process and Outcome.**

Destigmatize Failure

Failure is a necessary part of uncertainty and innovation, but this must be made explicit to reinforce the invitation for voice. Consider the implications of the failure typology in Table 7.2 for designing a productive response to news of a failure. Leaders who respond to all failures in the same way will not create a healthy environment for learning. When a failure occurs because someone violated a rule or value that matters in the organization, this is very different than when a thoughtful hypothesis in the lab turns out to be wrong. Although obvious in concept, in practice people routinely get this wrong.

Table 7.4   Destigmatizing Failure for Psychological Safety.

	Traditional Frame	Destigmatizing Reframe
Concept of Failure	Failure is not acceptable.	Failure is a natural by-product of experimentation.
Beliefs About Effective Performance	Effective performers don't fail.	Effective performers produce, learn from and share the lessons from intelligent failures.
The Goal	Prevent failure.	Promote fast learning.
The Frame's Impact	*People hide failures to protect themselves.*	***Open discussion, fast learning, and innovation.***

I frequently ask managers, scientists, salespeople, and technologists around the world the following question: What percent of the failures in your organizations should be considered blameworthy? Their answers are usually in single digits – perhaps 1% to 4%. I then ask what percent are *treated* as blameworthy. Now, they say (after a pause or a laugh) 70% to 90%! The unfortunate consequence of this gap between simple logic and organizational response is that many failures go unreported and their lessons are lost. As shown in Table 7.4, the primary result of responding to failures in a negative way is that you don't hear about them. And that, as Mark Costa noted in Chapter 2, should be your biggest fear.

A productive response to a complex failure at Children's Hospital is embodied in the FEA process, described in the Leader's Tool Kit section. All of the people whose work or role touched the failure in question are invited to sit around the same table to share their observations, their questions, and their concerns related to the events that unfolded. Everyone listens intently to what others saw, felt, and did. More often than not, individuals were doing their tasks in prescribed ways, but a host of factors came together in a new way to produce a mishap. The FEA is not a fun activity, but it is deeply meaningful and gratifying. People gain understanding of how various systems and roles in the hospital intersect, and they leave with a deeper appreciation of system complexity and interdependence. They do not feel blamed but instead empowered to go back out and make the system better so as to prevent a similar failure in the future. Most importantly, they feel psychologically safe enough to keep reporting what they see, to keep asking for help or clarification, and to offer ideas for improvement.

In fact, a productive response to intelligent failure can mean actually celebrating the news. Some years ago, the chief scientific officer at Eli Lilly introduced "failure parties" to honor intelligent, high-quality scientific experiments that failed to achieve the desired results.[33] Might this be a bridge too far? I don't think so. First, and most obvious, it helps build a psychologically safe climate for thoughtful risks, which is mission critical in science. Second, it helps people acknowledge failures in a timely way, which allows redeployment of valuable resources – scientists and materials – to new projects earlier rather than later, potentially saving thousands of dollars. Third, when you hold a party, people tend to show up – which means they learn about the failure. This in turn lowers the risk that the company will repeat the same failure. An intelligent failure the first time around no longer qualifies as intelligent the second time.

In brief, a productive response to preventable failures is to double down on prevention, usually a combination of training and improved system design to make it easier for people to do the right thing. However, there are instances in which a preventable failure is the result of a blameworthy action or a repeated instance of deviation from prescribed process, impervious to prior attempts at redirection. In such cases, usually rare, there is an obligation to act in ways that prevent future occurrence. This may mean fines or other sanctions, and in some cases even firing someone.

Sanction Clear Violations

Yes, firing can sometimes be an appropriate and productive response – to a blameworthy act. But won't this kill the psychological safety? No. Most people are thoughtful enough to recognize (and appreciate) that when people violate rules or repeatedly take risky shortcuts, they are putting themselves, their colleagues, and their organization at risk. In short, psychological safety is reinforced rather than harmed by fair, thoughtful responses to potentially dangerous, harmful, or sloppy behavior.

In July 2017, Google engineer James Damore wrote a 10-page memo railing against the company's diversity stance, arguing that biological differences explained why Google had fewer women engineers and paid them less well than men, and circulated it widely within the company.[34] Someone then leaked the memo, creating a public firestorm.[35]

How did Google respond? Damore was promptly and publicly fired a month later, earning the company both praise and criticism. Thoughtful arguments have been made on both sides of the firing debate. Rather than coming out on one side or the other, let's step back to consider *when* firing constitutes a "productive response," and when it doesn't.

Take this specific case. To begin, it is a shame that Damore chose to share his personal concerns electronically and widely within the company, all but ensuring that someone who disliked the memo would share it publicly. Ideally, an employee with an opinion to express related to an important work issue or policy would first solicit feedback from colleagues, especially with those who might be likely to have a different view. The person might want to first learn more about the potential impact of those ideas and the forms in which they could be expressed. Very few of us are able to see complex issues from multiple perspectives and consider the potential consequences well enough to make good decisions about them alone. This doesn't matter when stakes are low. But stakes are high when a document that affects your colleagues, customers, or company may be read by millions.

But, once the inflammatory memo has been made public, how should a company respond? My intention is not to illuminate the specifics of Damore's memo at Google but rather to suggest a general strategy for productive responses to actions or events in your organization that you wish had not occurred.

If there are clear policies against the use of company email addresses or social media platforms for the expression of personal opinions, then an employee who violates these policies commits what we can call a blameworthy act. In this case, a productive response indeed involves tough sanctions, which may include terminating the employee. A tough response is productive because it lets people know that the company is serious about its policies and values, which shapes future behavior, and because it constitutes a fair response to a stated violation.

If policies are unclear, however, a productive response is one that turns the unfortunate event into a different kind of learning opportunity – for the company and sometimes for the interested public. In the Damore case, executives might express dismay at the employee's opinion (and perhaps dismay at his ignorance of a larger set of societal forces that have systematically diminished advancement opportunities for certain demographic groups over decades). They might then go on to explain their plans for educating employees on what they believe to be the value of a diverse workforce. As part of this organizational learning process, company managers at all levels would elicit and listen to ideas, questions, concerns, and frustrations. They might create opportunities for engaging in perspective taking, building empathy, developing inquiry skills, and more. The organization might also seek ways to come up with new, improved ways to leverage employee diversity to build better products and services.

In short, a productive response is concerned with future impact. Punishment sends a powerful message, and an appropriate one if boundaries were clear in advance. Indeed, it is vital to send messages that reinforce values the company holds dear. However, it is equally vital not to inadvertently send a message that says, "diverse opinions simply won't be tolerated here," or "one strike and you're out." Such messages reduce psychological safety and ultimately erode the quality of the work. In contrast, a message that reinforces the values and practices of a learning organization is, "it's okay to make a mistake, and it's okay to hold an opinion that others don't like, so long as you are willing to learn from the consequences." The most important goal is figuring out a way to help the organization learn from what happened. And so, if there is ambiguity about public self-expression related to company policies, then a productive response is one that engages people in a learning dialogue to better understand and improve how the company functions. Table 7.5 shows how a productive response to failure in an organization should vary for different failure types.

Table 7.5   Productive Responses to Different Types of Failure.

	Preventable Failure	Complex Failure	Intelligent Failure
Productive Response	– Training – Retraining – Process improvement – System redesign – Sanctions, if repeated or otherwise blameworthy actions are found	– Failure analysis from diverse perspectives – Identification of risk factors to address – System improvement	– Failure parties – Failure awards – Thoughtful analysis of results to figure out implications – Brainstorming of new hypotheses – Design of next steps or additional experiments

Leadership Self-Assessment

The practices described in this chapter are dominated by complex interpersonal skills and thus not easy to master. They take time, effort, and practice.[36] Perhaps the most important aspect of learning them is to practice self-reflection. A set of self-assessment questions, provided in a sidebar, can be used to do just that. The questions map to and operationalize the framework introduced in this chapter.

Leadership Self-Assessment

I. Setting the Stage
   Framing the work

- Have I clarified the nature of the work? To what extent is the work complex and interdependent? How much uncertainty do we face? How often do I refer to these aspects of the work? How well do I assess shared understanding of these features?
- Have I spoken of failures in the right way, given the nature of the work? Do I point out that small failures are the currency of subsequent improvement? Do I emphasize that it is not possible to get something brand new "right the first time?"

   Emphasizing Purpose

- Have I articulated clearly why our work matters, why it makes a difference, and for whom?
- Even if it seems obvious given the type of work or industry I'm in, how often do I talk about what's at stake?

II. Inviting Participation
   Situational Humility

- Have I made sure that people know that I don't think I have all the answers?
- Have I emphasized that we can always learn more? Have I been clear that the situation we're in requires everyone to be humble and curious about what's going to happen next?

Proactive Inquiry

- How often do I ask good questions rather than rhetorical ones? How often do I ask questions of others, rather than just expressing my perspective?
- Do I demonstrate an appropriate mix of questions that go broad and go deep?

Systems and Structures

- Have I created structures to systematically elicit ideas and concerns?
- Are these structures well designed to ensure a safe environment for open dialogue?

III. Responding Productively
Express Appreciation

- Have I listened thoughtfully, signaling that what I am hearing matters?
- Do I acknowledge or thank the speaker for bringing the idea or question to me? Listen thoughtfully

Destigmatize Failure

- Have I done what I can to destigmatize failure? What more can I do to celebrate intelligent failures?
- When someone comes to me with bad news, how do I make sure it's a positive experience?
- Do I offer help or support to guide the next steps?

Sanction Clear Violations

- Have I clarified the boundaries? Do people know what constitute blameworthy acts in our organization?
- Do I respond to clear violations in an appropriately tough manner so as to influence future behavior?

Chapter 7 Takeaways

- Three interrelated practices help create psychological safety – setting the stage, inviting participation, and responding productively.

- These practices must be repeatedly used, in interactive, learning-oriented ways, to create and restore a climate of candor in an ongoing way.

- Building and reinforcing psychological safety is the responsibility of leaders at all levels of the organization.

Endnotes

1. This quote is from Gelb, M.J. *Thinking for a Change: Discovering the Power to Create, Communicate, and Lead.* Harmony, 1996. Print, pp. 96.

2. The details on Julie Morath at Children's Hospital draw from a case study that I conducted with my colleagues Mike Roberto and Anita Tucker: Edmondson, A.C., Roberto, M., & Tucker, A.L. Children's Hospital and Clinics (A). Case Study. HBS Case No. 302-050. Boston: Harvard Business School Publishing, 2001.

3. For additional details on framing, see Chapter 3 of Edmondson, A.C. *Teaming: How Organizations Learn, Innovate, and Compete in the Knowledge Economy.* San Francisco: Jossey-Bass, 2011. Print, pp. 83–113.

4. Edmondson, A.C., Nembhard, I.M., & Roloff, K.S. Children's Hospital and Clinics (B). Case Study. HBS Case No. 608-073. Boston: Harvard Business School Publishing, 2007.

5. Edmondson, A.C. *et al.* Children's Hospital and Clinics (A). 2001, op cit.

6. One version of the famous fable is found in an 1872 poem by John Godfrey Saxe, which includes these lines: "And so these men of Indostan disputed loud and long, each in his own opinion exceeding stiff and strong. Though each was partly in the right, and all were in

the wrong." The full poem can be found here: https://en.wikisource .org/wiki/The_poems_of_John_Godfrey_Saxe/The_Blind_Men_ and_the_Elephant Accessed June 12, 2018.

7. Teller, A. "The Unexpected Benefit of Celebrating Failure." *TED.* 2016. https://www.ted.com/talks/astro_teller_the_unexpected_benefit_ of_celebrating_failure Accessed June 8, 2018.

8. This quote comes from a talk Teller gave at Stanford University on April 20, 2016 as part of Stanford's Entrepreneurial Thought Leaders series. You can watch the full talk at Stanford's eCorner: https://ecorner .stanford.edu/video/celebrating-failure-fuels-moonshots-entire-talk/.

9. Lafley, A.G., & Charan, R. *The Game-Changer: How You Can Drive Revenue and Profit Growth with Innovation.* 1st ed. Crown Business, 2008. Print.

10. Catmull, E. & Wallace, A. *Creativity, Inc.: Overcoming the Unseen Forces That Stand in the Way of True Inspiration.* New York: Random House, 2013. Print, pp. 123.

11. Bryant, A. "Christa Quarles of OpenTable: The Advantage of 'Early, Often, Ugly." *The New York Times.* April 12, 2016. https://www .nytimes.com/2016/08/14/business/christa-quarles-of-opentable- the-advantage-of-early-often-ugly.html Accessed June 14, 2018.

12. Bennett, J. "On Campus, Failure Is on the Syllabus." *The New York Times.* June 24, 2017. https://www.nytimes.com/2017/06/24/ fashion/fear-of-failure.html Accessed June 14, 2018.

13. *Ibid.*

14. For more on different types of work, see Chapter 1 of *Teaming: How Organizations Learn, Innovate, and Compete in the Knowledge Economy.* San Francisco: Jossey-Bass, 2012. Print, pp. 11–43.

15. Edmondson, A.C. "Strategies for Learning from Failure." *Harvard Business Review.* April 2011. https://hbr.org/2011/04/strategies-for- learning-from-failure Accessed June 14, 2018.

16. This table presents a modified version of a table that appeared in Chapter 5 of Edmondson, A.C. *Teaming: How Organizations Learn, Innovate, and Compete in the Knowledge Economy.* San Francisco: Jossey-Bass, 2012. Print, pp. 166.

17. To cite just one example, Wharton professor Adam Grant and a team of researchers conducted a study in which they arranged for a group of university call center workers, tasked with the tedious and frustrat- ing work of trying to raise money for the university's scholarship fund, to meet the actual scholarship recipients funded by the donations they solicited. By seeing how their work contributed to the lives of others,

the callers subsequently increased both the time they spent on the phone and how much money they brought in, compared to callers who did not meet the scholarship recipients. See Grant, A.M., Campbell, E.M., Chen, G., Cottone, K., Lapedis, D., & Lee, K. "Impact and the Art of Motivation Maintenance: The Effects of Contact with Beneficiaries on Persistence Behavior." *Organizational Behavior and Human Decision Processes* 103.1 (2007): 53–67.

18. Schein, E.H. *Humble Inquiry: the Gentle Art of Asking Instead of Telling.* 1st ed. Berrett-Koehler Publishers, Inc., 2013. Print, pp. 11.

19. Owens, B.P., Johnson, M.D., & Mitchell, T.R. "Expressed Humility in Organizations: Implications for Performance, Teams, and Leadership." *Organization Science* 24.5 (2013): 1517–38.

20. Anne Mulcahy, HBS class comments, October 11, 2017.

21. *Ibid.*

22. Cable, D. "How Humble Leadership Really Works." *Harvard Business Review.* April 23, 2018. https://hbr.org/2018/04/how-humble-leadership-really-works Accessed June 14, 2018.

23. Tucker, A.L., Nembhard, I.M., and Edmondson, A.C. "Implementing new practices: An empirical study of organizational learning in hospital intensive care units." *Management Science* 53.6 (2007): 894 –907.

24. Hirak, R., Peng, A.C., Carmeli, A., & Schaubroeck, J.M. "Linking Leader Inclusiveness to Work Unit Performance: The Importance of Psychological Safety and Learning from Failures." *The Leadership Quarterly* 23.1 (2012): 107–17.

25. Ross, L. & Ward, A. "Naive Realism: Implications for Social Conflict and Misunderstanding." In *Values & Knowledge.* Ed. T. Brown, E.S. Reed, & E. Turiel. Lawrence Erlbaum Associates (1996): 103–35.

26. Adapted from "The Art of Powerful Questions." World Café. http://www.theworldcafe.com Accessed July 27, 2018.

27. For great work on advocacy and inquiry, the Actionsmith group posts this paper: http://actionsmithnetwork.net/wp-content/uploads/2015/09/Advocacy-and-Inquiry-Article_Final.pdf. Accessed June 21, 2018.

28. Bryant, A. "Bob Pittman of Clear Channel, on the Value of Dissent" *The New York Times.* November 16, 2013. https://www.nytimes.com/2013/11/17/business/bob-pittman-of-clear-channel-on-the-value-of-dissent.html Accessed June 14, 2018.

29. Schein, E.H. *Humble Inquiry: The Gentle Art of Asking Instead of Telling.* 1st ed., Berrett-Koehler Publishers, Inc., 2013. Print.

30. "Guide: Create an Employee-to-Employee Learning Program." *re:Work.* https://rework.withgoogle.com/guides/learning-

development-employee-to-employee/steps/introduction/   Accessed June 14, 2018.

31. For more on Danone's knowledge marketplaces, see the following case study I conducted with David Lane: Edmondson, A.C. & Lane, D. Global Knowledge Management at Danone (A) (Abridged). Case Study. HBS No. 613-003. Boston, MA: Harvard Business School Publishing, 2012.

32. For more on Dweck's fantastic work on fixed vs. growth mindsets, see Dweck, C.S. *Mindset: The New Psychology of Success*. Updated ed. Random House, 2016. Print.

33. Burton, T. "By Learning From Failures, Lilly Keeps Drug Pipeline Full." *The Wall Street Journal*. April 21, 2004. https://www.wsj.com/articles/SB108249266648388235 Accessed June 14, 2018.

34. The memo was first leaked to the public here: https://gizmodo.com/exclusive-heres-the-full-10-page-anti-diversity-screed-1797564320 Accessed June 15, 2018.

35. See, for example:

- Wakabayashi, D. "Contentious Memo Strikes Nerve Inside Google and Out." *The New York Times*. August 8, 2017. https://www.nytimes.com/2017/08/08/technology/google-engineer-fired-gender-memo.html Accessed June 14, 2018.

- Molteni, M. & Rogers, A. "The Actual Science of James Damore's Google Memo." *WIRED*. August 15, 2017. https://www.wired.com/story/the-pernicious-science-of-james-damores-google-memo/ Accessed June 14, 2018.

36. The late HBS Professor David A. Garvin, a friend and colleague, was fond of telling students that any word in the English language that ends in the suffix "ing" is a *process*, which means first, that it's not a one-and-done, and second, that a leader can get better at it with practice. In that vein, creating psychological safety in an organization is a messy process that requires leaders to set the stage, invite participation, and respond productively each and every day. It never ends! But just like you can optimize a manufacturing process, you can definitely improve at it.

8 | What's Next?

The greatest enemy of learning is knowing.

—John Maxwell[1]

By now it should be clear that psychological safety is foundational to building a learning organization. Organizations that seek to stay relevant through continuous learning and agile execution must cultivate a fearless environment that encourages speaking up. In any company that thrives in our complex and uncertain world, leaders must be listening intently, with a deep understanding that people are both the sensors who pick up signals that change is necessary and the source of creative new ideas to test and implement.

Continuous Renewal

We've seen that leaders have many tools at their disposal to create and nurture a workplace conducive to learning, innovation, and growth.

187

Through their words and actions, and through designing systems that engage people in useful conversations, leaders help bring fearless workplaces into being. We've also seen that psychological safety is fragile and needs continuous renewal. When we set out to create organizations where people can bring their full selves to work, we're swimming upstream against deeply ingrained psychological currents.

The basic asymmetry of the psychological and societal forces favoring silence over voice, or self-protection over self-expression, will always be with us. But the rewards of voice and silence are also asymmetrical. Self-protection remains a hollow victory compared to the fulfillment that comes from actively serving an inspiring purpose and being a part of a team that's able to accomplish an ambitious goal. It's the difference between *playing not to lose* and *playing to win*.[2] Playing not to lose is a mindset that focuses, consciously or not, on protecting against the downside; playing to win, in contrast, is focused on the upside, seeks opportunity, and necessarily takes risks. When we're playing not to lose, we play it safe.

Stop to consider which mindset is in charge when you're at work. How often do you find yourself truly playing to win? It can be challenging to make this shift, because when you play not to lose, you're likely to succeed (in not losing). But you miss opportunities to grow, to innovate, and to experience a deeper sense of fulfillment. When you make up your mind to play to win, the rules change. Yes, you might fall flat on your face publicly sometimes. But you also will become more able to contribute to something that makes a difference in the world.[3] Perhaps the best way to experience psychological safety is to act as if you have it already. See what happens! The chances are you'll be creating a safer and more energizing environment for those around you as well. Exercising a small act of leadership.

Leadership is a vital force in making it possible for people and organizations to overcome the inherent barriers to voice and engagement, so as to gain the emotional and practical rewards of fully participating in an inspiring shared mission. As noted in Chapter 7, leadership is not constrained to the top of an organization but rather can be exercised at all levels. Leadership at its core is about harnessing others' efforts to achieve something no one can achieve alone. It's about helping people go as far as they can with the talents and skills they have. As I hope this book convinces, substituting candor for silence and engagement for fear are essential responsibilities for leaders today.

The stories throughout this book capture specific moments in time in organizations around the world. We saw organizations where a lack of psychological safety contributed to significant business failures as well as to human physical harm. A contrasting set of cases provided glimpses into workplaces characterized by candor and engagement. These cases showcased unusual workplaces where failure was not stigmatized, and people understood that risk taking and learning were integral to how work gets done. Nonetheless, it's not easy to predict what will happen next in any of these organizations. Nor is it accurate to characterize the entire organizations based on the individuals and groups portrayed in these cases. Psychological safety is dynamic. A workplace with unusual candor may shift in the face of new leaders or new circumstances. One dominated by fearful silence also can change, becoming conducive to thoughtful input and deliberative decision-making. Often such shifts happen as the result of a deliberate effort to learn from an organization's painful past failures. A few, merely illustrative, examples follow.

Deliberative Decision-Making

Recall Nokia, the Finnish company with centuries of contribution to its nation's GDP and identity. Its downfall, as we saw in Chapter 3, had to do with a dance of fear between senior executives and engineers. Corporate headquarters didn't want to hear the bad news that Symbian, Nokia's operating system, was about to become obsolete, outperformed by Apple's iOS and Google's Android platforms. The engineers, whose antennae were tuned to what was coming from Silicon Valley, were afraid to break the news to their superiors; their attempts to speak up seemed routinely silenced from above.

Fast forward to 2013. Nokia's strategic comeback was to divest its mobile phone business and focus instead on manufacturing network equipment and software, acquisitions and partnerships, patent licenses, and the Internet of Things. In this dramatic shift, Nokia leaders had to have sustained, thoughtful conversations to make tough choices. For this to work, they needed to divest themselves of their previous dance-of-fear moves and embrace the candor of Pixar's Braintrust. They needed to begin from Eileen Fisher's place of not-knowing.

Professors Timo Vuori at Alto University in Finland and Quy Huy at INSEAD (originally an acronym for the French "Institut Européen d'Administration des Affaires") conducted 190 interviews at Nokia, including 9 board members and 19 top managers, to find out how the company's executives, many of them newly installed, managed to work together to make these strategic decisions. One of the first things the board did was to establish rules for discussion that included some of the basic norms of psychological safety – for example, that everyone's voice must be heard and respected. However, it wasn't enough to merely draw up a new set of conversational rules. Habits and culture do not change overnight.

A board member told the researchers that "after he had made a hostile comment to a top manager, the chairman made him apologize to the top manager in the next meeting."[4] In other words, the new chairman had to consciously *reinforce the rules* to increase trust between individuals and in general create a culture where people could feel psychologically safe to speak openly. This was no exercise in playground civility, no effort to "play nice." In contrast, the future of the company depended on fearless, creative input and open discussion from its leaders. And apparently, that's what they were able to do. As a top manager told the researchers, "with [the new chairman] we are not afraid, we don't have to think about what we say too much. It's pretty easy to discuss things with him and throw in ideas and think out loud."[5] Over a period of years, that process – of throwing in ideas, and thinking out loud together – yielded new perspectives, strategies, data collections, options, scenario analysis, and so on. Like Pixar's filmmakers, Nokia managers were able to reject strategies they found unusable and continue to brainstorm new ones until their deliberative decision-making process came up with a strategy the board and top management felt was right.

Hearing the Sounds of Silence

We must be realistic about the fact that "driving fear out" of any organization, as W. Edwards Deming (the father of total quality management who helped transform manufacturing practices around the world) put it, will be a journey.[6] We don't have a magic wand to make psychological safety happen overnight, but by committing to the aspiration to build it, one conversation at a time, leaders take the first step of a perpetual journey toward building and nurturing organizations that can innovate and thrive in the knowledge economy.

In the decade following the *Columbia* shuttle's final mission, I had been using a powerful multimedia case study that my colleagues and I developed from public sources to teach in leadership programs at Harvard Business School and around the world.[7] One day, in 2012, my office phone rang. To my surprise, the caller announced that he was from NASA. "We know what you're doing," he said. As I swallowed, he continued, "and we think it's great." The caller was Ed Rogers, and he was the Chief Knowledge Officer at NASA's Goddard Space Flight Center. This was a striking moment for me. In our research, we had had the opportunity to interview Diane Vaughn, the sociologist and Columbia University professor known for writing the definitive book on the ill-fated Challenger launch decision of 1986.[8] Back in the early 1990s, Vaughn's book had unexpectedly catapulted her into the limelight, and she received many invitations to speak to business executives and policy makers. As she humorously put it, "*everyone* called," and she went on to name several top corporations, as well as the US Congress. Vaughn laughed, "my high school boyfriend even called! But NASA never called . . ." So the simple fact of "NASA calling," to me, signaled a shift.

Rogers volunteered to visit my next on-campus class, bringing Rodney Rocha with him. Later, he did just that, and it was a powerful experience for the students and for me. Rogers went on to explain that he was organizing a day-long workshop, called the Sounds of Silence, and he wanted me to speak. (Of course, I cleared my schedule.) With three outside speakers and eight senior insiders, the workshop discussion ranged from the need to create a "no fear" federal workplace to the terrible dangers of silence to the power of studying near misses to avoid catastrophes.

Held in a large and packed auditorium, the workshop was only one of the many ways that NASA was taking seriously the desire to alter its culture. Several new structures had been implemented, including a formal dissenting-opinion mechanism to lower the bar to speaking up, a new safety reporting system, and an ombudsman program. New awards were created, like the "Lean Forward, Fail Smart Award" to recognize that in "a culture of innovation, failure is seen as merely a stepping stone to success."[9] Insiders wrote a detailed case study on *Columbia* and were teaching it throughout the agency, as well as making it publicly available.[10] This was a far cry from the organization I had studied, where managers had been fiercely committed to ensuring that no bad news escaped the organization walls. Rogers emphasized, in our personal conversations, that "communication is key to our success" and that a "listening culture" was as important as a speaking up culture, connecting to our discussion in Chapter 4 of Roger Boisjoly's unsuccessful efforts to speak up. "Communication involves transmitting and receiving," he explained. Rogers called Christopher Scolese, the then-new director of NASA's Goddard Space Flight Center, "the finest leader I've ever worked for." When I asked why, he explained it was because "he cares about people. He has a strategic perspective. He cares about Space and NASA" (as a whole, rather than favoring a given facility). He went on to talk about how much Scolese demonstrated respect for, and interest, in others' contributions.

I tell this story not as proof of culture change but rather as an illustration of the many ways in which organizations are waking up to the need for psychological safety for achieving excellence in a complex, ambiguous world.

When Humor Isn't Funny

"Can you stay late today to work on the project with me?" asked a female Uber employee to her male colleague.

"I will if you'll sleep with me." And then, after a beat. "Just kidding."

It sounds like a bad joke. After Harvard Business School Professor Frances Frei began a nine-month tenure at Uber as an executive on loan to change the culture, she describes this incident as one of many that belong to a category she labels "Just Kidding."[11] As she explained, if someone felt the need to add the tagline "just kidding," after a comment, it probably meant the person knew the comment was at risk of being unwelcome or inappropriate. Frei's insights into what went wrong at Uber to create the toxic culture described in Chapter 4, along with the measures she initiated to help after the onslaught of negative publicity, show how psychological safety can be created in organizations that had been blatantly unsafe.

Frei points out that people needed new skills to respond to these "just kidding" moments – especially until the time when such moments would become unacceptable in the organization's culture. Her suggested response to the exchange described above was, "Wow, that felt super-inappropriate. Can we have a do-over?"[12] Ideally, new responses would percolate throughout the organization, until eventually the "just kidders" would begin speaking appropriately and inclusively. These kind of "bottom-up" changes – enacted by people without formal power throughout a company – are most effective when accompanied by clear cultural directives set by leadership. When Uber's new CEO, Dara Khosrowshahi, came on board in August 2017, one of his first actions was to solicit employee input for a new set of company values. Signaling a shift to integrity from the company's previously valued "toe-stepping," Number 4 now reads, "Do the Right Thing. Period."[13]

Uber's hypergrowth as a ride-hailing company meant that managers were quickly getting promoted to positions beyond their capability. They did not have the experience or training to lead effectively. As Khosrowshahi put it, "we were probably trading off doing the right thing for growth, and thinking about competition maybe a bit too aggressively, and some of those things were mistakes."[14] In keeping with the more psychologically safe culture his leadership portends, Khosrowshahi explains, "mistakes themselves are not a bad thing. The question is, do you learn from those mistakes?"[15]

Some behaviors contributing to a climate of fear can be remedied by simple rule changes. For example, Frei recounts that when she first arrived, common behavior during meetings with senior team members included everyone on his or her phone – texting one another about the meeting![16] It was the equivalent of being whispered about behind your back in high school and obviously lowered whatever psychological safety might be in the room. Contrast this behavior with Dalio's injunction for transparency throughout the organization and his rather unattractive term "slimy weasel" for those who might violate the transparency norm. What's more, the behavior was indicative that no one felt safe enough to speak up or state honestly to the group what was on his or her mind. As Liane Hornsey, Uber's new head of Human Resources, put it, "there was no sense of trust, no sense of 'We're building this together.'"[17] In this case, the remedy was fairly straightforward: mandate that people put down their phones! Only then could people begin to look up, listen, and collaborate. In other words, the journey out of fear and toward psychological safety had begun.

Recall, also, from Chapter 4 that it was Susan Fowler's act of speaking up, early in the #MeToo movement, that first exposed Uber's culture of fear. While this is not the place to trace the fascinating trajectories and subtle cultural shifts that MeToo spawned, it's worth mentioning that the sheer act of speaking up eventually did lead to actionable change, and not only at Uber. For example, the National Women's Law Center founded a "Time's Up" Legal Defense Fund to enable more women to come forward and be assured of legal support.[18]

Change is possible. It may be hard work, but cultures can, and must, change if organizations are to thrive in a knowledge-intensive world. The hard, rewarding work of creating an environment where people can bring their full selves to work can be supported by outside facilitators and coaches, if desired. As we have seen in Chapter 7, a network of internal coaches can also be created to work with individuals and teams to build and restore psychological safety, as was done at Google with the g2g network. Of course, these approaches also can supplement each other. To help with this journey, next I offer a few additional thoughts triggered by questions from people working in organizations around the world.

Psychological Safety FAQs

Over the past 20 years I have led many leadership programs in business and public-sector organizations. Although myriad topics are covered in these sessions, psychological safety always plays a crucial role and often generates questions from participants. And so I want to provide some of the answers I've offered these audiences, with the hope that they will address your questions as well.

Can You Have Too Much Psychological Safety?

This is probably the question I am asked most often. When I talk with people in companies, hospitals, government agencies, and non-governmental organizations (NGOs) around the world, they intuitively recognize the need for psychological safety to allow learning and innovation to take hold. Yet many worry, understandably, that by releasing the brakes on voice, people will just plain talk too much. Uninformed, unhelpful comments will derail projects. Good ideas will get lost in a sea of chatter. People will be sloppy.

My short answer? No. I don't think you can have *too much* psychological safety. I do think, however, that you can have *not enough* discipline. Psychological safety is about reducing interpersonal fear. Making it less heroic to ask a question or admit an error. It doesn't mean you automatically have a good strategy for getting the work done. It also doesn't mean your employees are sufficiently motivated or well-trained.

People asking this question are often wondering where the level of psychological safety should be set to have the best results. I have sympathy for the concerns that motivate them to ask. But I want to suggest a solution that doesn't involve figuring out the optimal level of interpersonal fear.

My view is that interpersonal fear is never particularly helpful at work. While it can be motivating to be afraid of missing a deadline, afraid of failing the customer, or afraid of the prowess of the competition, being afraid of one's boss or colleagues is not only unhelpful in an environment where technologies, customers and solutions are in flux, it's downright risky. The potential costs of not speaking up in a timely way are simply too great.

What today's leaders need to understand is that people spontaneously set an invisible threshold that governs when they speak up and what they speak up about. The problem is that most people set the level too high when they're at work. We err on the side of holding back information or questions – even when we believe they might matter, that they might have the potential to add value. In fact, it's extremely rare to find people erring on the side of voice. I'm not saying that it isn't possible for the threshold to be set too low, thereby unleashing all kinds of unhelpful or inappropriate voice, but rather that this occurs less often than one might expect. Even so, this particular risk (of excessive voice) is not best addressed by reducing psychological safety but rather by providing feedback to give the speaker insight into the impact he or she had.

I do not see psychological safety as a panacea. Far from it. Psychological safety is only one of many factors needed for success in the modern economy. As discussed in Chapter 2, psychological safety is better thought of as an enabler that allows other factors like motivation, confidence, or diversity to have the desired effects on work outcomes. Psychological safety makes it possible for other drivers of success (talent, ingenuity, diversity of thought) to be expressed in ways that influence how work gets done.

Won't Having a Psychologically Safe Workplace Take Too Much Time?

This question – along with the very similar, "How will we get anything done if people are always talking?" – clearly overlaps with the question about having too much psychological safety but adds explicit attention to time and efficiency. And time and efficiency are such important issues in the modern organization that it's worth stopping to consider them directly.

Mirroring the concern about a low threshold for voice is the concern that meetings will go on and on because everyone must have his or her say. This confuses psychological safety with bad process. Just as discipline is needed for excellence in general, managing effective meetings – for decision-making, problem solving, or mere reporting – is a matter of skill, discipline, and smart process design. There are many good sources of advice on how to have effective, efficient meetings, complete with practical tools for ensuring input without unleashing chaos.[19] And none of these tools is at odds with establishing a climate of candor, where people are able to focus on the task rather than on face-saving and self-protection.

To take it a step further, I argue that psychological safety can save rather than consume time. Although not a hard and fast rule, psychological safety can be a source of efficiency. For instance, I've studied senior management teams in which a lack of psychological safety contributed to long-winded conversations (indirect statements, with veiled criticisms and personal innuendo, take longer than candid ones), elongated meetings, and an inability to come to a resolution about crucial strategic issues.[20] Decisions that could have been resolved in hours stretched over months.[21] In short, the lack of psychological safety can be deeply inefficient, in addition to being ineffective. Also recall from Chapter 3 how a lack of psychological safety at the Federal Reserve Bank of New York led issues to be discussed at length without resolution. By way of contrast, I have worked with teams in which clear process combined with direct and open dialogue to produce efficient, smart conversations and clear decisions.

You Advocate a Psychologically Safe Workplace. Does That Mean We Have to Be Transparent About Everything?

To say that psychological safety can't be too high is not the same as saying more transparency is always better. Different situations likely call for different levels of transparency. In the surgical operating room, I'd venture to say that full transparency is excellent practice. Please share any observations you have! If they are wrong or unhelpful, I hope (and expect) others to respond with appreciation and transparency to that effect as well. But there are times where it simply isn't all that helpful to share each and every one of your workplace thoughts – for example, about someone's attire or presentation style. I think reasonable people can disagree about whether Ray Dalio's aggressive transparency would work in their own companies or industries. Decisions about what aspects of personal growth and feedback are fair game in your organization, for instance, can be thoughtfully made.

But very few of us would voluntarily seek to work in an environment where we don't feel psychologically safe. So why should we want this for others? None of us does our best work when distracted by mild worries about how our colleagues or bosses will react if we speak up with a work-relevant idea or question. The goal is to figure out how much transparency, and about what, you need (and this will probably take some experimentation to get it right) to do the best possible work in your company or in your industry. In the meantime, it's important to keep working hard to make sure people are not holding back on work-relevant thoughts due to fear of embarrassment.

I'm All for Psychological Safety at Work, but I'm Not the Boss. Is There Anything I Can Do?

While it is true that bosses – team leaders, surgeons, department heads, etc. – play an outsized role in shaping expectations and behaviors in the workplace, anyone can help create psychological safety. Sometimes, all you have to do is ask a good question. This is truly a great place to start. A good question is one motivated by genuine curiosity or by a desire to give someone a voice. Questions cry out for answers; they create a vacuum that serves as a voice opportunity for someone. Especially when a question is directed at an individual (and expressed in a way that conveys curiosity), a small safe zone is automatically created. By asking a question, you have conveyed, "I am interested in what you have to say." In so doing, you have created a safe space that helps one or more others to offer their thinking.

Additionally, with or without having asked a question, you can create psychological safety by choosing to listen actively to what people say and by responding with interest, building on their ideas, or giving feedback. True listening conveys respect – and in subtle but powerful ways reinforces the idea that a person's full self is welcome here. Note that this does not mean you have to agree with what someone said. You don't even have to like it. But you do have to appreciate the effort it took for her to say it.

Saying things to frame the challenge you see ahead is another helpful practice. Reminding people of what the team is up against – for example, by talking about how the work is uncertain, challenging, or interdependent – helps paint reality in ways that emphasize that no one is supposed to have all the answers. This lowers the hurdle for speaking up. It reminds people that their input is welcome – because it's needed.

Finally, I would like to suggest a few simple, uncommon, powerful phrases that anyone can utter to make the workplace feel just a tiny bit more psychologically safe:

I don't know.
I need help.
I made a mistake.
I'm sorry.

Each of these is an expression of vulnerability. By being willing to acknowledge that you are a fallible human being, you give permission to others to do likewise. Removing your mask helps others remove theirs. Of course, this means acting as if you feel psychologically safe, even if you might not be fully there yet. Sometimes, you have to take an interpersonal risk to lower interpersonal risk.

Similarly powerful in shaping the climate even if you are not the boss are words of interest and availability. For example, most of us face many opportunities to say things like these:

What can I do to help?
What are you up against?
What are your concerns?

The personal challenge for all of us lies in remembering, in the moment, to be vulnerable, as well as to be interested and available. To do this you will have to take on the small interpersonal risk that your attempts may be ignored or, worse, rebuffed. But in my experience, the odds are low. Assuming a modest level of good will in your organization, most of the time your colleagues will respond well to genuine expressions of vulnerability and interest. So, give it a try. Pause; look around. Whom can you invite into the safe space for learning and contributing to the shared goal? See what happens.

What I hope is clear at this point is that you don't have to be the boss to be a *leader*. The leader's job is to create and nurture the culture we all need to do our best work. And so anytime you play a role in doing that, you are exercising leadership.

What's the Relationship Between Psychological Safety and Diversity, Inclusion, and Belonging?

This question, increasingly common, almost answers itself. So let me start by saying that a workplace that is truly characterized by inclusion and belonging is a psychologically safe workplace. Today we know that although diversity can be created through deliberate hiring practices, inclusion does not automatically follow. To begin with, all hires may not find themselves included in important decisions and discussions. Going deeper, a diverse workforce doesn't guarantee that everyone feels a sense of belonging. For instance, when no one at the top of the organization looks like you, it can make it harder for you to feel you belong.

Each of these three terms represents a goal to be achieved. The goals range from the relatively objective (workforce diversity) to the highly-subjective (do I feel that I belong here?). Inclusion is more likely to function well with psychological safety because diverse perspectives are more likely to be heard. But it is not easy to feel a sense of belonging if one feels psychologically unsafe. As goal achievement becomes more subjective, psychological safety becomes more valuable; there is no way to know if you're achieving the goal without broad input from people in different groups.

Although I've been studying psychological safety for more than 20 years, it's only recently that I've been asked to consider its relationship to diversity, inclusion and belonging at work. As issues related to diversity at work have moved to the forefront of the agenda in organizations aspiring to excellence, in response to current news and other societal factors, I have begun to consider the central role that psychological safety plays and can play. A fearless organization realizes the benefits of diversity by fostering greater inclusion and belonging. A recent tidal wave of harassment claims highlights the costs of failing to create a psychologically safe workplace for women.

At the same time, a singular focus on psychological safety is not a strategy for building diversity, inclusion, and belonging. These interrelated goals must go hand in hand. Great organizations will continue to attract, hire, and retain a diverse workforce because their leaders understand that that is where good ideas come from, and talented applicants will be drawn to work for those organizations. These leaders also recognize that hiring for diversity is not enough. They also must care about whether or not employees can bring their full selves to work – whether they can belong in the fullest sense to the community inside the organization. In short, leaders who care about diversity must care about psychological safety as well. It's that extra ingredient, as discussed in Chapter 2, that allows diversity to be leveraged.

Is Psychological Safety About Whistle-blowing?

Whistle-blowers are organizational insiders who expose wrongdoing they've observed (and often tried unsuccessfully to alter) by reaching out to external authorities or to the press. By reporting activity that may be illegal or unethical – from fraud and corruption to public safety or national security risks – whistle-blowers take on the risk of retaliation from those they accuse of wrongdoing. They demonstrate courage. Whistle-blowing, however, is not a reflection of psychological safety but rather an indication of its absence. In companies with psychological safety, whistle-blowing should not be needed because employee concerns will be expressed, heard, and considered.

Speaking up and listening, which go hand in hand in a healthy organizational culture, reinforce standards of professionalism and integrity. When valid concerns are expressed, changes can be made in a timely way. Of course, it is possible for an employee to fail to fully explore the options for internal discussion of concerns – and blow the whistle prematurely. It is possible even in a climate where internal learning would have been welcomed. By and large, however, in a psychologically safe climate, an employee's first instinct is not to go outside the organization to report perceived wrongdoing.

It's in any organization's best interest to foster an environment that facilitates speaking up internally rather than to leave people feeling they have no choice but to go outside the organization with their concerns. It is far better to respond to early signals that there may be problems, so as to address them through meaningful changes, rather than to end up with visible public reports of wrongdoing or harm. To make this process easier, ombudspersons can help internal voices be expressed in a specific context that is designed to be safe. Ombudspersons offer confidentiality and support for those with ethical and safety issues and also can trigger a process of making necessary changes in an organization to mitigate concerns through genuine improvement.

What About Those Successful Companies Run by Arrogant Top-down Dictators Who Don't Listen to Anyone and Sometimes Reduce People to Tears?

I've been asked this question more times than I can count. It comes from smart people who step back and think, "wait a minute! If psychological safety promotes excellence in an uncertain world, how come I can point to counterexamples – that is, to stories of extremely successful companies that seem very much to lack psychological safety?"

I want to respond in two parts to this important question. First, let's remember the fallacy of sampling on the dependent variable, a classic error in research. In other words, the success in question may in fact be explained by the leader's arrogance and top-down approach; conversely, it may be explained by other factors: good timing, a market vacuum, a genius idea, or even just plain luck.

Second, there's a lack of ready access to counterfactual data. In other words, we don't know what would have happened in the successful company had more of the talent it contained been put to good use. We simply have a case of low psychological safety and high company performance for a particular period of time. The first variable may, or may not, explain the second. It's possible that the company would have failed had more people felt able to express their ideas; it is also possible, and perhaps even likely, that the upside for the company could have been even higher than it was. Finally, the company's success may ultimately prove to be short lived because it is at risk of failing to make necessary changes when early warnings of the successful formula's wane in a changing marketplace are not heard or heeded. Not to mention the possibility that smart, talented people who are not being heard may leave for other opportunities.

Finally, the companies motivating thoughtful people to ask this question may be one of those rare cases of a genius at the helm who indeed has all the answers. Steve Jobs comes to mind. To the extent that you feel you fall into that category – a rare genius who has perfect pitch in terms of what the market wants – you may be able to specify the work that needs to be done clearly enough for others to merely execute. In that case, go for it! You will be able to forfeit seeking or listening to the input of those who work below you in the organization. Henry Ford, after all, was said to have complained, "why is it every time I ask for a pair of hands, they come with a brain attached?"[22] But for the rest of us, I wouldn't recommend that approach. Few business leaders today can afford to squander the brainpower available in their companies. At the very least most of us need an honest sounding board. But better yet, we need people to bring their ideas to work to help us create better products and a better organization.

Help! My Colleague Is Bringing His True Self to Work and It's Driving Me Crazy!

I think most of us can empathize with this one. Perhaps there are people we wish felt a little less psychologically safe at work so that they'd stop expressing themselves! Tempting as it is to want to solve this kind of problem with a sprinkle of interpersonal fear, in the long run it's not a productive solution. The most important reason is this: a colleague who is not being helpful and productive needs – and deserves – our feedback. Psychological safety doesn't guarantee effectiveness. It just makes it easier to find out what people have to offer. Sometimes, that's a happy surprise. But when people feel able to express themselves, and you find that what they say is not adding value, then you have a responsibility to help. To coach. And even though it's not fun to give people that kind of feedback, it's better to know that someone is in need of it than to remain in the dark. Moreover, it's only fair to let your colleagues know that the impact they're having is not what they're hoping it is.

Help! I've Started Bringing My Whole Self to Work and No One Likes Me (Anymore)!

I suspect if you're reading this book, the odds of the situation implied by this question are low because you're probably thoughtful, curious, and intent upon making your organization a better place. And, if so, others similarly intent on learning are likely to welcome hearing what you have to say. Nonetheless, let's consider the two basic possibilities. One is that your ideas are just not getting the positive reception you had expected. In this case, just as others deserve your feedback, you deserve others' feedback. Consider this a learning opportunity – an opportunity to find out what it is about what you're saying or doing that is falling short of the mark.

The other possibility is that you're learning something about your colleagues or your organization that suggests that you're not in a job that is a good fit with your personal values and goals. If you're sharing sincere concerns, ideas, and ambitions for the organization, and others are indifferent, turned off, or disparaging, then you may want to look for an opportunity where you will have colleagues who appreciate your commitment to making a positive difference at work.

What Advice Would You Give to the People Who Report to Managers Who Can't or Won't Change?

I would start by recommending curiosity, compassion, and commitment. You see, we all need to remind ourselves, whether we're the boss or not, that no one can actually change another person. We can't force people to change how they think and act, *even* when we have formal responsibility over them – let alone when we don't. We can only influence them. The good news is that anyone can influence others by modeling the three Cs listed above. Start with curiosity, which leads us to ask questions. When we ask genuine questions, people feel they matter (whether boss, peer, or subordinate), especially when we listen and respond thoughtfully to their answers. (Meanwhile, we just might learn something, which can also be helpful).

Compassion is the self-discipline to imagine and remember that everyone faces hurdles. All people are up against something – small or large – that frustrates them or keeps them up at night. The more you understand what others are up against, the more you spontaneously do things that help build work relationships that are resilient and strong, as needed for getting the work done. Finally, commitment matters because if you demonstrate your dedication to achieving the organization's goals, it can be contagious. When people, especially managers, believe you really care about the work, they'll also cut you some slack.

A related, oft-raised issue is captured in the following comment: "but the people above me don't do this, so I'm stuck." With great empathy, my response is first to let people know how widespread this experience is and that I recognize how frustrating it feels. Then, I go on to point out that people have a natural tendency to look up – to look in the direction of the managers above us in the hierarchy. We have to train ourselves to look down and across instead. As noted earlier, each of us can shape the climate in which we work in small ways. Creating a pocket of excellence, candor, and learning in *your* group is worthwhile, no matter what those above you are doing. It may be contagious! As an aside, I've been struck by how many times the people articulating this concern are near the very top of enormous companies. They may be among the top 200 managers in a global corporation, and yet their natural tendency is still to look upward and bemoan their powerlessness. And so I also remind them gently that there are a great many more people looking up and pointing to them as the problem than there are above them.

Can Anyone Learn to Be a Successful Leader of Psychological Safety?

My view is that, yes, most people can learn. And that includes learning to better understand the positive and negative effects that one's mindset and behavior is having on others. Most people would prefer to have positive rather than negative effects on others, and most are also able to gain insight on how to do that, with training and coaching. Will some people be harder to help? Yes, of course. Narcissism, borderline personalities, low emotional intelligence, and other limitations will make it more difficult to behave in ways that build psychological safety and, in some cases, impossible. Nonetheless, there is very little downside to starting with an open mind about the ability of anyone to change to become more effective. You might win, and you likely lose very little, with that open mind.

What About Cross-cultural Differences? Is It Possible to Create Psychological Safety in China? In Japan? In [you name the country here]?

Many people believe that in some countries expecting employees to speak up at work is simply unrealistic. Indeed, research shows that workplace psychological safety is lower in countries with greater "power distance," the extent to which a society accepts that power is distributed unequally between high-status and low-status members.[23] Trying to promote candor or error-reporting, for example, they claim, would be a fool's errand in Japan. Of course, this impeccable logic bumps up against the reality of the Toyota Production System – an approach to continuous improvement and flawless execution that depends on every employee, up and down the hierarchy, to continuously, energetically, willingly point out errors! Is this typical of the Japanese culture? No. Is it deeply embedded in the Toyota culture? Yes.

In other words, it can be done.

Of course, it's not easy to create a culture like Toyota's. But it is worthwhile – if excellence and continuous improvement are goals of your organization. And cultural differences in power distance does mean that the job of creating psychological safety is harder in some countries than others. Nonetheless, this does not make it any less necessary. If the work an organization does involves uncertainty, inter-dependence, or high stakes, success depends on creating some degree of psychological safety. Without a willingness to speak up about prob-lems and errors, quality cannot improve. Without willingness to ask for help, employees will underperform. Without a willingness to chal-lenge a decision, organizations are at grave risk of preventable failures, both large and small. So roll up your sleeves; you have work to do! It may involve swimming upstream against cultural forces, but it can be done. The good news is that, when done well, your efforts can create a powerful source of competitive advantage in a playing field where average psychological safety is low.

What the Questions Reveal

In closing, I am sometimes struck by the anxiety people seem to feel about creating psychologically safe organizations; perhaps we're natu-rally comfortable living with the devil we know – organizations where self-protection quietly crowds out much of the creativity, learning, or belonging that lies under the surface without our noticing. And the devil we don't know – unusual workplaces where people can be and express themselves, confronting greater conflict and challenge but greater fulfillment as well – awaits.

Tacking Upwind

If you set out to build psychological safety in your organization, it's somewhat like setting sail on journey for which much is known and much is unknown. Just as skippers and crew on a sailboat must communicate and coordinate to stay the course facing shifting tides and winds, you and your colleagues must do likewise. The sailing metaphor is apt as well because it's impossible for a sailboat to head directly to an upwind mark (almost always set as the first destination in a regatta). The boat can head at a 45-degree angle off from the target, getting closer, and then "tacking" – switching to head at a 45-degree angle on the other side. Zigzagging upwind in this manner, the boat eventually arrives at its destination, having made large (tacks) and small (sail adjustments) pivots along the way.

You speak up about newborns' need for prophylactic lung medication, comment on a weak plot twist in an animated film-in-progress, suggest clearance heights for forklifts, or advocate for physical safety in a large South African mine. Zig left. Smooth sailing ensues. Your superiors are too busy to listen, do not respond, tell you it can't be done, pass you over for promotion. The wind leaves your sail. If you happen to be the CEO of a mine, you can close the mine to make your point. Or ask a simple question that's motivated by genuine curiosity. Zag right. Ask nurses if everything was as safe as they would have liked. Assure miners that speaking up about safety issues will not endanger their jobs. Admit you don't know. Confess failure. Apologize. Call for help. Sailing will be smooth, at least for a while.

Creating psychological safety is a constant process of smaller and larger corrections that add up to forward progress. Like tacking upwind, you must zig right and then zag left and then right again, never able to head exactly where you want to go and never quite knowing when the wind will change.

Endnotes

1. Maxwell, J. *Beyond Talent: Become Someone Who Gets Extraordinary Results*. Thomas Nelson, 2011. Print, pp. 184.
2. This dichotomy between seeking gains vs. avoiding losses has been called many things in different circles. In business, we talk about managers or companies "playing to win" vs. "playing not to lose." Similarly, Daniel Kahneman and Amos Tversky spearheaded the field of behavioral economics partly through their research on "loss aversion," the idea that the pain of a loss outweighs the pleasure of an equivalent gain.

In psychology, Columbia University Professor E. Tory Higgins distinguished between individuals with a "promotion focus" vs. those with a "prevention focus" in describing what motivated people to make certain decisions or take certain actions. And Stanford educational psychologist Carol Dweck has written extensively about students with "fixed mindsets," who believe they must avoid looking dumb, vs. those with "growth mindsets," who are motivated by learning and improvement. Whatever one calls this dynamic, the verdict is clear: sustainable individual, team, and organizational performance come from seeking to gain, not through fear of loss.

3. See Wilson, L. & Wilson, H. *Play To Win!: Choosing Growth Over Fear in Work and Life*. Revised ed., Bard Press, 2013. Print., for a truly useful guide to making the mindset shift this entails.

4. Vuori, T. & Huy. Q. "How Nokia Embraced the Emotional Side of Strategy." *Harvard Business Review*. May 23, 2018. https://hbr .org/2018/05/how-nokia-embraced-the-emotional-side-of-strategy Accessed June 14, 2013.

5. *Ibid.*

6. Deming, W. E. *Out of the Crisis*. Cambridge, MA: Massachusetts Institute of Technology, Center for Advanced Engineering Study, 1986. Print.

7. Interested readers can find the case study here: Bohmer, R.J., Edmondson, A.C., & Roberto, M.A. *Columbia's* Final Mission (Multimedia Case). Case Study. HBS No. 305-032. Boston, MA: Harvard Business School Publishing, 2005.

8. Vaughan, D. *The Challenger Launch Decision: Risky Technology, Culture, and Deviance at NASA*. Chicago, Illinois: University of Chicago Press, 1996. Print.

9. See https://nasapeople.nasa.gov/awards/eligibility.htm Accessed June 14, 2018.

10. The case study that was taught, as well as several other NASA case studies, can be found here: https://www.nasa.gov/content/goddard-ocko-case-studies. Accessed June 1, 2018.

11. Frei described her experience at Uber in the following podcast: Harvard Business School. "Fixing the Culture at Uber." *HBS After Hours*. April 2, 2018. http://hbsafterhours.com/ep-6-fixing-the-culture-at-uber. Accessed June 1, 2018.

12. *Ibid.*

13. Kohlatkar, S. "At Uber, a New CEO Shifts Gears." *The New Yorker.* April 9, 2018. https://www.newyorker.com/magazine/2018/04/09/at-uber-a-new-ceo-shifts-gears Accessed June 14, 2018.
14. *Ibid.*
15. *Ibid.*
16. *HBS After Hours,* April 2, 2018, op cit.
17. Kohlatkar, S. April 9, 2018, op cit.
18. "TIME'S UP Legal Defense Fund." *NWLC.* https://nwlc.org/times-up-legal-defense-fund/ Accessed June 14, 2018.
19. One of the best sources I know is Schwarz, R. *The Skilled Facilitator: A Comprehensive Resource for Consultants, Facilitators, Managers, Trainers, and Coaches.* 2nd ed., San Francisco: Jossey-Bass, 2002. Print.
20. Edmondson, A.C. & Smith, D.M. "Too hot to handle? How to manage relationship conflict." *California Management Review* 49.1 (2006): 6–31.
21. Edmondson, A.C. "The local and variegated nature of learning in organizations." *Organization Science* 13.2 (2002): 128–146.
22. Herrero, L. "The Last Thing I Need Is Creativity." *Leandro Herrero.* April 14, 2014. https://leandroherrero.com/the-last-thing-i-need-is-creativity/ Accessed June 14, 2018.
23. For early research on power distance, see: Hofstede G. *Culture's Consequences: International Differences in Work-related Values.* Beverly Hills, CA: Sage, 1999. Print. For studies that have found differences in psychological safety between high vs. low power distance groups, see:

   - Anicich, E.M., Swaab, R.I., & Galinsky, A.D. "Hierarchical Cultural Values Predict Success and Mortality in High-Stakes Teams." *Proceedings of the National Academy of Sciences* 112.5 (2015): 1338–43.

   - Hu, J., Erdogan, B., Jiang, K., Bauer, T.N., & Liu, S. "Leader Humility and Team Creativity: The Role of Team Information Sharing, Psychological Safety, and Power Distance." *Journal of Applied Psychology* 103.3 (2017):313–23.

Appendix: Variations in survey measures to Illustrate Robustness of Psychological Safety

Source	Survey Items	Cronbach's Alpha
Garvin, Edmondson, & Gino (2008)[1]	1. In this unit, it is easy to speak up about what is on your mind. 2. If you make a mistake in this unit, it is often held against you. (R) 3. People in this unit are usually comfortable talking about problems and disagreements.	.94

(Continued)

Source	Survey Items	Cronbach's Alpha
	4. People in this unit are eager to share information about what *doesn't* work as well as to share information about what does work. 5. Keeping your cards close to your chest is the best way to get ahead in this unit. (R)	
Tucker, Nembhard, & Edmondson, Management Science (2007)[2]	1. People in this unit are comfortable checking with each other if they have questions about the right way to do something. 2. The people in our unit value others' unique skills and talents. 3. Members of this NICU are able to bring up problems and tough issues."	.74
Nembhard & Edmondson (2006)[3]	1. People in this unit are comfortable checking with each other if they have questions about the right way to do something. 2. Members of this NICU are able to bring up problems and tough issues. 3. If you make a mistake in this unit, it is often held against you. 4. It is easy to ask other members of this unit for help.	.73

Source	Survey Items	Cronbach's Alpha
Edmondson (1999)[4]	1. If you make a mistake on this team, it is often held against you. (R) 2. Members of this team are able to bring up problems and tough issues. 3. People on this team sometimes reject others for being different. (R) 4. It is safe to take a risk on this team. 5. It is difficult to ask other members of this team for help. (R) 6. No one on this team would deliberately act in a way that undermines my efforts. 7. Working with members of this team, my unique skills and talents are valued and utilized.	.82

Endnotes

1. Garvin, D. Edmondson, A., & Gino, F. "Is yours a learning organization?" *Harvard Business Review* (March 2008): 109–116.
2. Tucker, A.L., Nembhard, I.M., & Edmondson, A.C. "Implementing new practices: An empirical study of organizational learning in hospital intensive care units." *Management Science* 53.6 (2007): 894–907.
3. Nembhard, I.M. & Edmondson A.C. "Making it safe: The effects of leader inclusiveness and professional status on psychological safety and improvement efforts in health care teams." *Journal of Organizational Behavior* 27.7 (2006): 941–966.
4. Edmondson, A.C. "Psychological Safety and Learning Behavior in Work Teams." *Administrative Science Quarterly* 44.2 (1999): 350–83.

Acknowledgments

Many have contributed to my research on psychological safety in the quarter century since I stumbled into the phenomenon by accident. First, there are the managers, nurses, physicians, engineers, frontline associates, CEOs, and other employees in the many organizations that opened their doors to this university researcher. I am grateful for their willingness to be interviewed and studied; their generous contributions of time and insight made the work summarized in this book possible. I also thank the Division of Research at Harvard Business School for generous financial support that funded this research. I have been gratified in recent years by the dozens of both new and experienced researchers who have picked up on the concept of psychological safety to include it in their studies, adding valuable discoveries to the growing literature on this topic; their diverse, creative, rigorous research lends immense support to the argument that psychological safety matters for excellence in organizations around the world.

I am especially grateful to Jeanenne Ray at Wiley for her confidence in my work and for her patience as I sailed right past our original deadline. Patrick Healy provided invaluable research assistance that contributed to the quality and depth of the evidence I can offer to readers. In particular, he conducted literature reviews of both academic and practitioner writings on psychological safety, painstakingly reading and making notes on hundreds of articles. He identified numerous case studies that helped bring these ideas to life.

His suggestions, edits, and enthusiasm for the topic truly contributed to making this a better book. Pat also took on the thankless tasks of managing references, permissions, and other endless details that go into a project like this with skill, precision, and remarkable good cheer. I received insightful feedback at different points in the writing process from three brilliant friends – Roger Martin, Susan Salter Reynolds, and Paul Verdin – that made crucial improvements possible. Sara Nicholson provided essential help with proofing, with her usual level of extraordinary competence.

Of the many people who contributed to getting this book into its final shape, Karen Propp is by far the most important. I am deeply grateful to been able to work with her on this project. Without her perceptive questions, insights, ideas, stories, and well-honed skills as a writer and editor, this book would never have been finished. I think it's fair to say that Karen, Pat, and I had fun teaming up – identifying the cases and ideas that made it into the final draft, along with those that didn't. I hope you will find our choices to have been good ones for capturing the richness and diversity of the settings in which psychological safety matters for learning and fulfillment at work.

Finally, my husband, George Daley, put up with me as I put more and more time into working and writing. His love and confidence sustained me and made it possible for me to devote every spare moment to getting this done. He was there every step of the way for the past 25 years, never losing faith in me or in my work. While I spend my days studying leaders who make a difference in the world, George is one – having taken on the challenge of leading a major organization two years ago. Humble enough to claim my ideas have helped him succeed, George has thus given me even greater confidence that they may help others as well. This book is dedicated to him.

About the Author

AMY C. EDMONDSON

Nearing graduation from Harvard College over three decades ago, Amy Edmondson took a leap of faith and wrote a letter to a personal hero, seeking advice about employment. To her surprise, Buckminster Fuller wrote back. His letter arrived barely a week later with far more than advice. The legendary inventor, architect, and futurist offered her a job. Spending the next three years as Fuller's "chief engineer," she developed an intense and enduring interest in what leaders and organizations can do to create a better world. Today, as the Novartis professor of leadership and management at the Harvard Business School, Edmondson studies leaders seeking to make a positive difference in the world through the work they do in organizations of all kinds. The research described in this book captures the central thread that has run through her academic career – creating work environments where people can team up and do their best work.

Edmondson has been on the Harvard faculty since 1996 and teaches courses in leadership, teaming, decision-making and organizational learning. Her more than 70 articles have been published in *Harvard Business Review* and *California Management Review,* as well as in academic journals such as *Administrative Science Quarterly* and the *Academy of Management Journal.* Before her academic career, she was director of research at Pecos River Learning Centers, where she worked with CEO Larry Wilson to design and implement change programs in large companies. In this role she discovered a passion for understanding how leaders can build organizations as places where people can innovate, learn, and grow. Edmondson's prior books – *Teaming: How Organizations Learn, Innovate, and Compete in the Knowledge Economy* (2012), *Teaming to Innovate* (2013), *Building the Future: Big Teaming for Audacious Innovation* (2016), and *Extreme Teaming* (2017) – explore the challenges and opportunities of teamwork in dynamic environments. Her first book, *A Fuller Explanation: The Synergetic Geometry of R. Buckminster Fuller* (1986), clarifies Fuller's mathematical contributions for a nontechnical audience.

Edmondson's contributions to management research have been recognized by the 2018 Sumantra Ghoshal Award for Rigor and Relevance in the Study of Management, the 2017 *Thinkers50* Talent Award, the 2004 Accenture Award for significant contribution to management practice, and the Academy of Management's Cummings Award for midcareer achievement in 2006. She has been named one of the most influential thinkers in management by the biannual *Thinkers50* list since 2011 (#13 in 2017). *HR Magazine* has listed her as one of the 20 Most Influential International Thinkers in Human Resources. Edmondson received her PhD in organizational behavior, her AM in psychology, and her AB in engineering and design from Harvard University. She lives in Cambridge, Massachusetts, with her husband, George Daley, and their two sons.

Index

Abilities, confidence, 168
"Accident," term (usage), 155
Advanced Management Program
    (Harvard Business School),
    168
Agile execution, 187
Alphabet, 117
Android (Google)
    operating system, 65
    platform, 189
Anglo American, work, 165
"Anything goes" environment,
    17–18
Apathy zone, 18–19
Appreciation, expression, 173–174
Argument, winning (avoidance),
    111–112
ATC clearance, 81
Aurelius, Marcus, 129
Authority, confidence (excess),
    83–86
Avoidable future, avoidance, 53,
    68–70

Bad, embracing, 105–107
Baer, Markus, 40
Bank personnel, sales goals, 62
Barry-Wehmiller, 135
    approach, 123
    "Guiding Principles of
        Leadership," 121

psychological safety, 120
union support, 120
values/methods systematization,
    121
Barry-Wehmiller University,
    founding, 121
"Be a Don't Knower" (Fisher), 168
Beim, David, 66–67
    nonconfrontational/deferential
        style, 67–68
Belonging
    building, 201–202
    psychological safety, relationship,
        201–202
Bennis, Warren, 12
Bezos, Jeff, 96
Bischoff, Klaus, 56
Blackberry, RIM introduction, 64
Black Lives Matter, 96
Blameless reporting, 157
Blameworthy,
        consideration/treatment,
        176–177
Boeing 747s, collision, 79–82
Boisjoly, Rogert, 192
Borderline personalities, impact, 207
Boss
    role, framing, 164t
    work psychological safety,
        199–200
"Bottom-up" changes, 193–194
Bradley, Bret, 44

221

Brainstorming, usage, 191
Braintrust, 105–109, 112, 118, 190
Bridgewater Associates, 123, 167
    employees, attrition rates, 111–112
    founding, 109–110
Bryant, Adam, 171
Bryndza, Jessica, 96
Business failures, 71, 189

Cable, Dan, 169
California Air Resources Board (CARB), 54
Camp, Garrett, 94
Candor
    creation, 206
    definition, 105
    extremeness, 109–13
    reality, 104–109
"Captain of Moonshots," 117
Care, permission, 115–116
Carmeli, Abraham, 169
Carroll, Cynthia, 138–142, 165, 170
    harm, reduction attempts, 166
Cassandra, 86, 90
Catmull, Ed, 105–108, 160
Cause-effect relationships, 174
Centers for Medicare and Medicaid Services (CMS) pilot program, usage, 137–138
Challenger (space shuttle), disaster, 86–87
Chaplin, Charlie, 58, 167
Chapman, Bob, 120–122, 135
Check pilot, ability (testing), 80–81
Chernobyl, disaster, 89
Children's Hospital and Clinics, 153, 170
    failure, productive response, 176–177
    focused event analysis, 157–158
    staff, silence, 156
China, psychological safety (creation), 207–208
Clean diesel engine design, inability, 62–63

Clean diesel vehicles, 54
    software code, 55
Cockpit Resource Management (CRM), 131, 134
Cockpit training, change, 82
Collaborative process, production, 115
Colleagues
    receptivity, 38–39
    true selves, 204–205
Columbia (space shuttle), disaster, 78–79, 191
Comfort zone, 18–19
Command-and-control hierarchy, 60
Command, direct line (benefits), 83
Commitment, recommendation, 205–206
Communication
    challenges, 43
    misunderstanding, 132
    requirement, 164
Community Banking
    division, employees (impact), 63
    employees, motivation, 61
Company
    email addresses, usage (avoidance), 179
    success, top-down dictators (impact), 203–204
    target goals, 59
Compassion, recommendation, 205–206
Compensation, decisions, 110
Confidence
    absence, overcoming, 39
    excess, 83–86
    gaining, 168
    problems, knowledge (sharing), 38–39
Conflict
    navigation, 44
    usage, 43–44
Constructive feedback, 106
Consumer Financial Protection bureau (CFPB), 61

Continuous growth, enjoyment, 113–114
Continuous improvement, 207
Continuous renewal, 187–189
Conversations, logic (enforcement), 111–112
Costa, Mark, 25–26, 176
Counterfactual data, access (absence), 203
Counterproductive workarounds, 38
Courage, impact, 82
Coworkers, communication frequency, 39
Creative energy, production, 115
Crew Resource Management (CRM), 82, 134
Criticism, risk, 114
Cronbach's alpha, 20, 213–214
Cross-cultural differences, 207–208
Cross-sell, 61
Cross-selling strategy, 69
    execution, 63
Culture, change, 192–193
Culture of telling, 170
Curiosity
    humility, combination, 167–168
    recommendation, 205–206
Customer accounts, Community Banking employee opening, 63

Dalio, Ray, 109–113, 123, 145, 167, 198
Damore, James, 178
Dana-Farber Cancer Institute, 83–85
Dangerous silence, 77
Data collection/analysis, 30
DaVita Academy, 137
DaVita Kidney Centers, 46, 135, 166
    teammates, importance, 137–138
    Total Renal Care, 136
DaVita University, 135
DaVita Village Network, 136
Debate, occurrence, 112

Decision making
    deliberative decision making, 189–191
    improvement, 165–166
        conflict, impact, 43–44
        productive decision making, 44
Deming, W. Edwards, 191
"Design Kitchen," 119
Detert, Jim, 31–32
Dieselgate, 54
    root cause, 57–58
Disaster, enabling, 91–92
Discipline
    impact, 196–197
    self-discipline, 206
Discretionary work, willingness index, 42
Diversity
    building, 201–202
    performance, negative relationship, 45
    psychological safety, relationship, 201–202
    stance, 178
    usage, 44–45
Don't knower, action, 113–116
Dudenhoffer, Ferdinand, 59
Dudley, Bill, 66
Duhigg, Charles, 40–41
Dweck, Carol, 174

Eastman Chemical Company, 25–26
Educational backgrounds, consideration, 41
Effectiveness, guarantee (absence), 204–205
Effort
    harnessing, 188–189
    motivation, 166–167
Eileen Fisher Leadership Institute, founding, 116
Electronic media, communication challenges, 43
Eli Lilly, failure parties, 177
Embarrassment, risk, 114
Emergency Response Center (ERC), 143–144

Emotional harm, conditions
    (creation), 77–78
Emotional intelligence, problems,
    207
Empathy
    building, 179
    place, 106
Employees
    care, 119–123
    engagement, measures
        (validation), 42
    failure, 45–46
    motivation, 58
    perks, absence, 26
    satisfaction, importance, 41–42
    survey, 169
Engagement
    barriers, overcoming, 188–189
    creation, 45
Errors
    absence, 35–36
    admission, 31
    open discussion, 155–156
    reporting, appeal, 17
Everybody Matters (Sisodia), 120
Excellence, creation, 206
Expertise-diverse teams,
        performance, 44
Extreme candor, 109–113

Failing to fail, 119
Failure
    archetypes,
        definitions/implications,
        163t
    avoidance, 53, 59–60
    culture, 192
    czar, 161
    data source, 160
    destigmatization, 175–177, 176t
    evaluation, 118–119
    failing, 119
    freedom, 108–109
    impact, 161–162
    intelligent failure, 117
    learning to learn, 160–161
    parties, 177

    prevention, 162, 208
        productive response, 177
    productive response, variation,
        180
    psychological pain, 108
    real failure, defining, 119
    reframing, 158, 160–162
    reporting, fear, 160
    role, 161
    safety, 117–118, 160
    success, 116–119
    types, productive responses, 180t
    typology, implications, 175
"Failure," term (usage), 155
Fareed Zakaria GPS, 45
FEA. See Focused event analysis
Fear
    absence, 192
    climate, behaviors (impact), 194
    culture, insidiousness, 59
    expulsion, 191
    impact, 14–15
    interference, 144
    interpersonal fear, 165, 172–173,
        196
    motivation, problem, 13–15, 58
    "No fear" federal workplace,
        creation, 192
    understanding, 138
Fearless organization, creation, 146
Fearless workplace, 103
Federal Reserve of New York
        (FRBNY), 60, 92, 198
    condemnation/criticism, 66
    consensus, striving, 67
Feedback, 110, 173. See also
        Constructive feedback
    group, people (impact), 106–107
    provision, 196
Fictional vignettes, design, 32, 34
Financial system, collapse, 68
Firing, decisions, 110
Fisher, Eileen, 113–116, 123,
        165–168, 190
Flight 1549, 130–131
    non-normal situation, 130
Focus, creation, 114

Focused event analysis (FEA),
    157–158, 177
Ford, Henry, 57, 204
"Foundry," 119
Fowler, Susan, 93–96, 194–195
Frei, Frances, 193–194
Frese, Michael, 40
Frontline staff, stress, 42
Fukushima Daiichi Nuclear Power
    Plant, 87–92, 142
  control, 144–145
Fukushima Daini Nuclear Power
    Plant, 142–145, 165
  damage, assessment, 143

Game-Changer, The (Lafley), 160
Gazetta, Frank, 116
Geographic dispersion, overcoming,
    43
Gibbs, Jennifer, 43
Gibson, Charlie, 79
Gibson, Cristina, 43
Glass, Ira, 67–68
Goffman, Erving, 4–5, 8
"Going for Gr-Eight," 61–63
Goldman Sachs, 67
Good, journey, 105–107
"Good news" stories, simplicity, 104
Googler-to-Googler (g2g) network,
    172–173, 195
Google team, Project Aristotle,
    40–41
Google X, 117–118, 123, 160, 165
Government bureaucracy,
    responsibility, 92
"Great East Japanese Earthquake," 87
Great Recession, 120
Green Car of the Year (2008), 53
Groupe Danone, 173
Group-level phenomenon, 12
Groupthink, 67
"Guiding Principles of Leadership"
    (Barry-Wehmiller), 121

Halbesleben, Jonathon, 38
Hall, Amy, 115
Ham, Linda, 79

Harris, Sydney, 77
Harten, Patrick, 131, 133
Harvard Business School
  Advanced Management Program,
    168
  leadership programs, 191
Hatz, Wolfgang, 54
Healthcare delivery, explanation, 155
Help, seeking (appeal), 17–18
"Here-and-Now Humility"
    (Schein), 168
Hewlin, Patricia, 30
Hierarchy
  de-emphasis, 114
  psychological pull, 82
Hirak, Reuven, 169
Hobbies, consideration, 41
Hooke, Casey, 172
Hornsey, Liane, 194
Hospital care, error-prone system,
    155
Huang, Chi-Cheng, 40
Hudson Miracle, value, 134
Human health/safety, fostering, 134
Human interactions, importance,
    133
Humble listening, 114–115
Humiliation, risk, 114
Humility
  confidence, contrast, 168
  curiosity, combination, 167–168
Humor, absence, 193–195

Ideas, withholding, 31
Impostor syndrome, 161
Incentives, decisions, 110
Inclusion
  building, 201–202
  psychological safety, relationship,
    201–202
Industries, learning, 133–134
Innovation
  culture, 192
  fostering, 43–44
  impact, 66
  psychological safety, relationship,
    40

Input
    requests, 122–123
    structures, design, 172–173
Inquiry, 170
    proactive inquiry, 167, 170–172
    skills, development, 179
Institut Européen d'Administration
        des Affaires (INSEAD), 190
Intelligent failure, 117
Interdependence
    appreciation, 177
    emphasis, 162, 164
    levels, attention, 166
Interdependent departments,
        priorities (conflict), 154
Interpersonal fear, 172–173, 204
    problem, 196
    sensibility, 165
Interpersonal risk
    micro-assessments, 134
    overcoming, 166–167
    perspective, 164
Inter-term reliability, 20
Interview data, coding, 20–21
Inviting Participation, 123, 154, 156
iOS (Apple), 189
iPhone, impact, 65
Ishibashi, Katsuhiko, 88
    Madame criticism, 88–89

Japan
    Active Fault and Earthquake
        Research Center, 90
    national energy security, goal, 92
    nuclear meltdown, 87–91
    psychological safety, creation,
        207–208
Jiang, Pin-Chen, 40
Jobs, Steve, 204
Jogan tsunami, 90–91
"Just kidding" moments,
    193–194

Kahn, William, 12
Kalanick, Travis, 94
    Uber exit, 95–96
Khosrowshahi, Dara, 96, 193–194
Knowledge
    marketplace, 173
    sharing, 38–39
    workers, 58
Kurokawa, Kiyoshi, 91
Kyoto Protocol, 89

Lafley, A.G., 160
Lasseter, John (harassment), 107
Leaders
    job, 200
    participation, invitation, 156–157
    productive responses, 157–158
    stage, setting, 155–156
    success, learning, 207
    tool kit, 154–158, 176–177
        usage, 159t
    VUCA interaction, 166
Leadership, 146
    effectiveness, 56–57
    self-assessment, 181–182
"Lean Forward, Fail Smart Award,"
    192
Learn-how, 36–37
    behaviors, 37
Learning
    anxiety, 12
    behavior, 35
        psychological safety,
            relationship, 39–40
    creation, 206
    increase, 169
    inhibition, fear (impact), 14–15
    mindset, 167–168
    natural part, 108
    opportunity, 205
    orientation, power, 174
    support, work environment
        (impact), 35–39
    zone, virtual team (impact),
        131–132
Learning to learn, 160–161
Learn-what, 36–37

Lehman, Betsy, 83–85
  chemotherapy, 83–84
Lehman, Mildred K., 85
Lekgotla, 140
Leningrad, flood (1924), 14
Leroy, Hannes, 35–36
Listening, 114–115
  impact, 199
  importance, 96
Los Rodeos Airport, 80
Lutz, Bob, 56–57

Madame, Haruki, 88
Mahfouz, Naguib, 153
Management risk, 21
Manager change (absence), people
  (interaction advice), 205–206
Marcus, Roy, 137–138
Mask, removal, 200
Masuda, Naohiro, 142–146, 165
Maxwell, John, 187
Meaning, environment (creation),
  121
Meaningful work/relationships,
  value,
  109
Medical errors, 85
Medical team, efforts, 136–137
Meetings, silence (usage), 114
Mental health, 42
Merchant, Nilofer, 5
Meritocracy, 95
#MeToo movement, 92–96, 107,
  194–195
Meurs, Klaas, 80–82
Milano, Alyssa, 92–93
Milliken, Frances, 30
Mindfulness, creation, 114
Mines, safety protocols (usage), 141
Mining
  harm, reduction, 166–167
  shutdown, 139–141
Minorities, engagement (creation),
  45
Mistakephobia, 111
Mistakes, learning, 35–36
Modern Times (Chaplin), 58

Moody-Stuart, Mark, 139
Morath, Julie, 153–157, 165, 170
  terminology, introduction, 155
Morrison, Elizabeth, 30
Morton-Thiokol, 86–87
"Motivator Report," 62
MTV, programming work, 172
Mulcahy, Anne, 168

Narcissism, impact, 207
NASA
  leaders, emphasis, 166
  space shuttle disasters, 78–79,
    86–87, 191
National Union of Mineworkers,
  141
National Women's Law Center, 195
Ndlovu, Judy, 140
Near-perfection, desire, 158
Nembhard, Ingrid, 36, 169
Neonatal Intensive Care Unit
  (NICU), 169, 173
  babies, delivery, 3
  nurse, speaking up, 154
  protocol, 7
  quality improvement project
    teams, 36–37
Nitrous oxide (NO_x), production,
  54–55
"No fear" federal workplace,
  creation, 192
Nokia, 60, 63
  avoidable failure, 64
  comeback, 190
  emotional climate, 64
  external market threats, 65
  operating system, 189
  R&D culture, 65
  rise/fall, 64
  success, 65–66
Non-governmental organizations
  (NGOs), 195
Not-knowing (Fisher), 190
Nuclear Accident Independent
  Investigation Commission
  (NAIIC), 91

Nuclear Industrial Safety Agency (NISA), policing hesitation, 89, 90
Nurses, study, 35–36

Off-site company sustainability conference, usage, 115
Oil shocks (1970s), 89
Okamura, Yukinobi, 90
Ombudspersons, confidentiality, 203
"One for All and All for One" motto, 135–138, 166
One-on-one mentoring, 172
Open-minded disagreements, 111–112
OpenTable, 160
Operational performance, improvement, 173
Organization
    fearlessness, 201
    strategy, framing, 70
Organizational learning
    process, 179
    requirements, 71
Osterloh, Bernd, 59

Paper trail, 25
Participation, invitation, 156–157
    process, 167–173
Patient Safety Steering Committee (PSSC), initiative, 157
Patton, George, 142
People
    responses, 167–173
    treatment, 121
People Experience, 96
Perfectionism, discussions, 161
Performance
    measurement, 40
    problem, 70
    psychological safety importance, reasons, 39–41
    sacrifice, 55
    unit performance, improvement, 169

Performance standards
    lowering, psychological safety (contrast), 17–19
    psychological safety, comparison, 18f
Personalities, self-assurance, 112
Personality
    factor, psychologically safety (contrast), 16
    traits, consideration, 41
    types/skills/backgrounds, mix, 41
Personal values/goals, 205
Physical harm, conditions (creation), 77–78
Piech, Ferdinand, 56–57
Pittman, Bob, 171–172
Pixar Animation Studios, 14, 46, 105–109, 118, 123, 160
    Braintrust, 105–109, 112, 118, 190
Power distance, 207
    cultural differences, 208
"Powerful questions" attribution, identification, 170–171
Power, impact, 169
Power plants, construction allowance (government records), 88
Predictive validity, 20
Presentation of the Self in Everyday Life, The (Goffman), 4
Price, Christina, 3–4, 6–8, 17
Pride, environment (creation), 121
Principles (Dalio), 109, 111, 145
Proactive inquiry, 167, 170–172
Process improvements, 122
Process-laden work, 121–122
Process, outcome (relationship), 175f
Productive conflict, 111–113
Productive decision making, 44
Productive responses, 180t
    process, 173–180
    variation, 180
Project Aristotle, 12, 40–41
    aftermath, 45
Project Foghorn, 116
Promotions, decisions, 110
Promotions/protections, 94–96

Psychologically safe employees,
   engagement, 41–42
Psychologically safe organizations,
   creation, 208
Psychologically safe work
   environments, 165
   impact, 134–135
   learning, 123–124
Psychologically safe workplace, 6–8
   advocacy, 198–199
   creation, 138, 146
   profile, 104
   time, usage, 197–198
Psychological safety, 8–12
   absence, 130, 203
   assistance, 43
   building, 195, 208–209
      leader tool kit, usage, 159t
   certainty, 26–29
   confusion, 197
   creation, 140, 146, 199, 209
   cultivation, 165
   defining, 15–19
   demonstration, 134
   diversity/inclusion/belonging,
      relationship, 201–202
   dynamism, 189
   effects, 28–29
   efficiency source, 197
   emphasis, 43–45
   establishment/enhancement, 169
   excess, 195–197
   failure, destigmatization, 176t
   FAQs, 195–208
   group building, 36
   groups, 29–30
   impact, 156
   importance, 12–13
      reasons, 39–41
   improvement, 21–22
   innovation, relationship, 40
   insufficiency, 69–70
   leader, success (learning), 207
   learning behavior, relationship,
      39–40
   measurement, 19–21
   media mentions, 27–28, 27f

niceness, contrast, 15–16
norms, inclusion, 190
organizational commitment,
   relationship, 42
panacea, 196–197
performance standards
   comparison, 18f
   lowering, contrast, 17–19
personality factor, contrast, 16
power, 119–120
practice, research (usage), 45–46
predictions, 37
presence/absence, detection,
   20–21
research, 29–30
restoration, 195
rewards, 120
robustness, survey measures
   (variations), 213–215
role, emphasis, 43, 195
stage, setting (process), 158–167
studies, 44
survey measure, 20f
team psychological safety,
   citations, 28f
trust, comparison, 16–17
whistle-blowing, relationship,
   202–203
work, framing, 160–166
Psychological/societal forces,
   asymmetry, 188
Public self-expression, ambiguity,
   180

Qatar, sovereign wealth fund, 59
Qualitative case-study research,
   20–21
Quality environment, 36–37
Quality improvement (QI) project
   teams, 36–37
"Quality of Sale" Report Card
   (Wells Fargo), 62–63
Quarles, Christa, 160
Questions
   power, attributes, 171
   "powerful questions" attribution,
      identification, 170–171

Questions (*continued*)
  reason, 85
  revelation, 208

Radical truth/transparency, 109
"Rapid Evaluation," 118–119
Ratatouille (film), 14
Rathert, Cheryl, 38
Real failure, defining, 119
Regulators, regulation, 66–68
Regulatory capture, 67–68
Reporting policy, blame (absence),
      158
*Report of Systemic Risk and Bank
      Supervision* (2009), 66–67
Research, usage, 45–46
Respect, conveyance, 199
Return on assets, longitudinal
      change, 40
Ride-sharing economy, 94
RIM, 64
Risk, mitigation, 168
Risk, taking, 116, 174
Rocha, Rodney, 78–79
Rogers, Ed, 191–192
Role model, 25
Roosevelt, Franklin D., 103
Rozovsky, Julia, 3, 41

Safety Summit, 141
Safe zone, creation, 199
Sales numbers, hitting, 62
Sallan, Stephen, 83
Schein, Edgar, 12, 168
Schmidt, Oliver, 53
Schreuder, Willem, 80–82
Scolese, Christopher, 192
Segarra, Carmen, 68
Self-assessment questions, 181
Self-confidence, 168
Self-discipline, 206
Selfish agenda, absence, 106
Self-protection, 188
  perception, 167
Self-report, 40
Senior executives, engagement, 71
Sexual attention, suffering, 92–93

Sexual harassment, experiences, 93
Siemsen, Enno, 39
Silence
  culture, 86–92
  impact, 30–35, 92–96
  importance, 79–82, 156
  reasons, 31
  rewards, 188
  selection, 35
  sounds, hearing, 191–193
  understanding, 138
  usage, 114
  victory, reason, 34t
  warnings, dismissal, 87–90
"Silence Breakers" (TIME
      Magazine), 96
Simmons, Rachel, 161
Sisodia, Raj, 120
Situational humility, 167–169
  demonstration, 168
Skiles, Jeffrey, 129–133
Smart failures, honoring, 119
Smart process design, 197
Smith College, 160–161
  Wurtele Center for Work and
      Life, 161
Smith, Diana, 44
Social media
  platforms, personal opinions
      expression, 179
  problem, 95
  silence, impact, 92–96
Solutions, develop-
      ment/commercialization
      (goal), 117
South African Department of
      Minerals and Energy, 141
Space shuttle
  Challenger disaster, 86–87
  Columbia disaster, 78–79
Speaking up
  automatic calculus, 34
  failure, 78–79
  psychology, aspect, 79
  risk, 32
Staff meetings, orchestration,
      165–166

Standards, importance, 54–60
Stanton, Andrew, 106–107
Strategy, agile approach (adoption),
  70–71
Stretch goal, stretching, 60–63
"Study," term (usage), 155
Stumpf, John, 61
Success
  innovation, impact, 66
  requirements, 71
Sullenberger III, Chesley, 129–133
Superstorm Sandy, 162
Symbian, 189
  operating system, 63
System complexity
  appreciation, 177
  problem, 154

Tacking, 209
Taken-for-granted rules, 33t, 34
Talent, unleashing, 146
Task-based conversations, 111
Team psychological safety
  citations, 28f
  concept/measure, 28
Teams
  diagnostic survey, 9
  error rates, 9–10
  member performance, rating, 40
Teamwork, importance, 161
Teller, Astro, 117–119, 160
Telling, culture, 170
Tertiary care hospitals
  complexity, 154
  operations, error-prone nature
    (re-explanation), 156
Thiry, Kent, 135–136, 166
Threat and error management
  (TEM), 134
Three Mile Island, accident, 89
"Time's Up" Legal Defense Fund
  (National Women's Law
  Center), founding, 195
Time, usage, 133
"Toe-stepping," 194
Toe-stepping value, 95

Tokyo Electric Power Company
  (TEPCO), 144
  risk acknowledgment, 89–91
Top-down culture,
  cheating/coverup
  (by-products), 70–71
Top-down dictators, impact,
  203–204
Top-down strategy, 69–70
Total quality management (TQM),
  38
Total Renal Care, 136
Toy Story (movie), 104–106
Toy Story 2 (movie), 105–106
Transparency, 198–199
  aggressiveness, 198
  injunction (Dalio), 194
  levels, 198
  norm, violation, 194
  radical truth/transparency, 109
  whiteboards, usage, 142–146
Transparency libraries, 110–111
Trust
  destruction, practices, 121
  environment, creation, 121
  increase, 190
  psychological safety, comparison,
    16–17
Truth
  fear, 63–66
  radical truth/transparency, 109
Tucker, Anita, 36, 37, 169
Turnover intentions, 42

Uber Technologies, Inc., 93–96
  problems, 193
  sexual harassment, experiences,
    93–95
Uncertainty
  emphasis, 162, 164
  levels, attention, 166
Unconscious calculators, 4–6
Union support, 120
Unit performance, improvement,
  169
US Airways, Cockpit Resource
  Management (CRM), 131

Value creation, impact, 70
Value (gaining), diversity (usage),
    44–45
van Zanten, Jacob Veldhuyzen,
    80–82
Vaughn, Diane, 191
Verdin, Paul, 70
Vigilance, importance, 161
Violations, sanctioning, 178–180
Virtual teams, 43
Virtual zone, usage, 131–132
Voice
    barriers, overcoming, 188–189
    implicit theories, 32, 34–35
    mission criticality, 39
    productive responses, process,
        173–180
    requirement, clarification,
        162–166
    rewards, 188
    threshold, 197
Voice at work, taken-for-granted
    rules, 33t
Voice-silence
    asymmetry, 34
    calculation, silence (victory), 34t
Volatility, uncertainty, complexity,
    and ambiguity (VUCA), 19,
    26–27, 60, 70, 166
    conditions, 174
    success, requirements, 71
    value creation, impact, 70
Volkswagen, 174
    command-and-control hierarchy,
        60
    compliance, 55
    coverup, denial, 55
    diesel engines, problem, 58–59,
        107
    emissions scandal, effects,
        59–60
    engineers, blame, 56
    failure, avoidance, 53
    standards, importance, 54–60
    stretch goal, stretching, 60–63
    terror, reign, 57
    truth, fear, 63–66

Volkswagen Group, 53
Vulnerability, expression, 200
Vuori, Timo, 190

Warnings, dismissal, 87–90
Wells Fargo, 60, 174
    cross-selling strategy, 69
    "Quality of Sale" Report Card,
        62–63
    success, 60–61
West Virginia University, Center for
    Alternative Fuels, Engines,
    and Emissions, 55
Whistle-blowing, psychological
    safety (relationship),
    202–203
Whiteboards, usage, 142–146
Why Worry? (Ishibashi), 88
Winterkorn, Martin, 54, 164
    company rules, strictness,
        59–60
    leadership, impact, 56–57
    soft spots, 58
    villian, role, 56
Words, usage, 130–134
Work
    colleagues, true selves, 204–205
    emotional commitment, 41–42
    engagement, 42
    error-prone nature, 156
    framing, 160–166
    interdependent work,
        communication
        (requirement), 164
    process-laden work, 121–122
    psychological safety, 199–200
    quality, erosion, 180
    self, supply (problems), 205
Workarounds
    occurrence, 38
    problems, 37
    reduction, 37–38
Work environment
    impact, 35–39
    knowledge, sharing, 38–39
    mistakes, learning, 35–36
    quality environment, 36–37

Workers
    fatalities, avoidance, 158
    safety, speaking up, 138–142
Workforce, diversity, 201
Workplace
    fearless workplace, 103
    nurturing, 187
    phrases, usage, 200
    psychologically safe workplace,
        6–8

psychological safety
    absence, 29
    manifestion, 104
psychological safety climate,
    permeation, 68
silence, importance, 79–82
Wrong-doing, speaking out,
    28

X (project). *See* Google X